The Sins of
G. K. Chesterton

By the same author
God's Apology
Goldenballs
John Stewart Collis: A Memoir
Piper's Places
Muggeridge: The Biography
The Life and Adventures of William Cobbett
My Friend Footy
Ludo and the Power of the Book

ANTHOLOGIES
Beachcomber: The Works of J.B. Morton
Cobbett's Country Book
Dr Johnson by Mrs. Thrale
Jesus: Authors Take Sides
Quips and Quotes

The Sins of
G. K. Chesterton

RICHARD INGRAMS

First published in 2021 by Harbour Books (East) Limited
PO Box 10594, Chelmsford, Essex CM1 9PB

A catalogue record for this book is available from the British Library

ISBN 9781905128334

Typeset by Tetragon, London

Printed and bound in Great Britain by TJ Books Limited, Padstow, Cornwall

For Sara

Contents

Introduction

Born in 1874, G. K. Chesterton was a prolific writer whose bibliography lists over a hundred books – poetry, plays, theology, novels, literary criticism and history. All have attracted their particular admirers. Yet he himself insisted throughout his life that he was a journalist, his journalism consisting not of the stories or features which we nowadays expect from newspapers but essays – two thousand or so words on a topical theme (literary, political or religious), many of them later reprinted in book form, a typical title *All Things Considered* summing up Chesterton's singular achievement.

The long essay, once so popular, was the form in which he excelled and when he wrote a book, even his autobiography (1936), it tended to be a collection of essays on a particular theme rather than a continuous narrative. As he himself wrote of his book on Browning (1903): "I will not say I wrote a book on Browning; but I wrote a book on love, Liberty, poetry, my own views on God and religion...and various theories of my own about optimism and pessimism and the hope of the world; a book in which the name of Browning was introduced from time to time, I might say with considerable art, or at any rate with some decent appearance of regularity."

Chesterton was famous in his day, almost as famous as his great friend and admirer Bernard Shaw. He was a character, literally larger than life, a man renowned for his wit who in his final years became even better known as a broadcaster on BBC radio. Inevitably, after his death, his reputation declined, though kept alive over the years by a regular succession of biographies and collections – notably those of P. J. Kavanagh and

W. H. Auden – in which his appeal and versatility could be better appreciated than in his fictional fantasies like *The Napoleon of Notting Hill*. Only his masterpiece the series of Father Brown stories achieved classic status and has remained in print ever since his death, part of the appeal lying in the way the hero Father Brown mirrors his creator – a figure ignored by bystanders as an irrelevant, faintly comic character but who proves to be, in reality, a profound and serious figure with an intuitive insight into everything.

Yet since his conversion to the Roman Catholic Church in 1922 Chesterton studies, which have been extensive, particularly in the USA, have been the concern of critics and biographers, almost all of them fellow Catholics, for whom his writings on religion, his books about Thomas Aquinas or St Francis, on Catholicism in particular, have taken precedence over his other work, while his conversion is treated as the highlight and climax of his life.

In the process a rather unreal image has been created of a serene, unworldly and benevolent figure leading a blameless life, intent on a mission to promote the Church. But many of his admirers, especially in America, were not satisfied with the idea that their hero was a good man and went a large step further, proposing that he had been a saint and was deserving of canonisation by the Pope. Thus a campaign was started which culminated in 2013 with the Bishop of Northampton, the Right Revd Peter Doyle, appointing Canon John Udris to decide the question of whether Chesterton had lived a life of 'heroic virtue' and whether he could be credited with miracles due to his intercession. To the great disappointment of his admirers, the Bishop announced in August 2019 that after a six-year investigation he was not going to proceed with Chesterton's Cause, instancing as major obstacles his 'anti-Semitism' and the fact he could find 'no pattern of personal spirituality' in Chesterton's life. The decision, it can be predicted, will not stop the campaign, though it is fair to assume that it would have come as a relief to Chesterton himself.

In his book about R. L. Stevenson, Chesterton referred to 'the first essential qualification of a great man: that of being misunderstood by his opponents', but went on very typically to identify 'the other essential qualification, that of being misunderstood by his admirers'. Chesterton's Roman Catholic admirers, not unnaturally, seized on his Catholicism as the most significant thing about him. Considering the generally defensive attitude of the Catholic Church in response to centuries of Protestant prejudice and persecution, there was no doubt that the Church's recruitment of Chesterton was of enormous value, the conversion of such a popular and respected figure being often compared to that of John Henry Newman in the Victorian age. No doubt it was reassuring for Catholics to welcome Chesterton into the fold but in the process many of his Catholic admirers, sidestepping the fact that most of his best-known books including the best-selling religious work *Orthodoxy* (1908) were written well before his conversion, sought to promote a new version of Chesterton as primarily a Catholic apologist, even a theologian or, as Marshall McLuhan (famous for 'The Medium is the Message') called him, 'a Metaphysical Moralist'.

Thus a false image of Chesterton was created which gave the non-Catholic world an excuse for ignoring him while even a revered critic like George Orwell could dismiss him as a writer whose every sentence 'had to demonstrate beyond possibility of mistake the superiority of the Catholic over the Protestant or the Pagan.'

Chesterton's admirers were not too concerned with refuting such ill-informed judgements. If Chesterton was to be a candidate for canonisation then it only helped the cause if he was seen as a champion of the Church with every word he wrote. His biographers had already cleared the path to sainthood by painting a picture of him as a benign genius who had gone through life in a spirit of childlike wonder, untroubled by all the worries and doubts that make life difficult for the rest of us. 'Sweet and virtuous' was Evelyn Waugh's description; Joseph Pearce titled his 1997 biography *Wisdom and Innocence*. The cause has been maintained by Chesterton's latest apologist Dale Ahlquist, a fervent believer in his hero's sanctity, who can write of Chesterton that he 'epitomises each of the beatitudes with his humility, his sympathy, his kindness, his thirst for justice, his charity to his enemies, his purity and goodness and his patience with those who attacked him.' Chesterton's goodness, he says, 'seeps through the pages like sweet perfume.'

This saintly picture of Chesterton painted by the Catholic biographers involved isolating, as far as possible, three people who exercised a powerful if not damaging influence on the course of his career – his brother Cecil, Cecil's wife Ada (always known as Keith) and, in particular, the friend and mentor of both brothers, Hilaire Belloc.

The names of Belloc and Chesterton have always been coupled together and so became in the eyes of many Catholics a kind of Peter-and-Paul duumvirate defending the faith in the pages of their countless pamphlets and books. No one has suggested canonisation for Hilaire Belloc, but his reputation, too, has been zealously protected by Catholic commentators who saw him as the champion of Catholicism, a man who had spent a lifetime in defence of the Church – belligerent, admittedly, but admirable and sincere. Only A. N. Wilson's masterly 1984 biography has challenged that perception, though even Wilson is generally sympathetic to Belloc.

Leading the field in the campaign to preserve the good name of both men were their respective official biographers – Maisie Ward (Chesterton) and Robert Speaight (Belloc). Ward, who wrote two books, *G. K. Chesterton* (1943) and *Return to Chesterton* (1952), was the wife of Catholic publisher Wilfred Sheed and a close friend of Chesterton's wife Frances. Her biography contains a valuable store of information but, as Graham Greene wrote in a review, 'It is too long for its material, too cumbered with affectionate trivialities... Mrs Ward has amiably supposed her readers to be all friends of her subject... One wishes too that she had remembered more frequently her non-Catholic audience.'[1]

The same criticism could well be levelled at other writers, including Chesterton's most recent biographer, Ian Ker, whose 747-page book, published in 2011, gives precedence, as Ward does, to Chesterton's Catholicism and his religious writings – not surprising perhaps in view of the fact that the author is a Roman Catholic priest.

As well as pursuing an openly Catholic agenda, in common with

Maisie Ward, Father Ker was also too ready to grant Chesterton absolution for his sins, for example his false statement that his brother Cecil was killed in battle in 1918 (in fact he died of natural causes after the war was over – see Chapter 7 below). 'Cecil had as good as died in battle,' Ker writes, 'and his brother cannot be blamed for a very excusable slight exaggeration.' Belloc's official biographer Robert Speaight, an actor by profession, shows the same regrettable tendency to sweep disobliging details under the carpet, for example the well-publicised fact that Charles Granville, owner of Belloc's paper *The Eye-Witness*, a paper devoted to the exposure of political corruption, was himself a bigamist and a crook.

Whilst not regarding Belloc as deserving of canonisation, Speaight nevertheless described him as a near saintly figure. 'Like every man he had his faults,' he writes, 'but it is not often that one can say of a man of genius, quite simply, that he was a good man. One can say of Belloc not only that he was good, but that he was supernaturally good.' When prefacing his book Speaight even feels obliged to apologise in advance for any criticism of Belloc that might follow. 'I hope,' he writes, 'that his friends will pardon me for any note of criticism that may from time to time have crept into this book. Such criticism is hardly to be avoided in dealing with a highly controversial figure.'[2] Belloc's admirers must have felt reassured by the notion of any criticism of their hero merely creeping into Mr Speaight's narrative, thereby, perhaps, escaping notice altogether.

In his concern to safeguard Belloc's reputation, particularly from the charge of anti-Semitism, Speaight was even prepared to suggest that Belloc was influenced by Chesterton's younger brother Cecil (rather than vice versa, as other accounts maintained). The same argument was advanced by another Catholic stalwart, the long-serving *Tablet* editor Douglas Woodruff, who described Cecil as an 'evil genius' who had led Belloc astray.[3] It is hard to imagine Belloc being influenced, let alone led astray, by anyone, least of all a volatile fellow journalist ten years his junior and a man who was one of his most dedicated disciples.

Cecil's only biographer, Brocard Sewell (another Catholic priest), could hardly have called him a good man, let alone a saint. Whilst praising his courage and humility he admitted that 'there was quite a lot about him that was not particularly endearing'.[4] But as a fervent admirer of Sir Oswald Mosley, Father Sewell prudently refrained from defining what precisely he was talking about.

Chesterton's Catholic biographers have been particularly keen to sideline Cecil, whose violent anti-Semitism could not be denied, as it could be, at least to a limited extent, in the case of Belloc and Chesterton. Maisie Ward did her best, referring tactfully to his 'rather fierce way of handling such matters as race questions', admitting only that there were times when her 'nerves jangled' as she leafed through the pages of Cecil's paper the *New Witness* – but without going into details. Father Ker may also have suffered from jangling of the nerves, as his account of the Marconi scandal follows Maisie Ward's example and avoids any quotation from Cecil Chesterton's viciously anti-Semitic attacks on Herbert Samuel and the Isaacs brothers.

Yet sidelining Cecil meant ignoring one of the most powerful influences on Chesterton's life: his slavish devotion to his younger brother both before and after Cecil's death at the age of thirty-two in 1918. It was left to Dudley Barker, the only non-Catholic to write a life of Chesterton, to spell it out, even if it was a theme he failed to pursue:

Cecil was fond of him no doubt, but Chesterton's devotion to Cecil was an obsession. In many important respects it altered his adult life. The youthful habit of usually deferring, in the end, to Cecil's opinions accustomed Chesterton to accepting and championing them, so that some of the political and social views with which Chesterton's name is identified were largely those which he took, without sufficient question, from his brother, and since Cecil Chesterton and Hilaire Belloc found in each other a kinship of minds, Belloc's prejudices were also accepted by Chesterton.[5]

If Cecil was to be sidelined by the official biographers, the same principle had to be applied in the case of his wife Keith. 'All personal memories of the Chestertons,' Maisie Ward writes, 'are unusually happy: there is none of the mixture of the bitter with the sweet that personal memories commonly hold.' Such a sunny reflection is vivid proof of the extent to which Maisie Ward was able, when it suited her, to banish from her mind unwelcome thoughts of Cecil Chesterton's widow, whose 1941 memoir *The Chestertons* was a very vivid mixture of bitter and sweet.

'Mrs Cecil,' she writes, 'was of course never in the intimacy of the family. She only married Cecil in 1917 – by which date Gilbert and Frances had been married sixteen years – and before that she was merely an acquaintance.' But there was not much 'of course' about it. 'Mrs Cecil' may have married in 1917, but long before that date she had been the constant companion of Cecil, knew Gilbert very well from working with him and had become, as she remained, a close friend of their mother Marie Louise. Her book may be full of inaccuracies and gibes at Frances yet it contains very valuable information about the family. But from Mrs Ward's point of view, she introduced a jarring note into the 'unusually happy' account she wished to give her readers. Besides which 'Mrs Cecil', as a non-Catholic[6] and fellow-travelling Communist, was deserving only of a walk-on role in the drama, and her important work, for example in helping to launch *GK's Weekly* in 1925, could be ignored. Thus you have the unusual situation in which an official biographer deliberately ignores one of the most fruitful sources of information about her subject. Belloc's biographer, Speaight, excludes Keith from his narrative altogether except to record that she married Cecil Chesterton in 1917, referring to her only by her pen-name of J. K. Prothero.

Anyone hoping to rectify the balance, however, is faced with what looks like a suspicious lack of material. After Cecil's death, Chesterton himself threw away most of his notebooks and letters and did much the same when their father died. Mrs Cecil Chesterton writes that her collection of papers and letters was (conveniently perhaps) destroyed in a bombing raid during the Blitz. Her husband's wartime career is thus a virtual blank and his correspondence with Hilaire Belloc fails to cover the crucial Marconi period of 1912–13. Prior to Chesterton's death in 1936 all records of the disputes that had wracked the Distributist League and *GK's Weekly* (see Chapter 9 below) were destroyed at the behest of Gregory Macdonald, who with his brother Edward had been responsible for the running of Chesterton's paper *GK's Weekly*. Like others, Macdonald was determined not to say anything to damage Chesterton's reputation, and never referred to his disputes or difficulties when subsequently writing about the paper. Following Frances Chesterton's death in 1938, her devoted secretary and archivist Dorothy Collins threw out a further cache of papers.

Such cover-ups were motivated not just by a desire to protect Chesterton's reputation but also that of the Catholic Church with which he was in his later years so strongly associated. But in an age like our own which has seen the Church having to grapple with cover-ups of a much more damaging nature, the smokescreen created around Chesterton has come to seem, by comparison, trivial and irrelevant.

*

I have always found it hard to trace back the history of any book I have written. Like a hazardous journey made with no maps and many wrong turnings, the process of how it was done seems to disappear from the memory once it is completed. I know that for some time in the past I had an ambition to write a book about Chesterton, though well aware that several critics and biographers had done it already and that, in any event, it would be difficult to combine my researches with all my other commitments.

I had been an admirer from my youth, my Catholic mother being a convert and the niece of Maurice Baring, fellow convert and lifelong friend of both Chesterton and Belloc. All three were revered and their books, many of them inscribed, lined the shelves – Baring's remaining, sadly, by me unread. Though now a Catholic I was brought up as an Anglican – my parents having agreed to have two Catholic and two Protestant sons – and the author of *Orthodoxy* attracted me as an ecumenical Christian but more so because of his insistence that he was a journalist, which is what I always wanted to be, and above all because he was funny. His parodies, his cartoons, his clerihews made a strong appeal and I accepted without questioning the image of the jolly journalist, the Toby Jug figure scattering aphorisms and paradoxes like a wittier and wiser Oscar Wilde.

In 1974, the centenary of Chesterton's birth, I wrote a tribute to Chesterton in the *Daily Telegraph* magazine (reprinted in *G. K. Chesterton: A Half Century of Views*, edited by D. J. Conlon, 1987), and later, in 1986 an introduction to a reprint of his *Autobiography* (Hamish Hamilton). Re-reading it now, I am shocked by the number of mistakes I made as well as my determination to exonerate Chesterton of any shortcomings – 'It should be stressed,' I wrote, 'that there is no question of any evasiveness in the many gaps that occur in Chesterton's account of his life. There are no skeletons hidden away in the cupboard.' I remember all the same a lingering feeling of disappointment about the autobiography which I was reluctant to put into words, as I had been commissioned to recommend the book. I had a sense of important things left unsaid and ought not to have overlooked important clues – the way he referred to 'my friends' without wanting to name Belloc and Cecil, the very cursory reference to his *Daily News* editor, A. G. Gardiner, the bizarre description of the Marconi Scandal as one of the major turning points in the history of England, if not the world. Such incongruities were inconsistent with the picture of the man I described in my introduction as 'a simple and saintly man.'

It was the first part of Professor Owen Dudley Edwards's long review of Dennis Judd's life of Lord Reading, published in the *Chesterton Review* in 1985, that opened my eyes to a world very different from the sunny picture I had hitherto accepted as the reality. Dudley Edwards was not only an admirer of Chesterton (particularly of the Father Brown stories) but he was a Catholic and so could not be accused of anti-Catholic bias. Yet his aim was to defend at some length the principal villain, in Chesterton's eyes, of the Marconi affair, Rufus Isaacs (Lord Reading), and to accuse both Chesterton brothers of inexcusable anti-semitism and Chesterton himself of being, at times, 'unhinged'.

I cannot now remember how I happened to read the Dudley Edwards article as I have never subscribed to the *Chesterton Review* and so must have come across it by chance. All the same it was instrumental in persuading me that there was an alternative Chesterton story, a story that had been deliberately suppressed and in some cases ignored altogether by Chesterton's Catholic biographers.

If these writers were concerned to play down, in particular, the burning issue of anti-semitism, I discovered that, apart from Dudley Edwards, there were historians and sociologists who felt no similar need for restraint. Colin Holmes had preceded Dudley Edwards with his *Anti-semitism in British Society 1876–1939* and has since been followed by Ann Farmer with *Chesterton and the Jews* (2015) a lengthy survey which makes it difficult, if not impossible, for any Chesterton enthusiast to defend him against the anti-semitism charge. There is further evidence, particularly regarding Hilaire Belloc, in Jay Corrin's *G. K. Chesterton and Hilaire Belloc: The Battle Against Modernity*. In *Reaction and the Avant-Garde: The Revolt against Liberal Democracy in Early Twentieth Century Britain*, Professor Tom Villis has explored the role of Belloc and the Chesterton brothers in the reactionary political movements of the Edwardian era. A further study, *British Catholics and Fascism*, takes his researches into the 1930s.

I am grateful to these authors for their insights and in particular to Professor Dudley Edwards for personally confirming my initial reservations about both Chestertons, but Cecil in particular. My thanks are also due to many people who have helped me over the years, including particularly A. N. Wilson, biographer of Hilaire Belloc, for his continual encouragement, and Dr Piers Brendon who advised about the historical background and who has read the manuscript and made a number of corrections. I am especially grateful to my brilliant sub-editor from the *Oldie* Deborah Asher for editing the text and verifying all the references.

I would also like to thank Professor Peter Hennessy, Aidan Mackey, Robin Brodhurst, Dr Tom Stuttaford, Louis Jebb, Christopher Silvester, Dr James Lefanu and the late Edda Tasiemka. I am immensely indebted to Abbot Geoffrey Scott of Douai Abbey who gave me the run of his magnificent library, which includes the Dominican Archive.

My greatest debt is to my wife Sara who has carried out a massive programme of research on my behalf and made a number of key discoveries in addition to typing out a scarcely legible manuscript. This book could not have been written without her.

I

A Legend in the Flesh

In the early years of the twentieth century a young man became a conspicuous and instantly recognisable figure in Fleet Street. Six feet two inches tall with long curly chestnut-coloured hair, he weighed about twenty stone, was dressed in a black cloak and carried a swordstick. From time to time he would stop to read a book or write something down, or he would pause in the middle of the road apparently struck by a sudden and important thought while the horse-drawn hansom cabs swirled about him. Much of the time he seemed to be chuckling over some unspoken joke of his own.

His great friend Charles Masterman recalled how Chesterton would write his column for the *Daily News* in a Fleet Street cafe while waiters hovered about him anxious that he might leave without remembering to pay for all the drinks he had had. One day the head waiter whispered to Masterman, 'Your friend – he very clever man. He sit and laugh and then he write. And then he laugh at what he write.'[1] Cecil Chesterton describes how his brother would sit for hours over a bottle of burgundy in one of his favourite haunts and how he would sometimes take a hansom cab 'half way up a street, keep it waiting for an hour or so and then drive half way down the street again'.

Many such stories were already circulating about him, mostly involving his absent-mindedness. He had for example been seen in a cafe talking animatedly to a young friend. He ordered two poached eggs but when they came he was so engrossed with the conversation that he swept them both into his lap, then summoned the waiter and ordered two more, saying, 'I seem to have lost the others.' Perhaps the best way of understanding

Chesterton's complex character is to liken him to a blind man. When it came to the practicalities of living he needed the constant help of other people – in early life his parents, and later his wife, Frances. He was so ignorant of day-to-day matters that he once expressed surprise on being told that you could buy pyjamas in a shop. The Catholic publisher and Tory MP Christopher Hollis describes meeting him at his room in a hotel and asking if they would use the lift or the stairs to go down. 'My wife will come,' he said, 'and she will decide.'[2]

The public knew Chesterton not just as a Fleet Street character but as one of the liveliest, most popular journalists then at work. He wrote a weekly column in the Liberal *Daily News* which was far and away the best feature of that outstanding paper. His *Daily News* articles, a selection of which were first published in book form in 1909 under the title *Tremendous Trifles*, gives us the essence of Chesterton at his greatest and his best. He never really deviated from the *Daily News* philosophy though inevitably with age and illness and disappointment his tone became less exuberant.

The titles of some of these articles advertise Chesterton's ability to write about almost anything – 'A Piece of Chalk'; 'What I Found in My Pocket'; 'On Lying in Bed'. This last one opened with a typical Chestertonian fancy: 'Lying in bed would be an altogether perfect and supreme experience if only one had a coloured pencil long enough to draw on the ceiling.' Another article contained his famous remark 'The only way of catching a train I have ever discovered is to miss the one before.' Behind such jokes lay a profound and serious message. Chesterton argued that even the most trivial things were significant: 'Either everything is interesting,' he once wrote, 'or nothing is.' It was the same message as Blake's 'To see a world in a grain of sand'. Chesterton did not see a world in a piece of chalk, but he saw something.

One thing that comes out of these articles most forcefully is Chesterton's abiding faith in democracy. A true democrat is a rare phenomenon and in Chesterton's day it was rarer still, especially among his contemporaries. Wells and Shaw, for example, proclaimed their faith in progress and socialism but had no special regard or sympathy for its supposed beneficiaries, the working classes – the so-called 'ordinary man'. Chesterton, however, championed democracy not as an abstract political concept but a practical reality, based on the good sense, even the wisdom, of these 'ordinary men'. The idea was made flesh in the jury system – then as now under attack – when the most important, even life-and-death, decisions were entrusted to twelve people taken off the street. He himself had recently been called for jury service on the basis, he says, that he lived in Battersea and his name began with C:

> The trend of our epoch up to this time has been consistently towards specialism and professionalism... Many Fabians have insisted that a greater part of our political work should be performed by experts. Many legalists have declared that the untrained jury should be altogether supplanted by the trained judge... the horrible thing about all legal officials, even the best, about all judges, magistrates, barristers, detectives and policemen, is not that they are wicked (some of them are good), not that they are stupid (several of them are quite intelligent), it is simply that they have got used to it. Strictly they do not see the prisoner in the dock; all they see is the usual man in the usual place. They do not see the awful court of judgment; they only see their own workshop. Therefore, the instinct of Christian civilisation has most wisely declared that into their judgments there shall upon every occasion be infused fresh blood and fresh thoughts from the street... Our civilisation has decided, and very justly decided, that determining the guilt or innocence of men is a thing too important to be trusted to trained men... When it wants a library catalogued or the solar system discovered, or any trifle of that kind, it uses up its specialists. But when it wishes anything done which is really serious, it collects twelve of the ordinary men standing round. The same thing was done, if I remember right, by the Founder of Christianity.[3]

That final sentence is a good example of Chesterton's journalistic skill. An idea which another man might have spread over a whole paragraph, he throws away almost as an afterthought. The effect is to bring the reader up with a jolt.

Democracy, he wrote in another article, 'is an attempt to bring the shy people out... Democracy means appealing to the diffident people. Democracy means getting those people to vote who would never have the cheek to govern: and (according to Christian ethics) the precise people who ought to govern are the people who have not the cheek to do it.'[4]

How had he come to this? The article began by describing how he had been about to board a train when he noted that some of his carriages had an 'Engaged' notice stuck on them. What was it all about? The answer became clear when the train stopped at a station near Cambridge and a group of men got out accompanied by a number of burly attendants: 'They were all dressed decorously in one colour; and they were chained together.' There was only one other person in the carriage – 'a small tired-looking man', and, to make conversation, Chesterton wondered aloud where the convicts were bound for. 'I don't s'pose they're goin' on an 'oliday at the seaside with little spades and pails,' the stranger replied. They both laughed and then after a short silence the stranger said, 'Well, I s'pose we 'ave to do it.'

'And in those three things,' Chesterton wrote, 'his first speech and his silence and his second speech, there were all the three great fundamental facts of the English democracy, its profound sense of humour, its profound sense of pathos and its profound sense of helplessness.'

Chance encounters with strangers – the favourite being a taxi driver – are the staple inspiration for columnists. Chesterton was no exception. Returning home from a trip on the Continent he falls into conversation on the train with an American lady on her first visit to England who remarks how much ivy there is – 'It covers the churches and it buries the houses. We have ivy but I have never seen it grow like that.' Chesterton begins to list all the things that are best about England in addition to the ivy – kippers, Free Trade, front gardens, hansom cabs, cricket and heavy breakfasts. After a pause he looks at the paper and starts reading the report of a speech in praise of the House of Lords by the Prime Minister, the arch-conservative Arthur Balfour. Balfour argues that the House of Lords should be preserved because it represents something 'in the nature of permanent public opinion of England, above the ebb and flow of the parties'.

Chesterton's rule before attacking somebody was always to begin by praising him. (As he wrote of the satirist in his book *Heretics*, 'He takes a pleasure in pointing out his enemy's strength before he points out his weaknesses.') So Balfour is 'a perfectly sincere patriot, a man who... thinks long and seriously about the public needs... moreover a man of exceptionable intellectual power.' Then comes the boot:

> In spite of all this, when I had read that speech I thought with a heavy heart that there was one more thing that I had to add to the list of the specially English things, such as kippers and cricket; I had to add the specially English kind of humbug. In France things are attacked and defended for what they are. The Catholic Church is attacked because it is Catholic, and defended because it is Catholic. The Republic is defended because it is Republican, and attacked because it is Republican. But here is the ablest of English politicians consoling everybody by telling them that the House of Lords is not really the House of Lords but something quite different, that the foolish accidental peers whom he meets every night are in some mysterious way experts on the psychology of the democracy; that if you want to know what the very poor want you must ask the very rich, and that if you want the truth about Hoxton, you must ask for it at Hatfield.[5]

A few quotations like this are enough to rebut George Orwell's absurd suggestion that every paragraph Chesterton wrote had to demonstrate the superiority of the Catholic Church. Not only are Catholics scarcely mentioned but there is little specifically about Christianity. What is true is that Chesterton's views about democracy were based on his religious beliefs, or possibly vice versa. Every individual was equal in the sight of God and the same principle ought to apply in politics. 'All men matter,' he wrote. 'You matter. I matter. It's the hardest thing in theology to believe.'[6]

'My main work was on the *Daily News*,' Chesterton wrote in his autobiography. The main organ of the Liberal Party, the paper[7] had been launched in 1846 with Charles Dickens its first editor (he lasted only two weeks). In 1901 it was acquired by the wealthy Quaker and cocoa manufacturer George Cadbury, primarily to air his heartfelt opposition to the Boer War, then raging in South Africa. Cadbury surprised the newspaper world when in 1902 he appointed a relatively unknown thirty-six-year-old provincial journalist, A. G. Gardiner, as his editor.

Passionately devoted to cricket, books and music (particularly Bach), A. G. Gardiner was a very English character. With his unassuming manner, moustache and glasses he might easily have been mistaken for a small-town bank manager. In reality he came to be one of the most successful and influential editors of his time, the friend and confidant of Liberal politicians who was regularly consulted by Asquith, Lloyd George and even President Woodrow Wilson's right-hand man, 'Colonel' Edward House. Gardiner was a self-educated man, the youngest of eight children of a Chelmsford cabinet maker who suffered from a drink problem and underemployment. Gardiner fought his way out of this unpromising background and, determined to be a journalist, he studied shorthand and joined the local paper, the *Chelmsford Chronicle*, before going to Blackburn to work on the *Northern Daily Telegraph*. He spent fifteen years there, becoming editor of its weekly edition in 1899.

Nobody can predict with any certainty whether someone will make a good editor. The qualities required – the capacity to make quick decisions, the ability to attract good journalists – are not always apparent until the editor takes charge of the paper. Typically for a newspaper proprietor, George Cadbury thought Gardiner would succeed because 'he was a very retiring man' – the last sort of person to make a good editor. But then the *Daily News* was not, as papers are today, devoted to exposures and scoops – it prided itself on its critics and columnists who, under Gardiner's editorship, included not only Chesterton, but Shaw, Wells, Belloc and Arnold Bennett. (Proving the fact that writers will contribute to a paper regardless of the fee if they like the editor, Wells wrote to Gardiner that he was happy to accept a lower fee than his usual 'out of affection for the editor of the *Daily News*'.)

Aside from his political interests, the self-educated Gardiner was exceptionally well read. A profile of the Prime Minister Asquith would include a reference to Tacitus by Lord Morley or a quote from Dr Johnson, as well as talk of Pitt, Fox, Gladstone and other political heroes – always included pointfully without the aim, so common with journalists, of showing off.

Gardiner became one of the most successful editors in the history of Fleet Street for a number of reasons. The first, perhaps the most important, was that the journalists liked him. E. C. Bentley, Chesterton's colleague and old school friend, wrote that he had 'a faculty of getting on good terms with people great and small'. His friend Frank Swinnerton wrote in his obituary of his 'mirth, kindness, wisdom and badinage'. Swinnerton, in his memoirs, also pays tribute to Gardiner's 'power to judge men', which in his view was the secret of his success. 'It is a power so rare that the majority of people daily show their lack of it. But Gardiner has only to look once at a man to know the essential things about him. I have never known him to be at fault and the list of men whom he first employed on the *Daily News* would in itself be a proof of his gift.'

Further proof of Gardiner's skill in assessing character was the series of profiles he contributed regularly to the Saturday edition of the *Daily News* and which were later published in book form.[8] These profiles included nearly all the major political and literary figures of the day, not forgetting the occasional cricketer, and the articles are still read by modern historians to gain an insight into the Edwardian period. In her famous book of essays about pre-First World War Europe, *The Proud Tower*,[9] the American historian Barbara Tuchman states that of all the sources listed, 'the most consistently informative and brilliant writer is A. G. Gardiner'.

Elsewhere she commends him as 'a particularly perceptive student of political character'.

Gardiner's insights into character were almost always accurate, proof of his powers of observation and often prophetic gifts, such as when he wrote of the young Winston Churchill, then a major force in the Liberal Party:

> Nothing is accidental about this remarkable man. Behind all his actions, however sudden or headlong, there is the calculation of a singularly daring and far-sighted mind – a mind that surveys the field with the eye of a strategist, weighs the forces, estimates the position and when the hour has come strikes with deadly sureness at the vulnerable place. 'Keep your eye on Churchill' should be the watchword of these days. Remember he is a soldier first, last and always. He will write his name big on our future. Let us take care he does not write it in blood.[10]

His ability to judge character was just as effective when it came to recruiting staff. Though some of his best men, including Chesterton himself, had already been chosen by his predecessor R. C. Lehmann, it was Gardiner who allowed them to exercise their talents to the full. They included Chesterton's oldest friend from his schooldays at St Paul's, Edmund Clerihew Bentley (1875–1956), later in life, according to Mrs Cecil Chesterton, 'suave and diplomatic with a suggestion of the city magnate'. At St Paul's Bentley was a natural ally for his fellow schoolboy Chesterton, sharing his love of jokes and foolery. 'He was remarkable,' Chesterton wrote, 'for the combination of an extraordinary gravity of visage with extreme agility and quickness of movement... It was a poetic pleasure to see him walk, a little pompously, down the street and suddenly scale a lamp-post like a monkey, with the alleged intention of lighting a cigarette, and then drop down and resume his walk with an unchanged expression of earnestness and serenity.'[11]

It was while bored in a chemistry lesson, according to Chesterton, that Bentley wrote his first Clerihew (so-called after his middle name):

Sir Humphrey Davy
Abominated gravy
He lived in the odium
Of having discovered sodium

It was the start of a craze. Chesterton and Bentley wrote several more and eventually published a book of clerihews, *Biography for Beginners*,[12] probably the only classic written by schoolboys. Chesterton provided the illustrations as well as writing some of the clerihews, including:

George the Third
Ought never have to have occurred
One can only wonder
At so grotesque a blunder

Bentley later wrote a famous detective story, *Trent's Last Case* (1913), and was responsible for reviving the popularity of the ballade, a poetic form enthusiastically taken up by Belloc, Chesterton and their followers, often to fill an empty space in a paper. It is difficult to do well as the structure is strict – three eight-line verses using the same rhyme scheme throughout, each verse ending with an identical one-line refrain, followed by a four-line 'envoi'. Bentley himself wrote one of the best examples, 'A Ballade of Vain Delight', which appeared in *One Hundred and One Ballades*, a collection by various hands published in 1931:

Howling the chorus of a comic song
I stagger home to bed at half-past three.
A spirited performance on the gong
Brings down my maiden-aunt in robe de nuit.
She tells me she considers it to be
Her duty to inform me that Miss Bliss
This morning saw me wink at Mélanie.
What is the use of going on like this?

Alone I wander mid the giddy throng.
Last Thursday evening, feeling like a spree
(Although my conscience told me it was wrong),
I put some strychnine in my parents' tea,
Alas! Alas! How now too well I see
My own improvidence and thoughtlessness.
Who is there now to love and comfort me?
What is the use of going on like this?

I'm growing deaf. My lungs are far from strong.
I stoop and shuffle like a chimpanzee.
My stories are interminably long.
I laugh at them myself consumedly.
I talk about my mother's pedigree.
I note a tendency to avarice.
These are thy wages, O debauchery!
What is the use of going on like this?

Envoi

Prince, what is that you're hiding? Let me see.
A note from Mr. Semitopolis!
He will be pleased to come and shoot, will he?
What is the use of going on like this?

After reading for the Bar, Bentley took to journalism, eventually becoming deputy editor to Gardiner as well as writing leaders for the paper.

A fellow leader writer, also literary editor, was Charles (CFG) Masterman (1878–1927). Like his great friend Chesterton, Masterman appealed to Gardiner partly thanks to his air of other-worldliness and his total lack of concern about his personal appearance – even when applying for a job at the *Daily News*: 'He wore an obsolete tall hat,' Gardiner remembered, 'and buttoned shoes that lacked half their buttons and he carried a derelict handbag tied round with a piece of rope in place of fastening.' His wife Lucy deplored his habit 'of cramming a large twelve and sixpenny book into each of his side pockets, accompanied very often by a six-inch pencil with a sharpened point and no protector, with disastrous effects on the appearance of any suit'. His school nickname was 'Wreck'.

Masterman inspired affection in his *Daily News* colleagues, especially Chesterton, who relished what he called his 'jovial pessimism' – Masterman confessed to Chesterton that he was 'the sort of man who goes under a hedge to eat an apple'.

Gardiner was fond of many of his contributors but his particular favourite was Chesterton, whose copy was always eagerly awaited at the paper's Bouverie Street office on Friday afternoons. 'It arrived in all sorts of shapes and by all sorts of means,' Wilson Harris, the paper's news editor records, 'occasionally in a text accompanied by its author, occasionally in a taxi unescorted, occasionally by post-office messenger. It was written on any kind of paper that might be at hand, once at any rate, when GKC was in the throes of moving house, on a piece of wallpaper.'

'What is really the matter with almost every paper,' Chesterton once wrote, 'is that it is much too full of things suitable to the paper.' In promoting Chesterton as he did, Gardiner seemed to be in agreement with him on this point. The Quaker-owned *Daily News* preached a message of pacifism and temperance, yet Chesterton wrote regularly about the military virtues, the joys of drinking and the wisdom of the Catholic Church. His pieces provoked a flood of angry letters from the non-conformist readers but Gardiner never objected, possibly aware of the truth of another of his columnist's observations – that 'if an editor can only make people angry enough they will write half his newspaper for nothing.'

Nothing, it seemed, could diminish Gardiner's devotion to his protégé: 'Mr Chesterton is the most conspicuous figure in the landscape of literary London,' he wrote in 1908,

> He is like a visitor out of some fairy tale, a legend in the flesh, a survivor of the childhood of the world... For all the ordinary material cares of life he has no taste, almost no consciousness. He never knows the time

of a train, has only a hazy notion of where he will dine and the doings of tomorrow are as profound a mystery as the contents of his pocket... He lives in a world of Romance peopled with giants and gay with the light laughter of fairies. The visible universe is full of magic and mystery. The trees are giants waving their arms in the air... It is well that he has his swordstick with him for one never knows what may turn up in this incredible world... I burst in on him one afternoon and found him engaged in a furious attack on a row of fat books, around which his sword flashed like the sword of Sergeant Troy around the figure of Bathsheba Everdene. His eyes blazed, his cheek paled and beads of perspiration – no uncommon thing – stood out on his brow.[13]

'Gardiner loved him dearly,' his biographer Stephen Koss writes,[14] as is confirmed by the fact that he named his youngest child Gilbert after him and invited Chesterton to be the boy's godfather. Chesterton became a friend of the family, and wrote these verses in Gardiner's little daughter's picture book:

> *This is the sort of book we like*
> *(For you and I are very small)*
> *With pictures stuck in anyhow*
> *And hardly any words at all.*
>
> *You will not understand a word*
> *Of all the words, including mine;*
> *Never you trouble; you can see,*
> *And all directness is divine –*
>
> *Stand up and keep your childishness*
> *Read all the pedants' screeds and strictures;*
> *But don't believe in anything*
> *That can't be told in coloured pictures.*

It was sad for both men that such intimacy, rare between an editor and a contributor, was not fated to last, and when Chesterton wrote his auto-biography in 1936 he made only a curt reference to Gardiner, describing him as a 'well-read and sympathetic editor'. Considering that Gardiner had done more than anyone to put the young Chesterton on the map this amounted to an insult which would have proved deeply upsetting to Gardiner. Typically reserved, he said nothing, but he must have known very well who was responsible for the parting of the ways.

2

THE INDULGED YOUNGER BROTHER

C ECIL CHESTERTON WAS BORN ON 12 NOVEMBER 1879 AND WAS
therefore five years younger than his brother Gilbert. Despite the age
gap the two boys developed an exceptionally close personal relationship,
though their characters were very different. Gilbert took after his father
Edward who, having retired early as head of the well-known estate agents
Chesterton & Sons (still in existence) on account of a heart condition,[1]
devoted much of his time to artistic hobbies – photography, watercolours,
stained glass, magic lanterns and toy theatres. Cecil had more in common
with his mother, Marie Louise. A more practical and forceful figure than
her husband, she recognised the exceptional qualities of her two sons and
did everything possible to provide them with a happy home. In this she
was so successful that Cecil never showed any inclination to fly the nest
until he was forced to do so when he joined the army in 1917.

As a result of their mother's indulgence and the emphasis she put
on encouraging their intellectual pursuits, both sons were peculiarly
indifferent to more practical matters like money or clothes. Cecil's wife
Keith writes:

> Gilbert and Cecil were, frankly, hopeless. They had literally no pride
> in their appearance: they were indeed quite oblivious and utterly indif-
> ferent as to what they looked like. Left to themselves, they would have
> worn a suit until it was shapeless, threadbare and incredibly ancient.
> Only the persistent removal of their garments for pressing and cleaning
> kept them fairly decent. A rigid discipline in their early youth might
> have inculcated a more desirable sense of fitness in these two bundles

of temperament and talent, but mercury is not easily handled, and though Gilbert affected dramatic cloaks and broad-brimmed hats and flourished swordsticks and daggers, he had no more sense of clothes than a steamroller. Cecil, I should say, had less.[2]

She adds that neither Chesterton had much money sense and that as a freelance journalist Cecil relied on frequent postal orders from his mother in order to survive.

Several witnesses refer to the way in which the Chesterton brothers were, from their earliest years, constantly arguing. There is not much evidence as to what they argued about though all insist that the arguments were always perfectly friendly. What is obvious is that the naturally benevolent Gilbert was not an argumentative type, which suggests that the arguments were instigated by Cecil, and that he was continually questioning his brother's opinions, thus gaining a hold over him.

The arguments of the two brothers were tolerated and even encouraged by their parents regardless of how long they lasted. There was a memorable occasion which Keith records of an argument lasting for over eighteen hours when the family were on holiday at Lowestoft. The boys were left undisturbed and continued wrangling even when their parents left them to it and went to bed. 'And then,' said Marie Louise, 'at half past two in the morning I heard Gilbert come down the stairs and go out at the front door which he shut firmly and quietly behind him.'[3]

The story, even if exaggerated by Keith, is remarkable but unsatisfactory in that there is no indication of what it was all about. It is the ending, when Gilbert walks out into the night, which suggests not so much that he had been defeated by Cecil but rather that he had given up trying to convince him. This is in accordance with his later description of his brother as a man of 'staggering obstinacy'. Whether or not there was some event in their childhood that caused Chesterton always to defer to his brother, he developed that habit, wrongly described as loyalty but more akin to subservience. Whatever the cause, it was an attribute that never changed and was to have tragic consequences for him.

After following his brother to St Paul's as a day boy, Cecil qualified as a surveyor and estate agent with the aim of working for the family firm. Finding the work uncongenial he became a freelance journalist, contributing to political journals like *The Outlook*, for which he also wrote theatre criticism.

It cannot have been easy being Cecil Chesterton. Like his brother he was highly intelligent, well read, a fluent writer and debater – but he suffered from two handicaps. One was that, unlike Gilbert, he was physically very unattractive and as short as his elder brother was tall. 'When one contrasted him with his dwarfish brother Cecil,' the historian Sir Denis Brogan wrote, 'it was easy to assert that the material for the Chesterton brothers had been divided in the proportion of one and a half to Gilbert and half to Cecil. No brothers could have looked less alike except in certain details of their features.'[4] Belloc's lawyer E. S. P. Haynes writes that 'his features were slightly fantastic and his voice was as loudly discordant as his laughter'.[5] The writer and notorious philanderer Frank Harris, who met Cecil as a contributor to the magazine *Vanity Fair* which he edited, describes him as 'a short stout man with round head and round red cheeks, a contradictory temperament and an extraordinary belief in his own ability'.[6] The conductor Thomas Beecham, later a backer of Cecil's paper the *New Witness*, writes in his memoir: 'I must confess that the first sight of him was a distinct shock... Here was one of the most ill-favoured and unprepossessing individuals I had ever looked on. His method of speech – or rather delivery of it – was hardly better for he stammered, stuttered and spluttered and seemed to swallow his tongue as well as his words when he became carried away by enthusiasm or indignation.'[7]

While Beecham quickly suppressed any feelings of disaffection because he greatly admired Cecil's journalism (suggesting also that he may have shared his less appealing prejudices), others were not so complimentary. The recollections of his contemporaries at St Paul's all attest that Cecil was a very unpopular boy, a fact that may have made his elder brother, who was correspondingly popular, develop a protective feeling towards him (if so, it was a feeling that was to persist in later life). Lucian Oldershaw told

Maisie Ward he detested Cecil because he would always monopolise the conversation when the others wanted to talk to Gilbert. 'An ugly little boy creeping about,' was Edward Fordham's brutal recollection. Another St Paul's contemporary, Leonard Woolf, long-suffering husband of Virginia, wrote in his memoir *Sowing* (1960): 'I never liked Cecil Chesterton partly because his physical appearance was so unprepossessing and partly because even then he had a streak of that kind of fanatical intolerance which seems to be fertilised, not by profound convictions, but by personal animosities. Gilbert was a very different kind of person... whereas Cecil seemed to have a grudge against the universe, the world and you in particular, G. K. gave one the immediate impression of goodwill, particular and general.'

Small wonder that the friendless Cecil, according to Keith, lavished his affection on his collection of cockroaches which he kept in a cardboard box, feeding them on bread and butter.

Cecil's second handicap, as he grew older, was not so easily surmounted. As a fellow journalist, Cecil could not help being known to the world as the brother of the better known, indeed famous, G. K. Chesterton. Whatever he did or wrote, his name, an uncommon one, was enough for his audience to connect him with Gilbert and inevitably to compare him, unfavourably, with the great man. 'There are two brothers,' an American journalist wrote in 1912, 'one is big and one is little, but both are decidedly portly... Gilbert is the bigger brother of the two in more ways than the one that meets the eye. He is a brilliant and far better and more widely-read writer.'[8]

Such comparisons were almost inevitable, so it is not surprising that in her memoir Keith is constantly at pains to point out that intellectually, the two brothers were equal, that Cecil was just as gifted and exceptional as Gilbert – a fact that the public seemed not to have appreciated. It was only natural that Cecil himself, particularly when encouraged by Keith and later by Belloc, should have come to the same conclusion.

Proof was provided by the publication in 1908 of a short book, *G. K. Chesterton: A Criticism*. No author was named on the title page though the informed reader would probably have guessed that Cecil had written the book. Whoever it was, the author certainly had first-hand knowledge of his subject: 'Both Battersea and Fleet Street are, I believe, adequately policed,' he wrote. 'But Mr Chesterton insists on traversing them armed with a sword-stick, and generally carrying a revolver in his pocket.' Then there was the impression Gilbert gave of being lazy:

> His extraordinary lavishness in the taking of cabs has tended to enforce that view... I know a man who met him in a little bookshop just opposite the law courts. A cab was, of course, waiting outside. GKC drove my friend to a neighbouring hostelry about six doors farther down, just opposite St Clement Danes. There they went in and talked over their wine for three quarters of an hour, the cab still waiting. The other man naturally thought that the cab was to take GKC back to Battersea. But he was in error. When they got out it appeared that the eminent journalist was only going to the office of the *Illustrated London News* which is just about another six doors down the Strand. The total distance traversed could not have been more than a hundred and fifty yards. The time occupied was something over an hour.

Such stories no doubt helped to foster the G. K. Chesterton legend, but it was not as if he wanted or even needed publicity. Chesterton was already very well known not only as a columnist on the *Daily News* but as the author of the novel *The Napoleon of Notting Hill* (1904) as well as books on Browning and Dickens, all of which had been highly praised. What purpose could be served by a book assessing his achievement and prospects by an unnamed author? If Chesterton himself had an answer, it can only be guessed at, as he never once referred to the book when writing about his brother. Did he infer, as others may have done, that Cecil was making a misguided attempt to assert himself as an authority on his brother's work whilst at the same time turning it into an elaborate private joke by concealing his identity?

In a short preface, Cecil makes an improbable claim to be the adviser and protector of youth, his brother being primarily a man of ideas, a preacher and a propagandist: 'What is quite clear is that at the present moment he is profoundly influencing a great number of people. How far he is influencing them for good and how far for evil is surely a matter well worth discussing.'

The possibility that Chesterton might be influencing his readers 'for evil' is obvious nonsense, but if Cecil was attempting a joke, it was one that misfired. Although much of what he writes could be interpreted as teasing badinage, the kind of thing one can imagine that Cecil went in for during the brothers' interminable arguments, there is no disguising the general tone of the book, a tone not of a younger brother but of an older one, an almost schoolmasterly tone, praising the good points but at the same time pointing out the areas where there is still more work to be done: 'Unless he controls his effervescent desire to write everything that comes into his head he will never write the best that he might have written.' The language of the school report is unmistakable. At the same time it gives a clue to the strange relationship of the two brothers. Cecil thinks he knows best what Gilbert should be doing, what he should think about politics or religion, and because the world has not recognised that he is the person best qualified to judge his brother's merits and demerits he does so at great length and publicly, *but anonymously*. And the reason for anonymity is that he is well aware that the world would find it bizarre for a younger brother publicly to exhibit an attitude of superiority to his better known, more talented sibling.

Keen to parade his knowledge of history and literature Cecil writes in ponderous prose about his brother – referred to throughout as 'Mr Chesterton' – giving praise where it is due but often in an aloof, slightly condescending and even a sneering way. Thus one of the stories in Gilbert's book *The Club of Queer Trades* (see below) 'showed not only Mr Chesterton's usual qualities of energy and humour, but a certain careful artistry *which is not so commonly his* [italics added]'. Likewise Mr Chesterton fails altogether to appreciate the genius of Ibsen thanks to his 'incurable inability (or, it may be obstinate unwillingness) to comprehend his method and meaning'.

It seemed as though Cecil's commendable urge to protect his unworldly elder brother had developed into a need to control and direct him. Central to Cecil's critique is the failure of Gilbert to make the transition from being a journalist to the more serious role of literary critic – he ought to be aiming higher, in other words. In response to what was at the time a growing demand for books about authors, Chesterton had already written *Robert Browning* (1903) and *Charles Dickens* (1906), both of which met with Cecil's general approval. His brother had ceased to be primarily a journalist and had become 'a man of letters'. In a tone almost of exasperation, Cecil urges his brother 'Mr Chesterton' to think of his legacy, his posthumous fame. A serious study of Browning or Dickens, he writes, 'ought to aim at permanence' and Chesterton had made the mistake of including in his studies of these two authors references to contemporary writers whose names would mean nothing to future generations.

It annoyed Cecil that his brother was so little concerned with what Belloc was later to call his 'place in English literature'. He could not understand how he could be so careless of his own reputation. It must have upset him when Chesterton wrote in 1905, 'I have no feeling for immortality. I don't care for anything except to be in the present stress of life as it is. I would rather live now and die, from an artistic point of view, than keep aloof and write things that will remain in the world hundreds of years after my death… It so happens that I couldn't be immortal; but if I could I wouldn't want to be.'[9]

Such a creed was consistent with Chesterton's lifelong insistence that he was not, as Cecil wanted him to be, 'a man of letters': 'I have always been and presumably will always be a journalist,' he wrote, and in what reads almost as a response to Cecil, Chesterton noted in the introduction to *All Things Considered* (1908), a collection of articles he had written for the *Illustrated London News*, 'I cannot understand the people who take literature seriously, but I can love them and I do.' He regretted, he said, that so many of the articles in this book were very serious:

It is so easy to be solemn; it is so hard to be frivolous. Let any honest reader shut his eyes for a few moments, and approaching the secret tribunal of his soul, ask himself whether he would really rather be asked in the next two hours to write the front page of *The Times*, which is full of long leading articles, or the front page of *Tit-Bits* which is full of short jokes. If the reader is the fine conscientious fellow I take him for, he will at once reply that he would rather on the spur of the moment write *The Times* articles than one *Tit-Bits* joke. Responsibility, a heavy and cautious responsibility of speech, is the easiest thing in the world: anybody can do it. That is why so many elderly and wealthy men go in for politics. They are responsible because they have not the strength of mind left to be irresponsible. It is more dignified to sit still than to dance the Barn Dance. It is also easier.

In one respect Cecil's book appeared to be prophetic when he wrote that Mr Chesterton 'is a lover of detective stories... it occurs to him, I should imagine, that it would be rather fun to write a philosophic detective story.' This suggestion looks like an inspired prediction, apparently foreseeing what was to be Chesterton's most famous and longest-lasting creation, Father Brown. It is possible that Cecil put the idea into Gilbert's head, as the first Father Brown story written at the time of Chesterton's move to Beaconsfield in 1909 followed closely on the publication of Cecil's book the previous year. It is more likely, however, that Cecil knew that his brother was already toying with the idea and could not resist making something out of his inside information.

Cecil was aware that Chesterton had previously created a Sherlock Holmes-like figure in his book *The Club of Queer Trades*, published in 1905. It is a collection of stories (which Chesterton himself illustrated) in which the part of the detective is played by a retired High Court judge, Basil Grant, whose brilliant legal career fizzles out as his behaviour on the Bench becomes increasingly eccentric: 'Things came to a head in that celebrated diamond case in which the Prime Minister himself, that brilliant patrician,[10] had to come forward, gracefully and reluctantly, to give evidence against his valet. After the detailed life of the household had been thoroughly exhibited, the judge requested the Premier again to step forward, which he did with quiet dignity. The judge then said, in a sudden grating voice: "Get a new soul. That thing's not fit for a dog. Get a new soul."'

Grant finally cracks up at the climax of a 'long and complex' libel action involving 'two very eminent and powerful financiers': 'At last, after weeks of work and rhetoric, the time came for the great judge to give a summing-up; and one of his celebrated masterpieces of lucidity and pulverising logic was eagerly looked for. He had spoken very little during the prolonged affair, and he looked sad and lowering at the end of it. He was silent for a few moments and then burst into a stentorian song. His remarks (as reported) were as follows: "O rowty-owty-tiddly-outy, Tiddly-outy, Highty-ighty, tiddly-ighty, Tiddly-ighty-ow." He then retired from public life and took the garret in Lambeth.'

In obscure retirement Grant spends his time, like Holmes, at the beck and call of people who find themselves in baffling and apparently dangerous situations, all of which are traced back to the Club of Queer Trades – 'a society consisting exclusively of people who have invented some new and curious way of making money'. The first story, 'The Tremendous Adventures of Mr Brown', is about a man who runs an agency which in exchange for an annual subscription will organise dramatic and unexpected adventures to liven up your otherwise humdrum existence. In the second story, 'The Painful Fall of a Great Reputation', impoverished Baronet Sir Walter Cholmondeliegh has hired himself out as a stooge to be insulted at society dinners by a man about town who has thereby acquired a reputation for brilliant Oscar Wilde-like repartee, all of it scripted in advance by Sir Walter.

Cecil makes no reference to what is most obvious about these inspired stories – the identification of Chesterton himself with the retired judge, Basil Grant, a man who the world considers to be eccentric or even mad but who turns out to be better able to explain life's mysteries than supposedly more worldly characters.

Using some of Chesterton's own props – setting out on an investigation with a revolver, a swordstick and an old cloak – Grant makes a number of observations which could easily have been found in one of Chesterton's essays. So, in an argument with his friend Professor Chudd about Zulus, Grant says, 'I am very far from being certain that the Zulu is at an inferior evolutionary stage, whatever the blazes that may mean. I do not think there is anything stupid or ignorant about howling at the moon or being afraid of devils in the dark… why should a man be thought a sort of idiot because he feels the mystery and peril of existence itself?'

The narrator of the stories, Swinburne, also sounds like Chesterton at times, describing how he first met Grant at the National Liberal Club and got into conversation about politics and God: '…for men always talk about the most important things to total strangers. It is because in the total stranger we perceive man himself: the image of God is not disguised by resemblances to an uncle or doubts of the wisdom of a moustache.'

Travelling on a bus through the dreary streets of North London, Grant tells Swinburne, 'You must always remember… that the very vileness of the life of these ordered plebeian places, bears witness to the victory of the human soul… I agree that they have to live in something worse than barbarism. They have to live in a fourth-rate civilisation. But yet I am practically certain that the majority of people here are good people. And being good is an adventure far more violent and daring than sailing round the world.'

If Cecil misses the comic self-portrait of Chesterton in Basil Grant he also fails to comment on the fact that Grant has 'a practical brother', Rupert, who acts as a foil, a Dr Watson to Grant's Sherlock Holmes. Like Watson, Rupert, who is described as a private detective but who has also been, like Cecil, a house agent and a journalist, has a way of getting the wrong end of most sticks, and pursuing any amount of red herrings: 'Rupert Grant was a clever young fellow, but he had that tendency which youth and cleverness, when sharply combined, so often produce, a some-what extravagant scepticism. He saw doubt and guilt everywhere, and it was meat and drink to him.'

The fourth story, 'The Singular Speculation of the House-Agent', concerns one Lieutenant Drummond Keith, an eccentric who tells wildly improbable stories about himself:

'He has one fault,' said Basil thoughtfully, 'or virtue as you may happen to regard it. He tells the truth in too exact and bald a style; he is too voracious.' 'Oh! if you are going to be paradoxical,' said Rupert contemptuously, 'be a bit funnier than that. Say, for instance, that he has lived all his life in one ancestral manor.' 'No, he's extremely fond of change of scene,' replied Basil dispassionately, 'and of living in odd places. That doesn't prevent his chief trait being verbal exactitude. What you people don't understand is that telling a thing crudely and coarsely as it happened makes it sound frightfully strange. The sort of things Keith recounts are not the sort of things that a man would make up to cover himself with honour; they are too absurd. But they are the sort of things that a man would do if he were sufficiently filled with the soul of skylarking.' 'So far from paradox,' said his brother, with something rather like a sneer, 'you seem to be going in for journalese proverbs. Do you believe that truth is stranger than fiction?' 'Truth must of necessity be stranger than fiction,' said Basil placidly. 'For fiction is the creation of the human mind, and therefore is congenial to it.'

It is obvious that in Rupert Grant we have a satirical portrait of Cecil Chesterton and a not altogether charitable portrait at that. 'Rupert Grant generally came down late in a rather lordly way to breakfast,' the narrator writes. 'He contrived, I don't know how, to achieve always the attitude of the indulged younger brother.' While Basil/Gilbert is calm and collected, quietly chuckling over life's absurdities, Rupert/Cecil is excitable and impatient, convinced of his own rightness, speaking occasionally 'in that sweet and steely voice which he reserved for great occasions and practised for hours together in his bedroom'.

If Basil Grant was Chesterton in disguise, the same could just as well be said of his successor, the amateur detective Father Brown. Chesterton made no secret of the fact that the character was inspired by his chance meeting in 1904 with a Catholic priest, Father John O'Connor, who became a close friend, particularly of his wife Frances. The idea that especially appealed to Chesterton, after talking to Father O'Connor, was the contrast between the public's view of a priest as an unworldly, innocent figure with a mind filled with beautiful religious thoughts and the reality of a man who as a result of hearing confessions was better acquainted than most with all the varieties of human frailty and wickedness.

O'Connor may have been the inspiration for Brown – his props (he wore a flat black hat, carried a large umbrella and usually several brown-paper parcels) were incorporated into the stories. But there was little else to connect him with the fictional priest. Nor was there much to connect Brown with his church:[11] he appears to have no fixed parish, popping up in all kinds of unlikely places including California and South America, and there is no description of him saying mass or hearing confessions, the sort of thing that Graham Greene describes in his novels.

Like Grant who had his brother Rupert, Father Brown has his own Dr Watson in many of the tales. His name is Flambeau and he is introduced to readers in the very first story, 'The Blue Cross'. At that stage Flambeau is a notorious French criminal, a mastermind who has baffled the police with a series of brilliant ruses, like altering all the numbers of the houses in a street overnight to confuse his pursuers. But in Father Brown Flambeau meets his match and is so impressed by his detective skills and his religious convictions that he abandons a life of crime and becomes the priest's constant companion. The strange thing about Flambeau (meaning flaming torch) is that though a Frenchman he speaks perfect English and never lapses into his native language. Even when excited, he uses typically English exclamations: 'By Jove!' 'By George!' and even 'Oh bosh!', but never a 'Mon Dieu!' or a 'Zut alors!'

When we learn that Flambeau has served in the French army and also owns a little boat, it seems obvious that the character is inspired by Belloc, a human *flambeau* in Chesterton's eyes and similarly a Frenchman with a perfect command of English. The interesting thing is that in both fantasies, the *Club of Queer Trades* and the Father Brown stories, the nature of the relationships has been reversed. Whereas in real life Chesterton was led by the nose by Cecil and Belloc, once he moves into the world of the imagination he becomes the dominant partner to whom Rupert and Flambeau, who generally reach the wrong conclusions, habitually defer. There may even be some implied criticism of Belloc, as when Brown suggests, 'Those who are quick in talking are not always quick in listening.'

There is nothing to suggest that Belloc ever read the Father Brown stories (he was known to have no liking for detective fiction). Although he wrote several public declarations of his great admiration of his friend's works, in private he made known his lack of sympathy with Chesterton's style. The only occasions on which Belloc wrote openly in praise of Chesterton was when he enthused about his drawings, which he considered to be better than his books and journalism: 'He would with a swift pencil capable of giving every gradation in emphasis, from the lightest touch to the dead black print and line, set down in gestures that were like caresses, sometimes like commands, sometimes like rapier thrusts, the whole of what a man or woman was and he would get the thing down on the paper with the rapidity which only comes from complete possession... He drew of such human beings and their emotions, even their full characters, presented at once hundreds upon hundreds. No one else has done this.'[12]

Belloc wrote a handful of satirical novels, mostly about politics, all of which Chesterton illustrated. He would arrive at Chesterton's Beaconsfield home with the plot of his next book, claiming that he could not possibly write the story until Chesterton had done the illustrations as the characters only came to life once they had been drawn. 'He is marvellous,' Belloc wrote to his friend Mrs Raymond Asquith, daughter-in-law of the Prime Minister. 'He is far better with his pencil than his pen. I delight in the talents of my fellow man and his drawing of the human face is amazing.'

Chesterton could draw long before he could write – even before he could read, being very backward at reading as a small child. He inherited his artistic talent from his father Edward who had recognised his gift at an early stage. When he failed to excel at St Paul's – he never went to university – Edward arranged for Gilbert to enrol at the famous Slade School of Fine Art in London. But here too he failed to prosper and left after only a year, the principal, Henry Tonks, telling his parents tactfully that they 'could not teach him anything without spoiling his originality'.

What Edward Chesterton had failed to realise was that his son – 'very short-sighted' according to his friend Bentley – was a largely self-taught cartoonist who had little or no interest in drawing from life. A photograph taken at the Slade shows the young Chesterton posed in front of his canvas, brushes and palette in hand. He looks uncomfortable and out of place. It is not surprising that none of his drawing from life survives. As he wrote when describing a walk on the downs with his chalks: 'Do not, for heaven's sake, imagine I was going to sketch from Nature. I was going to draw devils and seraphim, and blind old gods... and seas of strange green, and all the sacred or monstrous symbols that look so well in bright colours on brown paper.'[13]

At St Paul's he covered his school books with doodles, a frieze of grotesques to ornament the text like the gargoyles on a cathedral: 'I like gargoyles,' he told Beachcomber, 'and every kind of grotesque thing, whereas Belloc likes diagrams and military maps.' This compulsion was to last throughout his life and there are several descriptions of him sitting at meetings, decorating the agenda and the blotting paper with his cartoons. Certain faces recurred: George III, Joseph Chamberlain, Whistler, Mr Gladstone and lean aquiline figures of the Sherlock Holmes or Don Quixote type. As a boy, his godson Nicolas Bentley, whose father Edmund was Chesterton's oldest friend, was inspired to become a cartoonist watching Chesterton draw. 'If any one person disposed me towards the profession of artist, it was Gilbert. To watch him at work, drawing forth handfuls of luminous powdery chalks from his pockets and sketching embattled Greeks and Persians, or perhaps it was Cyrano or the Cid or Mephistopheles or Mr Balfour – watching him put them down on brown paper with clear deliberate strokes, suggested that it was the easiest thing in the world.'[14]

A typical Chesterton doodle, done at a *GK's Weekly* board
meeting in 1929 (Douai archive). See page 205 also.

When authors describe the physical appearance of their characters they no doubt have in mind an image of a real person. Chesterton more probably saw them as drawings out of his head, and once you have seen his work it is hard not to picture them in that same satirical style, for example the characters described at the opening of *The Man Who Was Thursday*: 'That young man with the long auburn hair and the impudent face... That old gentleman with the wild, white beard and the wild white hat... That scientific gentleman with the bald egg-like head and the bare bird-like neck...'

Cecil makes no mention in his book of his brother's artistry, the drawings in the *Club of Queer Trades* or the fact that he had illustrated his friend Bentley's clerihews when he was still at school. In his urge to make Chesterton think of his posthumous fame, he misses altogether his vision of humans not only as extraordinary but essentially comic, in keeping with the characters he doodled on any paper surface. His pictorial imagination is evident in much of his writing. Man is 'a strange animal with two legs' who makes himself look even more ridiculous by putting a top hat on his head. His writing is full of these graphic insights, as in *Heretics* when he writes: 'The supreme adventure is being born. There we do walk suddenly into a splendid and startling trap. There we do see something of which we had not dreamed before. Our father and mother do lie in wait for us and leap out on us like brigands from a bush. Our uncle is a surprise. Our aunt is, in the beautiful common expression, a bolt from the blue.' It is easy to imagine a series of Chestertonian drawings to illustrate these sentences – the parents crouching behind the bush waiting to pounce on the unsuspecting baby, the stout aunt hurtling through the sky. It is a series of cartoons in words.

Sadly, with the exception of his first books of nonsense verse, Chesterton illustrated only one of his subsequent works, *The Club of Queer Trades*. *The Innocence of Father Brown*, the first volume of the series, has eight full-page plates, the work of one Sidney Seymour Lucas. His drawings, in the style of Sherlock Holmes illustrator Sidney Paget, show the priest, described by Chesterton as bustling and untidy, as a sleek, slim figure with nicely polished shoes. The remaining Father Brown books were not illustrated.

The Father Brown stories were never intended to be conventional detective stories and the ingenious plots do not stand up to any kind of scientific analysis. As an anonymous reviewer in the *Nation* wrote of the first volume, 'The central idea in each case is so striking as to hide the inherent flaws... None of the mysterious cases that Father Brown solves by his infallible insight could have occurred as stated... Readers of literal minds, and readers who have been taken captive by the meticulous methods of Sherlock Holmes may find these detective stories unsatisfying, but in literary brilliance and originality of thought they must rank above the ingenious structures of Mr Conan Doyle.'[15]

Chesterton himself always insisted that the solution to any murder mystery had to be something simple. He had no time for those detective stories which relied on a complicated explanation, the kind of thing he parodied in his 1925 essay 'How to Write a Detective Story':

> The vicar's first curate did indeed intend to murder him and loaded and then lost his pistol, which was picked up by the second curate and placed on a particular shelf in the vestry to incriminate the third curate, who had a long and lingering love affair with the niece of the organist, who is not really the niece of the organist but the long-lost daughter of the vicar; the organist, being in love with his ward, transfers the pistol to the coat pocket of the second curate, but the coat is accidentally put on by the first curate, who pulls out the pistol in mistake for a pocket handkerchief, and the vicar mistaking him for the real owner of the coat (who had done him a deep and complicated injury twenty years ago in Port Said) rushes furiously upon him (the pronouns are getting mixed like everything else) so that the holder of the pistol (whoever he may be by this time) is forced to fire in self-defence and the vicar falls dead.[16]

Just as their characters can be visualised as Chesterton drawings, so the settings of the Father Brown stories often call to mind the toy theatre which so fascinated Chesterton from childhood onwards. The landscapes or streetscapes are pictured more like stage scenery than realistic settings; the skies, often described in lurid and improbable colours, are backcloths against which, in many of the stories, a group of characters are imagined with Father Brown inevitably hovering unnoticed in the shadows: 'In the cool blue twilight of two steep streets in Camden Town, the shop at the corner, a confectioner's, glowed like the butt of a cigar.'[17] In the mind's eye the curtain rises on the stage of the toy theatre, and the drama begins.

Father Brown became Chesterton's most popular creation and magazines were prepared to pay substantial sums for a new story featuring the famous priest. This proved a valuable source of income whenever his paper, *GK's Weekly*, which he kept going in memory of Cecil, ran into financial difficulties. As Dorothy Collins, Chesterton's faithful secretary for the last ten years of his life, remembered: 'To the large printers' bills for *GK's Weekly* we owe some of the Father Brown stories. I would say, "We have only got £100 in the bank." "Oh well, we must write another Father Brown story," and this would be done at lightning speed a day or two later from a few notes on the back of an envelope.'

It was ironic that Cecil, who had pontificated in his 1908 book about 'the need to aim for permanence', should end up after his death as the direct cause of Chesterton's resorting to potboilers in order to find the money to preserve his brother's legacy.

3

KEITH AND FRANCES

R EADERS WHO REACH THE END OF MAISIE WARD'S OFFICIAL
biography of Chesterton published in 1943 may be surprised by
Appendix C on page 559 when Miss Ward, who has maintained a cautious
considerate note throughout the book, changes gear and becomes savage
and satirical.[1]

Her target is a rival Chesterton chronicler, Cecil Chesterton's widow,
whose book *The Chestertons* had appeared two years earlier in 1941 when
the author was in her seventies. Mrs Cecil Chesterton, as she called herself in later life, had a wide variety of different names, some male, some
female. She was born Ada Eliza Jones but never used the name Ada and
later changed Eliza to the grander-sounding Elizabeth. She wrote novels
using the name Margaret Hamilton and drama criticism and other journalism as J. K. Prothero, the J standing for Johnny, the K for Keith, the name
by which she was most commonly known. She was born on 30 June 1869
(not in 1888 as she stated in *Who's Who*) and so was ten years older than
her husband-to-be, Cecil. She died aged ninety-two on 20 January 1962,
having outlived almost all her contemporaries.

Keith, as we shall call her, was a remarkable character, the only person
in the Chesterton entourage to have experienced life in its rougher
aspects. Both her father, described in the *Oxford Dictionary of National
Biography* as a 'manufacturer of braces', and her brother were journalists
and she had earned her living as a freelance since the age of sixteen, at
a time when women journalists were almost unheard of – one reason
why she used a male pseudonym. Short and dark-haired, she was 'one
of the boys' in the tough but generally high-spirited, hard-drinking Fleet

44

Street world, prepared to turn her hand to reporting, theatre and book criticism and romantic love stories serialised in newspapers and women's magazines. In his autobiography, Chesterton paid tribute to her versatility: 'It marked a sort of sublimation of the Fleet Street spirit in my sister-in-law that, within healthy limits, she not only could do everything, but she would do anything. Her work was patch-work of the wildest and most bizarre description… She would turn easily from a direct and demagogic, though quite tragically sincere, appeal in a Sunday paper against official oppression of poor mothers to an almost cynical modern criticism of the most sophisticated modern plays.' Chesterton told the story of how Keith once received an urgent telegram from the editor of a Scottish newspaper who was featuring one of her romances: 'You have left your hero and heroine tied up in a cavern under the Thames and they are not even married.'

'She had seven or eight years of frantically hard hackwork to support practically a whole family,' Cecil told Belloc in 1911, when the two men first collaborated on *The Party System*, 'a mother, an invalid sister and brother who is dying of consumption. It is one of the hardest cases of a person being sacrificed to necessity that I know of.' Cecil, who was besotted with her, became a friend of the Jones family and a regular visitor to their home in Hammersmith, always bringing with him a bunch of carnations for Keith. He pestered her with proposals of marriage and wrote her love poems in the style of Swinburne:

> *Dearest, your royal heart*
> *Puissant and strong*
> *Bids all the hosts of night*
> *Break into song*
> *Hark! Where the clear stars wheel*
> *In dark employ*
> *Are not the sons of God*
> *Shouting for joy?*

Keith rejected his initial proposals but, like many women, including Belloc's wife, Elodie, she was attracted to Cecil, unaffected by the physical ugliness described by his male acquaintances. 'He had the same wavy hair as Gilbert,' she wrote, 'and his head was finely shaped. He was short but at that time slim, with a very charming smile, a plain face and highly critical eyebrows.' Above all she admired his skill as a fellow journalist and debater. 'He was an amazingly swift worker with a capacity for prolonged effort which I have never found equalled.'

If ever a man needed the restraining influence of a level-headed woman it was the rash, conceited Cecil. But Keith was not fitted to play that role. Though a fearless and resourceful reporter who later trekked round Stalin's Russia enduring all manner of squalor and discomfort, she was as prone to erratic judgements and inconsistency as was Cecil. At the same time she did nothing to dampen his overweening self-confidence. As Cecil's sweetheart she persuaded herself that he was just as clever and as talented as his famous brother – that in every way they were equals and, in some respects, when it came to editing a paper, for example, Cecil was far superior to his brother. She joined forces with him in his various activities, encouraging him to take risks and, in the view of Belloc's worldly and eccentric lawyer E. S. P. Haynes, dominating him. There is no evidence that they were lovers prior to their marriage in 1917 and little evidence that Keith was greatly interested in men.

Maisie Ward's attack on Keith is primarily concerned with convicting her of inaccuracy. She begins by citing Keith's claim that Chesterton liked red-headed women and though married to Frances Blogg was secretly in love with her sister Gertrude. Ward is able to state, categorically, that Gertrude's hair was definitely not red.

Auberon Waugh writes that in his experience complaints about inaccuracy invariably conceal 'a deeper unease'. Beneath her point-by-point denunciation of Keith's narrative one can sense a general disapproval of the way in which an interloper and an unbeliever has broken into the calm and Catholic Chestertonian world, revealing unseemly family tensions and even – horror of horrors – details of Chesterton's sex life (or rather his alleged lack of it). Maisie Ward is especially critical of the way in which Keith writes about Chesterton's devoted wife Frances, whom she knew well.

Frances and Keith had nothing in common apart from their respective love for the two Chesterton brothers. Frances, who had married Gilbert in 1901, was born Frances Blogg, eldest of seven children of a one-time diamond merchant George Blogg who died when Frances was fourteen.[2] She had been educated at an Anglican convent school in Windsor, was devoutly Anglo Catholic, wrote poetry, and suffered from ill health of one kind or another throughout her life. When Chesterton visited her family in the arty-crafty London suburb of Bedford Park he fell instantly in love with her and remained so until his dying day. The basis of what he called his 'indefensibly fortunate and happy life', his friend Bentley wrote, 'were the devotion of his mother and the devotion of his wife. He moved directly from the care of one to the care of the other.'[3]

Unlike Cecil, Chesterton had very limited experience of women and was almost certainly a virgin when he married Frances in 1901. But that did not stop him writing copiously on the subject of women, marriage and even sex. He was not the only writer to base his view of all women on one particular woman – in this case his wife. But the fact that he did so gives us a few insights into the character of Frances Chesterton.

Quite apart from Keith she has not had a very good press. Belloc's sister Marie Belloc Lowndes calls her 'narrow-minded and penurious'[4] and Christopher Hollis remarks, rather snootily, that 'she was not a woman of especially outstanding intellectual power'.[5] Such criticism made little allowance for her mental and physical frailty. 'I don't get to London very often,' she told Lucy Masterman. 'I so easily get attacks of neuritis which attack my back and neck and make me almost helpless.'[6] Like her mother and her brother, she suffered from depression (her brother Knollys committed suicide) and all her life struggled against a variety of ailments – a painful limp, arthritis of the spine, rheumatism, neuralgia, pneumonia – 'recurrent problems of pains and depressions', according to Chesterton, who called her life 'in many ways a very heroic tragedy'.[7]

When Chesterton wrote about his wife (disguised as the entire female sex) he had two images in his mind – one of the woman summoning her husband from the pub where he was enjoying himself with his male friends ('the eternal voice of woman summoning man from the tavern') and the second of a wife practising the virtue of thrift while her man squandered the money he had earned. The two ideas were inter-related because the money tended to be squandered in the pub – and not only money, but time: 'These women are not exasperated merely at the amount of money that is wasted in beer; they are exasperated also at the amount of time that is wasted in talk.'[8]

This picture, written in 1910, exactly matches the complaints made public many years later by his sister-in-law Keith who, along with Belloc and Cecil, resented the way Frances had taken over the organisation of every practical aspect of her husband's life (his one-time secretary Mrs Meredith remembers Chesterton at meal times asking Frances, 'Do you think I should have a little more?'). Neither Cecil nor Keith seems to have recognised that given Chesterton's inability to deal with even the most basic issues it was inevitable that he would be as reliant on Frances as would a child – inevitable too that he would come to regard her as his controller. But it was not a situation that he especially resented: 'There is no hope for men,' he wrote, 'who do not boast that their wives bully them.' In this respect he persuaded himself that Frances was typical of all her sex, concluding, 'The average woman is a despot! The average man is a serf.'[9]

Frances, according to Keith's account, had not joined in what she calls the 'Fleet Street junketings' – the Doctor Johnson evening with Chesterton dressed as Johnson, the Pickwick evenings and the parties at the Chesterton family home in Warwick Gardens – but still it came as a shock when in 1909, after one such congenial dinner with Keith and Cecil, Chesterton made the ominous announcement, 'Frances wants to leave London.'

Gilbert and Frances moved from Battersea to Beaconsfield in Buckinghamshire and remained there for the rest of their lives. It was the cause of intense resentment on the part of Cecil and Keith, who never forgave Frances for, as they saw it, taking Chesterton away from them, away from all their happy London get-togethers and, in their opinion, virtually imprisoning him in a suburban backwater where his genius was stifled. It might have been better, in Cecil's view, if she had chosen a really rustic retreat where Chesterton could sit in a country pub 'talking to country folk and drinking country ale'. But Beaconsfield was the haunt of stockbrokers and solicitors commuting to London from the newly built railway station, and a far cry from the colourful unpredictable world of Fleet Street.

Frances's overriding motive in leaving London was to improve her husband's health and provide him with a routine and an environment in which he could do what she wanted him to do, which was to write books. In this she was partially successful. In the years that followed the move to Buckinghamshire, Chesterton produced a stream of books including studies of Stevenson, Cobbett and St Francis as well as his most successful religious work, *The Everlasting Man*. At the same time he continued to lecture and write journalism, notably a 2,000-word weekly essay for the *Illustrated London News*. It is doubtful whether he could have been so productive if faced with all the distractions of London life. In addition, Frances was able to control his diet and his drinking, with the result that his health improved.

In a more important sphere, however, Frances must have known she was powerless to influence her husband. She could separate him from his brother but she could not diminish the powerful influence that Cecil exercised over him. Unlike Keith, Frances left no memoir and even told Chesterton when he wrote his autobiography that she wanted to be kept out of it. She therefore remains, rather like William Cobbett's wife as described by Chesterton, 'in the background of his life in a sort of powerful silence'.[10] What she felt about Cecil she kept to herself, but her close friend Lucy Masterman wrote later: 'Frances Chesterton could have no more than tepid feelings for him because he was constantly borrowing from GKC when they were not well off.'[11] (It seems likely that when Cecil later launched a vicious campaign against Lucy Masterman's husband Charles[12] the temperature of her feelings would have dropped from 'tepid' to uncomfortably cold.) Once or twice in the ensuing years when Chesterton, who had taken on Cecil's responsibilities following his death, became overburdened with financial and other worries, Frances tried to intervene on his behalf but was always rebuffed, so that even when he was dead Cecil managed, in the long run, to frustrate her campaign to preserve her husband's health and save him from a premature death.

As for money, Belloc who, like Cecil, borrowed money from Chesterton, said that he spent it 'like water'. Chesterton's habit, in his Fleet Street days, of hiring hansom cabs to cover short distances and then making them wait outside cafes and pubs sometimes for an hour or so confirms that money had little or no meaning for him. Quite often he would arrive with his copy at the *Daily News* without any money at all and the commissionaire would have to pay his taxi fare. It was only natural that a wife would be worried, and eventually Frances took over all the financial arrangements, issuing Chesterton, as she would a schoolboy, with a regular sum by way of pocket money. What Father Vincent McNabb later wrote about Frances was perfectly true: 'So greatly did he need her that she had to be to him almost more mother than wife.' Chesterton persuaded himself that her concerns about money were common to all her sex, writing, 'Thrift is not a timid or provincial thing. It is part of that great idea of the woman watching on all sides out of all the windows of the soul and being accountable for everything.'[13] Keith however insists that Chesterton was made to feel ashamed by his wife's control over his expenses, particularly when, surrounded by his friends on one of his occasional visits to Fleet Street, he discovered that he hadn't sufficient cash to buy a round of drinks when his turn came.

Cecil Chesterton, who once wrote a ballade with the refrain 'It was in Fleet Street that I learned to drink', was a heavy drinker and smoker. 'When Cecil Chesterton stayed with us,' Belloc's daughter Eleanor remembered, 'he smoked and coughed all the time.' Bill Titterton, a freelance journalist and assistant editor of the *New Witness* and *GK's Weekly*, wrote, 'Cecil Chesterton's true place of business was the pub, there you met him to talk over articles.' The poet Theodore Maynard, a regular contributor to the *New Witness*, records, 'It was Cecil who used to edit the *New Witness* in the George or the Essex Arms, producing in the noisy bar his beautifully lucid prose' –a fact that perhaps helps to explain some of Cecil's more outrageous and less lucid outbursts. As for Keith, Titterton wrote, 'I have drunk in all the pubs of Fleet Street with Mrs Cecil Chesterton.'

Such a routine owed much to the influence of Belloc, who constantly harped on the benefits of drink. He was a connoisseur of fine wines, wrote poems in praise of inns, wine and beer, and attacked any attempt by the government to restrict opening hours, whilst pouring scorn on all Quakers, puritans and teetotallers. Both Chesterton brothers dutifully joined the campaign though neither had the iron constitution of Belloc. Chesterton drank with the same carelessness as he spent money but, whereas Belloc kept fit with constant walking, he lived a sedentary life and was consequently overweight (P. G. Wodehouse in one of his stories once likened a very loud noise to 'G. K. Chesterton falling on a sheet of tin').

Chesterton had little or no concern for his health and believed that worrying about such things was itself a sign of sickness: 'Of all human things the search for health is the most unhealthy.' As for drink, he advised his readers: 'Drink because you are happy, but never because you are miserable.' Naturally high-spirited, he was never in danger of alcoholism, but Frances fretted about his intake, especially when he was in the company of Cecil, Keith and fellow journalists. Deprived of their company, he was bound to drink less and feel better as a result. But Cecil would have none of it. 'Comradeship,' he had written in his book about his brother, 'is a necessity of life for him. He enjoys the sound of his own voice, he laughs openly at his own jokes. The atmosphere really native to him is still the atmosphere of Fleet Street, and he is never more at his ease, never more amusing, never more wholly himself, than when he is talking to his old brothers of the craft.'

Keith insisted that Chesterton was bound to suffer, particularly as by achieving the move to Beaconsfield Frances had made it difficult for him to travel to London and enjoy the company of his friends: 'We felt that his excursions would grow fewer and fewer and become more difficult and that he would find himself gradually cut off from those deep draughts of stimulative discussion which were so large a part of his mental existence.' But the likelihood is that it was Cecil and Keith who suffered more from Chesterton's retreat to suburban Buckinghamshire. Cecil, as the comments of his contemporaries suggest, was never a very popular personality, but accompanied by his brother he could be sure of attracting convivial company in the Fleet Street taverns where 'the brothers of the craft' congregated. And with his own brother at his side he could bask in his company and experience the old pleasure of arguing – the 'stimulative discussions' that Keith describes.

Chesterton was perfectly happy to indulge Cecil and Keith but as far as his work was concerned there was nothing much to choose between Battersea and Beaconsfield. What he wrote of his alter ego Basil Grant in *The Club of Queer Trades* could just as well have been applied to himself: 'Very few people knew anything of Basil; not because he was in the least unsociable, for if a man out of the street had walked into his rooms he would have kept him talking till morning. Few people knew him because, like all poets, he could do without them; he welcomed a human face as he might welcome a sudden blend of colour in a sunset, but he no more felt the need of going out to parties than he felt the need of altering the sunset clouds.'

There is a similar character in *The Wisdom of Father Brown* (1914) in a story titled 'The Strange Crime of John Boulnois'. Boulnois is an obscure scientist living in an Oxfordshire cottage who, rather than watch his actress wife performing in *Romeo and Juliet* opposite their famous neighbour Sir Claude Champion, prefers to stay at home drinking port, smoking cigars and reading a book called *The Bloody Thumb*. 'I can't analyse myself well,' he tells Father Brown, '…it was not only a peace but a plenitude.'

So long as he had his wife, Chesterton was perfectly content: 'Where's Frances?' he once asked anxiously. 'I don't want her now, but I might want her any minute.' He had come to rely on her not only for all the practicalities but also as a constant companion. But Cecil and Keith were both intensely resentful of the hold that Frances seemed to have over her husband. Cecil cared so much about the Chestertons' break from London that he began to fantasise with Keith about how to rescue his brother from his abductor. They would hire an aeroplane, fly to Beaconsfield and invite Chesterton to join them for a 'short spin'. 'We even went so far as to enquire when and where a plane could be secured and what it would cost us,' Keith writes. If that is true, and there is no reason why Keith should invent the story, it is vivid proof of the strength of Cecil's resentment.

Belloc, in Keith's account, joined in the anti-Frances campaign, inviting himself to Beaconsfield, saying to Frances, 'Have you any beer? If not, I'll bring some with me.' Even Elodie Belloc became involved, expressing her sympathy for Chesterton, cut off from his closest friends: '"Why on earth does Gilbert stand for it?" Cecil asked. "He loves her," Elodie replied. "But really he should beat her. Hilary would beat me if I behaved like that."'[14]

Keith was to harbour hostility towards Frances well into old age. In her memoir published in 1941, three years after Frances's death, she cannot stop herself from making what Graham Greene, reviewing her book,[15] called 'little gibes': 'She looked charming in blue or green, but she rarely wore those shades, and usually affected dim browns and greys'; 'She did not like food, except cakes, chocolate and similar flim-flams and her appreciation of liquor stopped short at tea.'

Such comments, Greene noted, were 'harmless and silly enough if it were not for the culminating passage of staggering vulgarity which purports to describe Chesterton's wedding night', and which illustrates very well her talent for writing Mills & Boon-type fiction. 'The opening chapters of the married life of Gilbert and Frances had gone strangely, pathetically awry'; Keith wrote:

He was fathoms deep in love, and in that first transcendent moment of their honeymoon when, far beyond time and space, they found themselves utterly, unbelievably alone, he must have heard the sun, the moon and the stars singing together. And then the whole world went crash. The woman he worshipped shrank from his touch and screamed when he embraced her. A less sensitive or more experienced man would have regarded the affair as distressing though by no means irremediable but he was haunted by the fear that his brutality and lust had frightened the woman he would have died to protect. He dared not contemplate a repetition.

She goes on to conjure up a picture of Chesterton, 'quivering with self-reproach and condemnation', appealing for help from his younger more experienced brother Cecil, who gives him some practical advice: 'Some citadels must be taken by storm while others yield only to long siege.' But all to no avail. Frances was unable to reconcile herself to 'the physical realities of marriage' and thus Chesterton was condemned to what she calls 'a pseudo-monastic life'.[16]

It is hard to imagine Chesterton quivering with self-reproach or confiding his sexual difficulties to Cecil, particularly as he habitually shied away from personal issues of that kind. It is not hard, however, to imagine Cecil in his quarrel with Frances embellishing or even inventing such a story to discredit her. It is perfectly possible, even likely, that the honeymoon was not a success. But as Maisie Ward points out, both Frances and Gilbert were very keen to have children and Frances had had an unsuccessful operation to make her capable of pregnancy which she would never have done in the tragic scenario described by Keith, who must have known about the operation when she wrote her story.

Keith never revised her low opinion of Frances as the wife who had not only failed as a lover but, more significantly, who had cast a blight on her husband's career by cutting him off from his 'brothers of the craft'.

One can see why she and Cecil came to think in this way as there is no question that from about 1911, two years after the move to Beaconsfield, there was a decline in the quality of Chesterton's writing. Amongst the many sympathetic critics of his work there is a general agreement that, with a few exceptions like *The Everlasting Man* (1922), his best books are those of his early years – *The Napoleon of Notting Hill, Orthodoxy, Charles*

Dickens, The Victorian Age in Literature, the first batch of Father Brown stories and the essays in books like *Tremendous Trifles.*

All these books had been praised by their reviewers. But for the first time, in 1910, a new book, *What's Wrong with the World,* attracted adverse critical comment. In November 1910 his greatest and earliest admirer Max Beerbohm wrote to his friend Reggie Turner, 'I thought GKC's *What's Wrong with the World* very cheap and *sloppy* though with gleams – gleams of gas lamps in Fleet Street mud and slush.' Three months later he added, 'Chesterton doesn't wear well at all, though I'm not sure whether it is that he has lost his quality or merely that he hasn't acquired a new quality to keep me interested.'[17]

Beerbohm was not alone. One or two of the critics of *What's Wrong with the World* made equally dismissive comments, the anonymous reviewer of the *Evening Standard* describing 'discussions that are so dreary and meaningless that nobody but a poor slave of a reviewer would make the attempt to follow them, into page after page of the thickest dotted nonsense it was ever our misfortune to read'.[18]

Beerbohm's criticism is more significant, coming as it does from a master stylist who appreciated, better than most, the wit and skill of Chesterton's early work, which he himself brilliantly parodied in his 1912 collection, *A Christmas Garland.* Chesterton was still writing his weekly column in the *Daily News* but there were fewer escapades, fewer flights of fancy. It was easy for Keith to attribute the change to the move to Beaconsfield and the dire influence of Frances. But there were other, far more powerful forces at work undermining Chesterton's seemingly invincible optimism. As Christopher Hollis has written, he had hitherto been able to see his little world 'to a large extent as a high-spirited debating society'. But Cecil – ex-imperialist, ex-socialist – was now promoting a more radical, more dangerous creed. Debating the rival merits of liberalism, conservatism or socialism was dismissed as irrelevant. Parliamentary democracy was terminally corrupt, undermined by dark and alien forces operating in secret.

Such a vision was a far cry from the heady optimism of the early years of Liberal government and it was one that Chesterton might well have refused to countenance, but for one thing: Cecil was no longer just his younger brother advising him on his literary career – he had a new master to whom he had grown utterly devoted, a master who was making a profound impression not only on Cecil but on Chesterton himself. His name was Hilaire Belloc and his influence on both Chestertons was to prove disastrous.

4

Baskets and Dead Cats

THERE ARE TWO QUITE DISTINCT PICTURES OF HILAIRE (HILARY to his friends) Belloc in the memoirs and biographies. One is of a handsome, thickset young man with tousled hair and eyes that Chesterton described as 'not without anxiety and that curious distant keenness that is seen in the eyes of sailors'.[1] The second is of an older, grim-faced, even surly-looking figure dressed in black, his hair cropped short, his face jowly. If shown the two portraits you would never guess that they were of the same person.

It was the first of these Bellocs that Chesterton met in 1902. Aged thirty-two he was already a famous figure. His father was a French lawyer who died when Belloc was only two; his English mother Bessie (née Parkes) was a descendant of the famous scientist and political radical Joseph Priestley. His only sibling, his devoted sister Marie (Belloc Lowndes), also became a successful writer. When his mother moved to England Belloc went to Cardinal Newman's school in Edgbaston. After working as a land agent and an architect and serving a year in the French artillery, he went up to Oxford at the age of twenty-three where he had a triumphant career, gaining a First in history, becoming President of the Union and making influential friends. He was already engaged in a long courtship of Elodie Hogan, an American friend of his sister Marie, a devout Catholic who felt a strong sense of vocation to become a nun. However, after a brief spell in a convent she decided against the religious life and eventually married Belloc in 1896. They were to have five children – three boys and two girls – but Belloc, an incurably restless man, was unfitted for family life, with the result that their marriage was punctuated by constant separation.

If Chesterton was 'the jolly journalist' (as he characterised himself), Belloc, with what Gardiner described as his 'square pugnacious face', was the gloomy one and it is hard to find a photograph which shows him smiling. His wife Elodie died aged forty-two in 1914 and Belloc wore black for the rest of his life in her memory. His eldest son Louis and many of his best friends were killed in the First World War and as he grew older he more and more began to relish the persona of the outcast, the man who had been made to suffer for his religious and political principles. 'You can't be happy,' he told a journalist who asked him for the secret of happiness. 'Don't try. Cut it out. Make up your mind to be miserable.'[2] He saw himself as a lonely victim – he never remarried – and affected a melancholy but stoical view of his lot, whistling to keep his spirits up but not without traces of self-pity:

> *A lost thing could I never find,*
> *Nor a broken thing mend:*
> *And I know I shall be all alone*
> *When I get towards the end.*
> *Who will there be to comfort me*
> *And who will be my friend?*[3]

After graduating, Belloc had pinned his hopes on a Fellowship at All Souls College, which would have given him the freedom to read for the Bar. All Souls was more like a highbrow club than a college and in addition to their academic ability candidates were judged by their social skills at a dinner with the Fellows. Tradition has it that Belloc did not endear himself to the Fellows by talking too much and showing off and so failed to be accepted, something he had not anticipated. He never got over his rejection, which left him with a permanent sense of grievance. He attributed it to the fact that he was a Catholic and so a victim of 'the fierce hatred which the Catholic Church provokes'. (Chesterton, he was later to write, 'would have known that hatred better if he had been to Oxford'.[4])

Rejected by All Souls and a number of other colleges including his own, Balliol, he went off on holiday to Scandinavia with his friend Lord Basil Blackwood and began to compose *The Bad Child's Book of Beasts* (illustrated by Blackwood), the first of a brilliant series of satirical verses, including *The Modern Traveller,* for which he is now best known. It was followed in 1902 by *The Path to Rome*, an account of his long walk across Europe which has all of his personality in it – his restlessness, fervent Catholicism, love of wine and didacticism, all combined with a poetic response to landscape. And as if this were not enough, he illustrated the book himself with accomplished pencil drawings.

'He had a wonderful life for say fifteen years,' his sister Marie wrote in 1947, long after his star had waned, 'perhaps only ten years if one leaves out the First War, but before '14... Hilary had a glorious life – nothing like him had been seen in the high little world in which he lived.'[5] Even George Bernard Shaw, while disagreeing with him about almost everything, had to admire his versatility: 'Hilaire Belloc, Catholic, militarist (late of the Gallic artillery) Irishman, Frenchman, Oxonian, historian, romancer, journalist, traveller, trouper, troubadour, devotee, scoffer and a dozen other things thrown in.'[6] A prolific writer – he claimed to be able to write (or rather dictate) 8,000 words a day – he was also from 1906 to 1910 the Liberal MP for Salford, mixing with most of the prominent politicians of the era.

His personality, both in public and private, was forceful, and he exercised a powerful influence over a great many people. Wilfred Sheed, Chesterton's godson and the son of his biographer Maisie Ward, refers to 'the quasi-hypnotic powers of Mr Belloc which were, so I am told, next thing to irresistible'.[7] His most faithful disciple, J. B. Morton (the famous columnist 'Beachcomber' of the *Daily Express*), who hailed Belloc as 'a great man and also the greatest writer of his day', describes 'the direct, unwavering, penetrating glance of the eyes... when he came into a room... he changed that room'. The first impression he gave 'was of power, of energy under command, of dignity, of distinction'.[8] The diplomat and author Maurice Baring, who was a close friend of both Belloc and Chesterton, became a Catholic as a result of Belloc's influence: 'But for you,' Baring wrote to him, 'I should never have come into the Church; you were the lighthouse that showed me the way.'[9]

And it was not only in the religious field that he exercised his powerful influence. Nicolas Bentley, another of Chesterton's godsons and the son of his oldest friend E. C. Bentley, describes how Belloc arrived one day in the offices of Shell where he was then working. He took one look round the crowded office and announced, 'If you don't get out of here pretty soon, my boy, you'll be tied to the wheels of commerce for the rest of your life. Clear out while you can, my boy.'[10] It was enough for Bentley to hand in his notice, rather in the spirit of those fishermen who abandoned their nets to follow Jesus. He later became a successful cartoonist and the illustrator of many books, including some of Belloc's satirical verses.

It was Belloc's talk that most of his contemporaries remembered. J. B. Morton, who wrote what is the best Belloc memoir, remembered 'the fullest, the most creative talk… I ever heard in my life… The subject was anything that came into his head: the breakdown of our civilisation, history, economics, politics, travel, military campaigns, the sea, physical science, poetry, wine, religion, the English character, international affairs. One thing would lead to another, and the whole would be seasoned with songs and jests and other digressions. It was not merely the variety of the talk that was so amazing. It came bubbling and boiling out of his richly stored mind… a boiling flood of anecdote…'

Those who described Belloc's talk often used watery imagery, but it was a one-way stream and some complained of the difficulty of holding a conversation with him. 'Talking to Belloc,' according to H. G. Wells, was 'like trying to break into a hailstorm,' while Belloc's lawyer E. S. P. Haynes wrote, 'The only drawback to Mr Belloc's conversation is that one often forgets what one wishes to say to him because one is whirled so quickly from one subject to another.' Nor were all his listeners mesmerised by the contents of the flow: 'When you really get talking, Hilary,' the famous satirist Max Beerbohm once told him, 'you're like a great Bellocking ram, or like a Roman river full of baskets and dead cats.'[11] Gardiner was another to resort to watery metaphors whilst feeling dubious about some of the things he was hearing. 'His talk,' he wrote, 'hard, brilliant, cocksure, thunders along in a ceaseless torrent... Authorities, facts, instances, proofs, tumble out in a torrent; they submerge you; they sweep you away; they fling you up a bruised and battered wreck. And all the while you suspect that if you only had time to think, time to turn round, time to stem that torrent, you would find some of his authorities a little shady, some of his facts a little thin. It is the impetus of the man that settles you.'[12]

If there were dead cats, as Beerbohm alleged, Chesterton was the last to notice them. The two men first met in 1902 at the Mont Blanc restaurant, a writers' haunt in Soho's Gerrard Street. Belloc 'talked into the night' while Chesterton listened enraptured. He had never before met anyone like this, a man who seemed to have been everywhere and knew everyone; who had served in the French army, had sired four children and could sail a boat and mow a meadow. In comparison, the Chesterton brothers had lived a sheltered life, with a comfortable home, devoted parents and limited experience of the world at large. Later Belloc was to claim that at his first meeting with Chesterton he had 'opened his eyes to reality'.[13] Unfortunately Belloc's conception of reality was dangerously wayward, a fact Chesterton never recognised, remaining for the rest of his life in awe of his friend. Maisie Ward wrote in her biography, 'A mutual friend has told me that Chesterton listened to Belloc all the time and said very little himself.'

Morton noticed how Belloc dominated his friends Chesterton and Baring in any gathering: 'They were no match for him,' he wrote, 'and that was due not only to his wide range of knowledge and his multiple interests, but also to the strength of his personality.' Morton himself was so greatly influenced by Belloc that he followed his example in almost every respect – moving to Sussex, walking in France and Spain, writing books about French history and, naturally, joining the Catholic Church.

Like Morton, A. G. Gardiner noted how his favourite columnist Chesterton had succumbed to the force of Belloc's personality. Gardiner, a lover of literature, greatly admired Belloc's poetry, his travel books, his nonsense verses – 'What wit there is, what vitality! What splendid joy of living sings through his pages.' But he must have had mixed feelings as he saw his protégé fall under Belloc's spell. Whereas previously he had written with delight of Chesterton's childlike innocence and exuberance, he now adopted a more mocking and satirical tone when describing his reliance on his new mentor. Chesterton is in thrall to Belloc, he writes, he follows him faithfully wherever he goes:

> His most miraculous quality is his loyalty to Mr Belloc. Wherever that impetuous Rupert rides he thunders after him with mighty trumpeting and vast perspiration, scattering death and destruction in his labouring path... It was the hero in Mr Belloc that captured Mr Chesterton's heart. For Mr Chesterton is the boy who refused to grow up. The world is for ever filled with knights and dragons and Dulcineas in horrid dungeons. Spiritually he is with the Rolands and the Amadises of old romance; but Nature has given his chivalrous spirit a vast and unadventurous envelope of flesh, and he cannot chase the dragons himself. But Fortune has provided him with a physical counterpart, and so he watches his volcanic leader flashing into the lists and he winds his mighty horn to cheer him on. There is in him that limitless devotion which Bardolph expressed so touchingly for Falstaff when someone said that the knight was perhaps in hell: 'Would I were with him whereso'er he be, whether in heaven or in hell.'[14]

Introducing Chesterton to 'reality' in 1902 will have involved Belloc putting him right about the Dreyfus affair. Chesterton, along with all Liberal opinion, had sided with the Dreyfusards. He wrote a poem in praise of Colonel Picquart, the only army officer to insist on Dreyfus's innocence, and another, 'To a Certain Nation', included in his first poetry collection *The Wild Knight*, published in 1900. That nation was France, and the theme of the poem was that this once great country which had earned our gratitude – 'For that hour's sake when thou didst wake all powers / With a great cry that God was sick of kings' – was now disgraced by the notorious Dreyfus affair. 'We who knew thee once,' it ended, 'we have a right to weep.'

Baskets and Dead Cats

The Dreyfus Affair rocked France for several years, creating storms and divisions in French society which were to last well into the 1930s and beyond. British opinion saw only the injustice in the story of the Jewish army officer Alfred Dreyfus, found guilty of spying for Germany by a secret court martial in 1894 and sentenced to life imprisonment in a stone hut on Devil's Island, a strip of rock off the coast of South America two miles long and five hundred yards wide, once a leper colony. The evidence on which he was convicted was later proved to have been forged.

In response to the vociferous campaign by supporters of Dreyfus, the French government at last capitulated and in 1899 he was released and court-martialled for a second time at Rennes. The new trial excited world-wide interest and when Dreyfus was found guilty yet again, the indigna-tion, particularly in England, was on an extraordinary scale. Boycotts of French foods were called for, travellers were urged to cancel their proposed visits and Queen Victoria herself telegraphed the Lord Chief Justice, Lord Russell, who had personally attended Dreyfus's trial, to protest at the injustice to the man she described as 'a poor martyr'. 'A cry will ring out over the world,' Georges Clemenceau, later the French president, declaimed. 'Where is France? What became of France?' Chesterton's 'we have a right to weep' was like an echo.

But Hilaire Belloc disagreed. 'During the Dreyfus agitation,' Dean Inge, the famous 'gloomy dean' of St Paul's, commented, 'Mr Belloc was almost the only man in England who did not take the part of the unfortunate prisoner.' The Dean was within his rights to name Belloc as almost the only Englishman to insist on Dreyfus's guilt. But con-sidered as a Frenchman, there was nothing exceptional about Belloc's standpoint. There were thousands of Bellocs in France, 'ninety-nine out of a hundred' men and women who he claimed were not concerned with the rights and wrongs of the case, but who saw the Dreyfusard campaign as a threat to France and especially its army. Uppermost in the thinking of these patriots was the memory of the defeat of their nation by Germany in the Franco-Prussian War of 1870, ending in the humil-iating surrender of the French army at Sedan. That war, which broke out a few days before Belloc's birth, led to the virtual destruction of his father's house at La Celle-St-Cloud, twelve miles from Paris, and it was natural that the Bellocs looked to those politicians promising *revanche* – resurgence, revenge and restitution of territory – all of it dependent on the French army.

Prominent amongst these was the soldier, poet and parliamentary deputy Paul Déroulède – 'long-legged and long-nosed like Don Quixote', according to historian Barbara Tuchman.[15] Déroulède, who served in the French army and had been captured by the Germans in 1870, founded his Ligue des Patriotes to campaign for *revanche* against Prussia for the defeat of France. He was a friend and neighbour of Belloc's parents and became a hero of their son, with whom Belloc later came to identify himself. 'I knew Déroulède well,' Belloc wrote, 'and Déroulède hammered away all his life at the expense of ceaseless insult and contempt, paying for the preservation of his honour the heavy price of an unbroken isolation, and dying without seeing any apparent fruit of his effort. It was his mission to proclaim to his French compatriots that until they had secured the defeat of Prussia in a war, they themselves were doomed to increasing decay, and Europe to increasing ills.'[16]

The young Belloc responded to Déroulède's call, and with his sister Marie, who likewise maintained a lifelong devotion to Déroulède ('the noblest, most selfless son borne by the France of his generation'),[17] joined the Ligue des Patriotes and sent some of his early poems to Déroulède's paper *Le Drapeau*. Together with their mother they attended a mass rally of the Ligue on the Champ de Mars in Paris.

Déroulède's *revanche* could only be achieved by the French army and it was the army's reputation that was, in the eyes of Belloc and the patriotic Frenchmen of the Ligue, under threat as a result of the Dreyfusards' campaign. At the height of the affair, following the sensational revelation that the evidence against Dreyfus had been forged by Hubert-Joseph Henry, an officer who had now committed suicide, the government submitted the case to a civilian court to investigate the army's evidence. The decision, which meant that the hitherto secret forged evidence would now be made public, caused a storm of protest on the Right and Déroulède, determined to uphold the honour of the army, attempted to lead a military coup to overthrow the Republic. The coup was timed for the state funeral of French President Félix Faure, who had died while engaged in sexual intercourse at the Élysée Palace with Madame Steinheil, the fun-loving wife of a well-known portrait painter. Déroulède with two hundred patriots intercepted the military cortège returning from the cemetery and catching hold of the bridle of the escort's commander, General Roget, cried, 'To the Élysée, General! To the Place Bastille! Save France!' Having no special wish to save France the General took no notice and Déroulède was arrested and charged with insurrection – which only increased his stature in the eyes of the youthful Belloc.

Unfortunately the patriotism of the anti-Dreyfus campaign was mired by the virulent anti-Semitism of many of the campaigners. Déroulède was not an antisemite but he had joined forces with the Anti-Semitic League (which was financed by the Duc d'Orléans) to bring about his aborted coup. Following a number of financial scandals in France involving Jewish financiers, anti-Semitism had become a powerful force in French politics and given that Dreyfus was a Jew, his alleged betrayal of France to Germany could be seen as evidence of a conspiracy by powerful Jews in France and elsewhere to destroy the French Republic and undermine the Catholic Church.

Such views were commonplace at all levels of French society and it is not surprising that Belloc was powerfully influenced by them. It was the Dreyfus affair which first put into his mind the notion of a threat posed by 'cosmopolitan' (in other words Jewish) finance operating independently of democratic governments and threatening all national institutions in France, particularly, but also in England. The central plank in Belloc's theory was the secrecy of the worldwide conspiracy. He convinced himself that in common with the Freemasons, the powerful Jews hatched their plots in secret, in the dark[18] – a fact that made it conveniently difficult if not impossible for Belloc to provide written (or other) evidence to support his various claims.

Following his experience of the Dreyfus Affair, all world events were to be explained by reference to this 'secret conspiracy' theory. Thus not only was the Russian Revolution brought about by Jewish Bolsheviks, the reason Western governments failed to confront the threat of Bolshevism was that they too were controlled by Jewish finance.[19] Likewise Jewish banks in America had 'worked hand in hand with the Bank of England in preventing our foreign policy from interfering with the Nazi movement'.[20] Hitler himself was a mere stooge of 'the clever yid [Alfred] Rosenberg', the so-called philosopher of Nazism later hanged at Nuremberg, thus making the Führer yet another product of a Jewish conspiracy – though Belloc might have given a moment to ponder why a Jew should be a notorious and vicious antisemite. (In fact there is not a shred of evidence that Rosenberg was a Jew, but for Belloc, his Jewish-sounding name was enough to condemn him.[21]) England was meanwhile ruled by an 'Anglo-Judaic plutocracy'. The press was controlled by Jewish millionaires. Jews had a monopoly over the stage, the fruit trade, the tobacco industry. As he grew older his obsession began to dominate his thoughts: 'The whole of English life,' he wrote in 1938, 'is interwoven with Jewry; our leading families are intermarried into it... most important of all the moral tradition of our society is inseparable from the Jewish money power throughout the world.'[22] And, again: 'Every English institution had its strong and active element of Jewish membership, especially the chief colleges of the older universities.'[23] (Had these Jewish dons been responsible for Belloc's rejection by All Souls?)

All this nonsense could be traced back to Dreyfus, who preyed on Belloc's mind throughout his life, so much so that he even managed to bring him into his book about Marie Antoinette. When the writers Hesketh Pearson and Hugh Kingsmill visited him in 1946, when he was seventy-six, he told them, 'It was the Dreyfus case that first opened my mind to the Jewish question.' He never accepted the proven innocence of Dreyfus, insisting that there were still plenty of doubts and that no one had the right to advance an opinion without first examining all the thousands of documents – 'even of the most technical terms of gunnery' – a difficult, even impossible, task.

Yet Belloc always denied the charge of anti-Semitism and in his 1922 book *The Jews* he described it as a 'mania', elaborating on how the anti-semite has to find the Jews at work in all financial and political scandals: 'His prejudices soon lose proportions altogether. He comes to see the Jew as everything and everywhere, and to accept confidently propositions which he would himself see to be contradictory, could he give a moment's thought to the matter.' Belloc seems unaware of how closely this description coincides with his own response to the so-called 'Jewish problem'. Either that, or he is only too well aware of the fact and is hoping to present an acceptable image to his readers, that of a rational, well-balanced individual, the last sort of person to be influenced by mania.

So although in private Belloc might tell his friends that Dreyfus was 'guilty as sin', in his public writings he fell back on a feeble compromise, claiming that he was no better qualified than anyone else to advance an opinion. 'For myself,' he wrote in pompous phraseology, 'I pretend to no certain conclusion in this matter' – a typical piece of Bellocian humbug and a dead cat if ever there was, Belloc being well known for his certain conclusions on every subject under the sun, except apparently on this one occasion.

When it came to Dreyfus, politics and patriotism were mixed with religion. Belloc was brought up as a Catholic and the Church in France was, and remained, deeply involved with French nationalism and notably with anti-Semitism. So in Belloc's mind the French nation, its army and its Church were threatened by Germans and Jews, making it incumbent on all true lovers of France to support the Church whenever it came under attack. This stance was not confined to France and extended to Belloc's take on history and current affairs in general. As Gardiner wrote:

When the conspiracy against Dreyfus was exposed, his voice rose like a hurricane in defence of the anti-Dreyfusards. When the Congo horrors shocked the world, he braved the storm on behalf of the wretched Leopold [King of the Belgians and a Catholic]. When Ferrer was shot after a secret trial for a crime he did not commit, it was he who justified the shooting. It was not that Dreyfus was a traitor to France or Ferrer a traitor to Spain; it was that both were outlawed by the Church. The one was a Jew, the other a rebel against the clericalism of Spain. Rome will tolerate no rival hegemony, whether of Jews or Freemasons or Socialists. And Rome never had a more gallant or less scrupulous champion than Mr Belloc.[24]

Belloc made frequent reference to his concern for truth, it being the goal of all writers like himself. 'To release the truth against whatever odds,' he once proclaimed, 'is a necessity for the soul.' But truth in terms of factual accuracy, the truth that journalists and scholars hopefully aspire to, was not what Belloc had in mind when he spoke of truth – which was perhaps why the Oxford dons had turned down his fellowship applications.

Liberal opinion, personified by Gardiner and almost all of Chesterton's colleagues and friends, supported Dreyfus. But now Chesterton, previously a Dreyfusard, appeared to break ranks. His *Wild Knight* had been a success, but when a second edition was published in 1905 he added a footnote to the Dreyfus poem: 'While not having been able to reach any final conclusion about the proper verdict on the individual, I have come largely to attribute the difficulty of doing so to the acrid and irrational unanimity of the English press…There may have been a fog of injustice in the French courts; I know that there was a fog of injustice in the English newspapers.' This clarification, as it would be called today, precisely echoes Belloc's evasive argument that it is impossible to reach a definite judgement for or against Dreyfus, this despite the well-attested fact that the evidence against him had been forged. As such it constitutes the first significant evidence of Chesterton's growing submission to Belloc's influence. The reference to the English press is less explicit but it undoubtedly refers to Belloc's conviction that the papers are controlled by Jews, hence their unanimity on Dreyfus. This, again, marks a change in tone as there is no trace of anti-Semitism in Chesterton's early works. Though there are plenty of Jewish characters in the later Father Brown stories, there are none in his early fiction *The Napoleon of Notting Hill* (1904) and *The*

Club of Queer Trades (1905).[25] His biography of Dickens (1906) takes no special interest in the character of the Jewish villain Fagin, and the earlier book on Browning (1903), while mentioning the theory that Browning may have had Jewish blood, dismisses the possibility as irrelevant. It was a view, he writes, 'which is perfectly conceivable and which Browning would have been the last to have thought derogatory', a view which the young Chesterton himself plainly shared.

The malign influence of Belloc is, however, apparent in Chesterton's first collaboration with him as illustrator. His satirical novel *Emmanuel Burden* (1904) introduced Chesterton to many of Belloc's most harped-on anti-Semitic themes: Burden himself is an honest businessman who is led astray and eventually ruined by a wealthy Jewish financier, I. Z. Barnett (later created Lord Lambeth), who typified Belloc's view that Jews have infiltrated and corrupted the aristocracy, thus gaining control over politicians and, in particular, the press. Chesterton was happy to draw Barnett as a hook-nosed patriarch, reassuring himself perhaps that Belloc was writing in a satirical spirit in keeping with his habit of speaking, in private, about 'yids', even when referring to St Paul. As his influence grew, Chesterton absorbed Belloc's belief in the existence of a sinister and secret Jewish conspiracy, and could refer, almost casually, to the 'secret society' of 'plutocrats who govern England'. Their influence extended to the press, as the suppression of the case against Dreyfus had clearly shown: 'I happen to be quite certain that in that case the British public was systematically and despotically duped by some power – and I naturally wonder what power... I can only guess about the traitor in France but I know about the tyrant in England.'[26]

Here Belloc's conspiracy theory is fully developed by Chesterton – the theory of a sinister force, 'a tyrant', working in secret to undermine the press. There was never any evidence provided. Chesterton writes that 'as a journalist behind the scenes' he soon found out that the truth about the Dreyfus case 'was not so simple'. When Chesterton says he 'soon found out' the truth, it is safe to assume that what he meant is that he was told what to think about the Dreyfus case by Belloc. Significantly, in the same passage he goes on to quote with approval Belloc's hero Déroulède: 'Dreyfus may or may not be guilty, but France is not guilty,' a fine sounding patriotic proclamation but one that assumes that there is a mystical entity called France, quite distinct from the French public, the government, the press, the army, the judiciary, the Church and so on.

The case of the Spanish anarchist Francisco Ferrer, referred to by Gardiner in his profile of Belloc, will have hastened Chesterton's gradual acceptance of his friend's view of the world, the 'reality' which Belloc claimed to have revealed to him at their first meeting. Now largely forgotten, it was, on a smaller scale, a repetition of the Dreyfus affair, Ferrer often being described at the time as 'the Spanish Dreyfus'. A wealthy intellectual and anarchist, Ferrer had renounced his early revolutionary views and devoted himself to promoting secular education as part of his obsessive atheistic and vehemently anti-Catholic bias. He was executed by firing squad on 13 October 1909 having been convicted by court martial of organising a week-long riot in Barcelona which had erupted after the conscription of troops to fight in Morocco – the so called *Semana Trágica*. It had resulted in the burning of several convents and churches and the loss of about one hundred and fifty lives. There was little or no evidence that Ferrer had been involved, and after his conviction there followed, as with Dreyfus, a wave of protest throughout Europe, with even the Pope petitioning the Spanish government to reprieve him. In England, liberal opinion, typified by Gardiner and the *Daily News*, took up the cause and Shaw's friend the theatre critic William Archer, famed as the translator of Ibsen, travelled to Spain and later published a detailed account of the Ferrer story exonerating him of any responsibility for the riot, whilst not seeking to confer heroic status on him.

As with the Belgian Congo,[27] Belloc was, once again, almost alone in defending the Spanish government and condemning Ferrer. He interrupted the Commons debate with a cry of 'Rubbish!' and in two long articles for the *Dublin Review,* another for the *Tablet* and later a pamphlet issued by the Catholic Truth Society in 1910, pooh-poohed the protests, which he claimed were not what they seemed. As with Dreyfus he discerned, without producing any evidence, dark, secret forces at work – 'very powerful though hidden agencies' – this time led not by Jews, but Freemasons – though even they inevitably had Jewish affiliations. In Belloc's version Ferrer was the emissary and agent of the Masonic lodge the Grand Orient, based in Paris. These powerful Masons, Belloc wrote, as part of their secret campaign to destroy the Catholic Church had later organised the synchronised pro-Ferrer protests throughout Europe. As for the charges against Ferrer he was plainly guilty – 'the soul of the business' – and the Spanish government's response to the week of rioting had been 'extraordinarily mild', 'almost comically small... There is perhaps no case in contemporary history of so serious a tumult involving so small a measure of punishment.'[28]

Though Belloc presented himself to the public as a journalist solely concerned with revealing the truth, Gardiner was right to see him as a propagandist whose principal aim was to defend the Catholic Church regardless. But his restless nomadic lifestyle was not one that allowed time for detailed research into a story like that of Francisco Ferrer. He would often seek to cover himself by maintaining that all he was doing was setting out facts that were already well known and accepted by everybody competent enough to take an interest – 'the educated and travelled reader' – someone like himself in other words. More often than not he was unable to mask his bluster. Belloc was the sort of man, H. G. Wells wrote, 'who talks loud and fast for fear of hearing the other side'. It was not so surprising in view of his fixed beliefs, which did not stand up too well if challenged by informed opponents. The most important could be summarised as follows:

GERMANY:	The enemy (always to be referred to as Prussia) of Christendom.
FRANCE:	Home of freedom, Catholicism, threatened by Prussia and Jewish conspiracies.
PARTY POLITICS:	A sham. No difference between Tories and Liberals.
SOCIALISM:	A plot to enslave the working man.

LLOYD GEORGE:	The arch enemy, seeking to enslave the working man by making him dependent on the State. Controlled by sinister press baron Lord Northcliffe.
JEWS:	Aliens, not British. Bankers and businessmen intent on infiltrating the political system to attain domination. Hence 'The Jewish problem'.
TSARIST RUSSIA:	A fine country allied to France. Later undermined by a Jewish conspiracy (Bolshevism).
MONARCHY:	A polite word for one-man-rule, or dictatorship.
PLUTOCRACY:	Government by the rich – bankers (mostly Jews).
POLAND:	The most important country in Europe. Catholic majority threatened by powerful Jewish minority.
DISTRIBUTISM:	Having rejected liberalism and socialism Belloc became an advocate of 'distributism', a political creed based on Catholic teaching and promoting the ideal of widely distributed property to counteract the power of capitalists (Tories) and the state (socialists). The attraction of this policy was partly that it had little or no chance of being widely adopted, thus absolving Belloc from any involvement in conventional politics. Although a Distributist League was later formed with a few hundred members, Belloc took little or no interest in its meetings and deliberations.

When Belloc boasted that he had 'opened Chesterton's eyes to reality' he was thinking of reality in some such terms as these. In awe of Belloc's powerful personality, both Chesterton brothers were to adopt the Bellocian manifesto almost without qualification or any awareness of the flimsy factual basis on which much of it was based. The results were disastrous for both men, but particularly for Cecil, as Gilbert, unlike Cecil, inhabited his own imaginative world in which Belloc had no say and which, in any case, he was not particularly interested in.

As he grew older, Belloc's political opinions moved sharply to the Right. The youthful Belloc had been an ardent Republican, a devotee of the makers of the French Revolution like Danton, the subject of his first historical work. In common with many who had campaigned against the Boer War he joined the Liberal Party and was elected as an MP in the 1906 election when the Liberals won by a landslide. Uncertain about his political ambitions he was later to claim, unconvincingly, that he had never thought much of Parliament: 'If I went in at all it would only be to add to my stock of experience.' Eventually, realising that he was making little impact as a backbencher, he gave up his seat and thenceforth denounced party politics as corrupt and doomed to decay as he had always thought.

Just as his rejection by All Souls and the other colleges had turned him against Oxford and its dons, so now he railed against the 'party system', ranting about the wretched tawdry game of professional politics: 'the futile vulgar and unreal verbiage... a universal toleration of bribery and blackmail among politicians... corruption had come on in a flood, taking every conceivable form, but all those forms proceeding from the immunity of the evil-doers'. Such lurid opinions, spiced up with talk of 'filth' and 'vomit' and taken in conjunction with his belief in the domination of European politics (including those of Russia) by a Jewish conspiracy, naturally left Belloc to look forward to the arrival of the dictators. 'What will save our society when it comes will be some new line of Dynasties sprung from energetic individual men who shall seize power,' he wrote in 1922, the year of Mussolini's March to Rome. Belloc hailed Mussolini's triumph as a momentous event which confirmed all his prophesies, spelling the end not only of parliamentary corruption but of all the decadence that went with it: 'All that crowd which we of the later nineteenth century have known to nausea, the "advanced" journalist, the highbrow reformer, the Earnest woman, the millionaire socialist, the party fund banker, the inevitable Jewish cabinet minister, the pimp secretary, were swept away in the common rubbish heap. It was high time!'[29]

Belloc secured a meeting with the Italian dictator in 1924 and was ecstatic. 'What a contrast with the sly and shifty talk of your parliamentarians! What a sense of decision, of sincerity, of serving the nation, and of serving it towards a known end with a definite will!'[30]

It was inevitable, given his anti-Semitic bias, that Belloc was going to find himself in unsavoury company. His hero Paul Déroulède died shortly before the outbreak of war in 1914, the war of revenge against Prussia that he had always hoped for but which, after four long years and a terrible death toll, had not brought about the end to the decay of France but rather had only accelerated its progress. Belloc mourned him and made a pilgrimage to his grave just after the Battle of the Marne. 'It is in a little, somewhat neglected churchyard, some three miles from the house he had inherited: a place windswept and overlooking from beyond its walls a great horizon to the north. The season being late summer, and the war having left the little place untended, the grass was rank and high around the mound and the slab which marked the place where he lay...'[31]

Chesterton had previously paid a poetic tribute to Déroulède, saluting the hero 'Who in the day of all denial blew / A bugle through the blackness of the world.'[32] Taking his cue, as so often, from Belloc, he would later acclaim the chivalry of Déroulède, 'who acted much in the military and Christian spirit as Belloc and my brother' – a far-fetched if not ludicrous comparison.

Belloc soon found a substitute hero, another more influential Frenchman in the person of Charles Maurras, the leader of the reactionary *Action Française* movement (also the name of his daily paper) and, like Belloc and Déroulède, a poet. A short, deaf, cultured intellectual with a goatee beard, Maurras, like Déroulède, was a veteran of the anti-Dreyfus campaign. A deeply unattractive individual, he had joined the nationalist movement *Action Française* and became its leader, advocating the restoration of the monarchy, by force if necessary, as a means of reviving the greatness of France which had been betrayed by the Revolution of 1789, and was now reduced to ruins by the Dreyfus affair – proof in the eyes of Maurras and his partners of the power of Jews, Freemasons and those he dubbed '*métèques*'[33] to undermine a once great nation.

This was a heady brew, but Belloc along with many intellectuals like T. S. Eliot responded to the call, praising Maurras while turning a blind eye to his vicious racism. Maurras was so violently anti-Semitic that whilst valuing the role of the Catholic Church as a conservative force he felt unable to join it himself as it had been founded by a Jew. (The Gospels he dismissed as the work of 'four obscure Jews'.) Maurras even composed a special marching song for the members of *Action Française*:

> *The Jew having taken all,*
> *Having robbed Paris of all she owns,*
> *Now says to France:*
> *'You belong to us alone.*
> *Obey! Down on your knees all of you.'*
> *Insolent Jew, hold your tongue*
> *Back to where you belong, Jew...*[34]

Maurras later became an ardent supporter of General Pétain and his wartime Vichy government's deportation of French Jews to German camps, deriding the French Resistance as 'Jew-lovers'. Sentenced to life imprisonment in 1945, he called his punishment, appropriately, 'the revenge of Dreyfus'. (Belloc's biographer Robert Speaight tactfully avoids referring to these sad events, saying merely that 'it all came to a sticky end', leaving his educated and travelled readers to speculate about precisely what that entailed.)

Belloc's high opinion of Maurras had been duly adopted by Chesterton and other disciples like 'Beachcomber' and historian F. Y. Eccles. Chesterton wrote that 'Maurras has been arguing all his life, lucidly, logically, largely triumphantly, and on his side there was nothing except his own strong and independent argument,'[35] while Eccles described Maurras as 'a man universally esteemed... a man of blameless life, conspicuous for his severe intrepidity and absolute rectitude and the greatest intellectual force in contemporary France'.[36] As Gardiner had realised, Belloc never bothered to look too closely into the political issues he talked and wrote about, or he would have been more circumspect in saluting a thug like Mussolini or a racist bigot like Maurras. Chesterton's tragedy was that he accepted, without questioning, almost all of Belloc's political opinions – idolising Déroulède, studying and extolling Maurras, and echoing his contempt for parliamentary democracy and admiration for Mussolini. He even followed in Belloc's footsteps to Rome and visited the Italian dictator, though the interview leant rather more towards farce than Belloc's had done. Chesterton did not speak Italian and Mussolini did not speak English so they ended up conversing in, particularly on Chesterton's part, rather poor French. Hoping to hear of Mussolini's plans for Italy, Chesterton was disconcerted when he found himself being questioned about the Church of England and the Revised Book of Common Prayer. When they parted Mussolini told Chesterton, 'Well I will go and reflect on what you have told me,' leaving Chesterton disappointed that he had 'nothing to report about the great Fascist's views on Fascism'.[37]

Cecil's progress to Bellocism had been slower but his conversion when it came was absolute and final. A natural hero-worshipper, his idol, prior to meeting Belloc, was Hubert Bland (husband of the better known E. Nesbit, author of *The Railway Children* and other classic tales), one of the founding fathers of the Socialist Fabian Society along with Shaw and the Webbs. Shaw, who frequently shared a platform with him, described Bland as 'a man of fierce Norman exterior and huge physical strength… never seen without an irreproachable frock coat, tall hat and a single eyeglass which infuriated everybody. He was pugnacious, powerful, a skilled pugilist and had a shrill, thin voice reportedly like the scream of an eagle. Nobody dared to be uncivil to him.'[38] Bland, who once described himself as an 'expert in illicit love', was also a man of voracious sexual appetite who according to Shaw had 'simultaneously three wives all of whom bore him children'. He managed to preach socialism whilst being strongly opposed to the suffragettes and also a supporter of the Boer War in South Africa, which he said 'would overcome national flabbiness and restore the manhood of the British people'. When it came to the Boer War, Cecil loyally followed him into the imperialist camp, even to the extent of praising the poet of Empire, Rudyard Kipling, a writer, he said, who 'gave to the silent movement of sentiment and opinion an articulate voice... to which no man with blood in his veins could refuse to listen', yet he managed to reconcile these jingoistic opinions with the socialism of A. R. Orage and Shaw. Shaw, who greatly admired Chesterton, describing him to Lawrence of Arabia as 'a man of colossal genius', seems also to have had a soft spot for Cecil.

In 1908 Cecil seconded Shaw in a public debate with Chesterton, giving vent to traditional socialist views: 'It seems to me impossible that the great mass of people in this country can very much longer continue to practise the extravagant altruism of the present time when they are handing over annually a sum of six hundred million pounds to support an idle rich class.' The following year he was writing in the *New Age* dismissing out of hand Belloc's policy of Distributism which by now his brother Gilbert had endorsed: 'A large and ever increasing section of the working class is socialist while I never in my life met or heard of a working man who was a Chester-Bellocian. Socialism is a real popular demand. Petty proprietarianism is, as far as England is concerned, a paper demand made by brilliant men of letters.' Cecil's friend and fellow Fabian Shaw was even more scathing about Distributism: 'The error is that proprietorship is good for the soul,' he wrote, 'and the nonsense is that a decent civilisation could be made by a hoard of small proprietors each squatting jealously on his own dunghill.'

For five years after leaving the Fabian Society, Cecil worked with A. R. Orage, the socialist editor of the *New Age*, a revered figure in radical circles who launched his paper in 1907. Orage attacked Fabianism and advocated a version of workers' control which was known as Guild Socialism, though, unlike Belloc, who shared many of his opinions, he was never a Believer, being an admirer of Nietzsche.

As with Gilbert, it was the 'quasi-hypnotic' personality of Belloc, nearly ten years his senior, which effected the change in Cecil, Belloc taking over the role formerly played by Bland and Orage. Like Maurice Baring and J. B. Morton, Cecil also converted to Roman Catholicism as a result of Belloc's influence and also that of his wife Elodie, who, according to Father Vincent McNabb, summoned Cecil, of whom she was very fond, to the Bellocs' home in Sussex and told him he had to join the Church. After a long talk lasting into the small hours, Cecil went to the Brompton Oratory the following day and was baptised on 7 June 1912.

For Belloc, the acquisition of a new disciple in the shape of Cecil Chesterton was a great stroke of good fortune. He was young, highly intelligent and energetic, knowledgeable of English history and literature and, in Belloc's view, one of the best writers in the country, superior even to his better-known brother. And now he was converted to the Bellocian cause he seemed the ideal man to assist Belloc and collaborate with him in some of the many assignments to which he had committed himself. Most pressing was an exposé of parliamentary corruption to be called *The Party System*, commissioned by the publisher Stephen Swift (real name Charles Granville), who was offering an advance of £100 which Belloc, in turn, offered to share with Cecil. Cecil was overwhelmed: 'My own feeling,' he wrote to Belloc, 'is one of considerable pride that you should think well enough of my work to make such a proposal.' Later, Cecil was to undertake an even more ambitious collaboration when Belloc was commissioned by an American publisher to produce an updated final volume to John Lingard's *History of England*, originally published in 1830. Cecil wrote almost all of the book without being given a word of credit. But he expected no reward, telling Belloc, 'You've given me an enormous gift of letting me collaborate with you.'

Belloc's patronage was to be the making of Cecil Chesterton but it was to have one very unfortunate consequence both for him and his brother. Prior to his association with Belloc, Cecil had shown no tendency towards anti-Semitism and had even, when a schoolboy at St Paul's, written a poem praising the Jews. But thanks to Belloc this sympathetic approach, shared by Chesterton, was to undergo a change.

At the heart of Belloc's neurotic obsession with Jewry was the concept of a 'Jewish problem'. But although it was, in Belloc's opinion, 'everywhere in this modern world' it was a problem of which the majority of the British public, including the Jews themselves, seemed unaware. Put simply, the problem was that Jews were foreigners ('aliens') owing their allegiance to another 'nation' and therefore could not be regarded as patriotic Britons like the majority. The existence of this problem and the need to propose a solution was accepted by Cecil and was to obsess him for the rest of his life, as it did Belloc.

By 1908, when Cecil published his anonymous book about his brother, the signs of Belloc's influence can already be discerned. Here he echoes Belloc's frequently expressed view that the English aristocracy has been corrupted by an incursion of Jews. 'The idea that brains were any part of the make up of a gentleman,' Cecil wrote, 'was never dreamed of in Europe until our rulers fell into the hands of Hebrew moneylenders.'[39] Writing later in 1916, without naming Belloc, Cecil looked back to his days of innocence when he worked for the Fabian Society: 'In those days I only thought of a Jew as an Englishman with an odd religion and I knew nothing of the sacred blood of the Liverpool pawnbroker or of the old moneylender's purchase of a peerage which was probably even then being negotiated.[40] ...If I had known when I was a Fabian all that I know now about the way in which England is governed, many things hidden from me would have been plain. Only perhaps in that case I should not have been a Fabian.'

Just as Gilbert had changed his view of the Dreyfus affair after listening to Belloc on the subject, Cecil was to follow in his footsteps, slavishly taking the Bellocian line when writing about Dreyfus. 'He was able to enlist on his behalf the influence of the rich Jewish political families,' he wrote, without stopping to explain how a man imprisoned on Devil's Island was able to do this. 'All the sources of the Hebrew money power could do for him was done, with the result that after many vicissitudes and another trial (at which he was again condemned) he received a free pardon.' There was a strong prima facie case against Dreyfus 'yet there was a weak point' – this presumably referring to the fact that the evidence against him was proved to have been forged.

Once he had shown himself a loyal devotee, Belloc saw Cecil as the ideal man to assist him when the publisher of *The Party System*, Charles

Granville, offered to finance a new journal, the *Eye-Witness*, which was eventually launched in 1911, the year following Belloc's departure from Parliament. The tone of the paper was serious and political. In shape it consisted of 32 pages of solid print with no illustrations of any kind, a lengthy leading article and an introductory feature (copied from Orage's *New Age*) called 'Notes of the Week' comprising a series of anonymous comments mostly dealing with politics – a useful format for Belloc. He had travelled far and wide to recruit contributors and was confident of achieving commercial success. But the paper never reached a circulation of more than about 1,500 copies, and Belloc was largely to blame, believing as he did that his name alone would be enough to attract large numbers of readers as well as contributors in the way that editors like Gardiner or Orage were able to do. Orage, however, was of the firm opinion that an editor's job was not to concern himself with his own articles but to encourage and foster other talents, whereas Belloc's primary aim was to have a platform for his personal opinions on national and international affairs. He had been ignored in Parliament but now he hoped to exercise his influence with the printed word. He did not consider he had a duty to concern himself with other writers or with marketing the paper, and in common with French journalists he was strongly opposed to advertisements, which he regarded as a corrupting influence.

His own combative character was also an obstacle. Unlike Gardiner and Orage, Belloc had a way of putting people's backs up. H. G. Wells had told Gardiner that he would write for the *Daily News* just because he liked him but did not feel the same way about Belloc, complaining that there was 'a sort of partisan viciousness about him'. D. H. Lawrence, who at one point considered sending an article to the *Eye-Witness*, told a friend, 'I think Hilaire Belloc is conceited, full of that French showing off.'

What is surprising about the *Eye-Witness* and its successor the *New Witness* is that they were strongest in areas in which Belloc had little interest. The famous music critic Ernest Newman wrote a full-page weekly article in the *New Witness* unsurpassed in any other paper, while the *Eye-Witness* theatre reviews were the work of the distinguished critic

Desmond MacCarthy, self-styled 'literary journalist', who later wrote under the pseudonym 'Affable Hawk' (based on his physical appearance). 'We began in two little rooms in John Street,' MacCarthy remembered,

> We did not stop long and we never seemed rid of carpenters and painters. It was quieter in the bar of the Adelphi Hotel so we moved to printers overlooking Covent Garden on the south side and then I made the important discovery that the only essential things when starting a paper are talent and a good-sized table. Writers always have fountain pens: the important thing is to get the stuff written and printed, and the nearer the table is to the machines the better. Our large round table (four could write at it comfortably) was in a sort of box, partitioned off from a long dusty room. The box also contained a greasy black sofa to seat agreeable interrupters and those lovers of work who, as Dan Leno used to say, can watch a man working all day long.[41]

MacCarthy was struck by the astonishing fluency of Belloc and Cecil, both of whom were capable of dashing off a piece if ever there was a page or two that needed to be filled at the last minute. A two-inch space, which frequently occurred, would invariably be filled by a ballade or a triolet, one example being remembered by MacCarthy:

> *We have to print a triolet*
> *When space is clamouring for matter*
> *We try to put it off and yet*
> *We have to print a triolet*
> *It is with infinite regret*
> *That we admit the silly patter – But*
> *We have to print a triolet*
> *When space is clamouring for matter.*

It might have been expected that Chesterton would write a regular column for the *Eye-Witness*, but it was a sign of Belloc's lukewarm view of his friend's journalism that he remained only an occasional contributor, mostly of poems and ballades (Cecil must have been aware of Belloc's indifference and perhaps gained confidence from the high opinion he had of his own writing in contrast to that of his better-known brother). As for Belloc himself, his role in the *Eye-Witness* was not that of the satirist but the serious political pundit, the man who knew what was going on. But now that he was no longer an MP he felt little personal involvement in the great political upheavals of the time: the wave of industrial unrest beginning with the transport strikes that coincided with the launch of the paper; the crisis over Asquith's Parliament Bill to abolish the Lords' power of veto and the sinking of the *Titanic* in April 1912 did little to engage the interest of Belloc, who continued to agitate about his pet obsessions, Lloyd George's Insurance Bill and the skulduggery of his land tax.

With serious competition from other magazines, notably the *New Age* and Ford Madox Ford's *English Review*, the *Eye-Witness* remained an ambitious venture, but Belloc persuaded himself that with Cecil installed in Essex Street handling the day-to-day business, he could make a success of it and still be able to fulfil all his other commitments. He had bought a country home, King's Land, near Horsham in Sussex, he was producing a flood of books (his bibliography for 1911–12 lists fifteen different titles) and at the same time he was dashing all round the country delivering lectures, something he was very good at. ('First I tell them what I'm going to tell them. Then I tell them. Then I tell them what I've told them.') The *Eye-Witness* staff struggled to work for an editor who was constantly on the move – his loyal assistant W. R. Titterton remembered sitting around the table with Desmond MacCarthy hard at it while Belloc 'might dash in and stand reading a sheaf of galleys' before dashing off again. With so much on his mind Belloc 'could at times be very difficult', Keith wrote. 'When he called to dictate his copy there was always a slight tension among the secretarial staff. Would he be amiable or temperamental? Very generous, indeed quixotic in many ways, his fine qualities were discounted by his moods. He was not understood by Fleet Street in general, though a small and fervent clique always adored him.'[42]

Keith herself was never a member of that clique, possibly due to her sex. Belloc's opinion of her is not recorded anywhere and their office correspondence is formal – 'Dear Mr Belloc', 'Dear Miss Prothero'. Still living with his parents in Kensington, Cecil was more than happy to hold the fort while Belloc hurried hither and thither often disappearing to the Continent for days and sometimes weeks on end. Whilst at home or on his travels he kept in touch with his loyal deputy, bombarding him with a non-stop stream of letters and telegrams, articles and leaders, not to mention constant instructions about meeting Belloc at one or other London terminus. In marked contrast to Chesterton, Belloc had an obsessive interest in railway timetables and making travel arrangements for himself and other people. A typical memo to Cecil ran:

> Your winter journey from Crowborough is not so easy as one of the summer, but if you leave Crowborough for Groombridge at 4.36 change at Groombridge for Three Bridges for Horsham and change at Horsham for Southwater, you get to Southwater at six-something-rather than seven. A quicker way for you, though rather late, is to take the Crowborough train for Brighton (where, if your train is punctual, you have about half an hour) and take the 6.45 from Brighton to West Grinstead. This gets into West Grinstead at about twenty minutes to eight. Let me know which train you come by – I suppose it will be the Brighton one, and remember that in that case you book to West Grinstead and not to Southwater.

Belloc must have been delighted by the way Cecil faithfully followed his instructions, both on the railways and in the office of the *Eye-Witness*. The difficulties arose when he was left to his own devices, as was inevitable given Belloc's nomadic tendencies and his lecturing engagements all over the country. Cecil, who later took over as editor, accepted all of Belloc's opinions – about Lloyd George, Dreyfus, the Jewish conspiracy – but he showed little restraint when advocating them in his own provocative terms.

Belloc was in two minds about this. On the one hand he admired Cecil's recklessness, the savagery of his attacks. On the other he was aware that there were a great many people whose good opinion he valued who were offended by them. The situation posed especial problems for Belloc when it affected his relationship with one of his closest aristocratic friends, Hon. Maurice Baring, who was offended, in particular, by the anti-Semitic tone which became increasingly strident as time went on. Belloc was at pains to reassure his friend that he had done his best to restrain Cecil but with little success. He had thought of writing him a letter but decided against it 'because it would look disloyal. Certain cardinal points which I emphasised have been quite abandoned, as for instance that you must never attack without knowledge.' (This was a bit rich coming from Belloc, who never bothered too much about knowledge when pontificating on such matters as the Dreyfus affair or the execution of Ferrer.)

As things turned out, the partnership of Hilaire Belloc and Cecil Chesterton was to have disastrous consequences for both men. It might have been different had Belloc been more circumspect, less obsessed by his various conspiracy theories – but his tendency to make wild assumptions about events and people, coupled with Cecil's indifference to public opinion and the laws of libel, often resulted in a dangerous mix of propaganda and half-truths.

G. K. Chesterton, cherishing an uncritical devotion to both men, remained blissfully unaware of all the risks involved.

5

GOING INTO THE OTHER CAMP

C HARLES MASTERMAN, CHESTERTON'S GREAT FRIEND AND *DAILY
News* colleague, was elected to Parliament alongside his fellow
Liberal Hilaire Belloc in 1906. Typifying the close links which then existed
between the literary world, radical politics and the Catholic wing of the
Church of England, Masterman, son of a failed engineer and fervent
nonconformist, had briefly considered becoming ordained after leaving
Cambridge in 1896. He campaigned with both Chesterton brothers in the
Christian Social Union, an Anglican lobby to help the unemployed, and for
a time lived with two friends in the working-class South London district
of Camberwell, describing his experiences in a book which showed he
could have been a poet instead of a politician:

> Here is Saturday night in one of the main arteries of the Abyss: an
> ineffaceable remembrance of sight, sound, scent and colour. The whole
> world is choking up pavement and street, tossing backwards and for-
> wards like an angry sea. A hum of many-voiced life rises to the quiet
> stars... Children with tattered clothes and tangled hair dancing in front
> of a street organ: a woman with compressed lips and the hectic flush
> of consumption: a little girl with the unique pinched beauty and bright
> eyes that blossom in the children of want and poverty – such impressions
> stand out sharply from a blurred background. The continual shouting
> of the vendors of varied goods: the perpetual hum of the moving mul-
> titudes... the slow-moving packed trams, continually rumbling down
> the roadway, gigantically exaggerated in the leaping lights and shadows:
> the visions down side streets of long avenues, dark, silent, lifeless: the

looming above of monstrous dwellings lost in the low-hanging clouds and the impenetrable darkness above this weltering human crowd...'[1]

Masterman was quick-witted, very hardworking and a brilliant speaker. 'In theory he is a collectivist,' Beatrice Webb wrote, 'by instinct an anarchic individualist – above all he is a rhetorician.'[2] His speeches in the House of Commons were so successful that it was not long before he was being tipped for high office. Gardiner described him as 'running neck and neck with Churchill as the man of the future'[3] and Ford Madox Ford, a great friend, records that when a group of fellow writers were campaigning for a government pension for D. H. Lawrence, who had contracted TB working in a state school in Croydon, they decided the man most likely to arrange it was 'Masterman, who was supposed to be scheduled as the next Liberal Prime Minister'.[4] Gardiner, as always more perceptive, took a cautious view, writing: 'It would be hazardous to cast the horoscope of Mr Masterman. He is the wind that bloweth where it listeth, indifferent to theories, impatient of slow processes, governed only by a compelling passion for humanity – the dreamer of dreams and the seer of visions.'[5]

Unlike Belloc, Masterman had been given preferment, first as Parliamentary Secretary to the Board of Local Government under John Burns, leader of a famous London dock strike in 1889, who defected to the Liberals and became the first working-class man to sit in the Cabinet, and then as Under-Secretary at the Home Office under Winston Churchill who, like others, had been overcome by reforming zeal. 'Winston is full of the poor, whom he has just discovered,' Masterman wrote. 'He thinks he is called by providence to do something for them – "Why have I been kept safe within a hair's breadth of death except to do something like this?"'[6] Masterman and Churchill formed a close bond – 'almost sentimental friends' according to Beatrice Webb. After Churchill returned from his famous appearance at the siege of Sidney Street, where a group of anarchists were besieged by the police, Masterman rebuked him. 'Now, Charlie, don't be croth,' Churchill lisped. 'It was such fun.'[7]

Like many men who enter Parliament eager for reform, Masterman was frustrated by the procedural delays – 'impatient of slow processes', in Gardiner's phrase. He had gone in for politics with high hopes but was playing little or no part in introducing the social reforms which he felt were badly needed. All this changed when he joined forces with David Lloyd George, the one radical figure in the Cabinet, a man of ferocious energy and brilliant political skills who had little time for the customary consultations and committees that stood in the way of reform. Unlike the aristocratic Churchill, Lloyd George appealed to Masterman partly because he had direct experience of the working class and was, like him, determined to make life more tolerable for the so-called common people. Until he fell out with him, as most of his admirers tended to do, Masterman worked happily alongside Lloyd George, doing most of the donkey work while telling his wife Lucy, 'You can get anything you want done in this life if you don't mind someone else getting the credit.'[8] The two men holidayed together with their wives, visiting France and Brighton and playing golf. For three or four years prior to the First World War, as the country was convulsed by a series of political crises, strikes and the violent protest of Ulstermen and suffragettes, Masterman was at the centre of events.

Lloyd George, Chancellor of the Exchequer since 1908, had already rocked the boat with his revolutionary 'People's Budget' of 1909, 'specifically designed,' in the words of historian A. J. P. Taylor, 'in order to transform the social order, designed, effectively or not, as an attack on the rich and particularly on the landlords.'[9] With its increase in death duties, introduction of a supertax on the wealthy and, most controversially, a new tax on the sale of land, the proposal caused a major political – and constitutional – crisis when it became clear that the House of Lords with its huge Tory majority would veto it. The government now introduced a Parliament Bill to abolish the House of Lords' power to veto financial legislation. It led to what was described as 'the most violent scene in the Commons within living memory'. The Prime Minister Asquith was shouted down with cries of, 'Who killed the King?' (a reference to the recent death of Edward VII, blamed by diehard Tories on the government's proposed reforms). For the first time in history the Speaker was forced to adjourn the House as a 'disorderly assembly'.

In the event, following threats by Asquith to create hundreds of new peers, the Parliament Bill was passed by the Lords and Lloyd George blithely continued his programme of reform, focusing on his National Insurance Bill, now seen as the first step in the creation of the Welfare State. The proposals resulted in furious protests not only from the Tory party but also the Northcliffe press, which included *The Times* and the best-selling *Daily Mail*. The Bill[10] was dubbed 'a gigantic fraud' by Northcliffe's *Weekly Dispatch* and the *Mail* organised a mass protest at the Albert Hall, where duchesses spoke of the indignity of having to lick stamps for their servants' insurance cards.

Like school bullies picking on a victim who they decide is weak, the powerful opponents of Lloyd George ignored the man himself, whose position seemed invulnerable, and singled out his faithful right-hand man, Masterman. With his languid self-deprecating mien, his watch chain, little gold cross and long black frock coat giving him, in the view of Irish MP T. P. O'Connor, 'something of a clerical air', he did not seem cut out for the rougher side of politics, particularly at election time. Masterman was well aware of the intense opposition from the Tories and the press, but what must have alarmed him was to find his old friends Hilaire Belloc and Cecil Chesterton now joining in the attack.

In 1911, at the height of the political crisis, the two men had published their book *The Party System*, crying 'a plague on both your houses', arguing that there was nothing much to choose between the Tories and the Liberals – a view famously expressed in Belloc's much-quoted verse:

> *The accursed power which stands on Privilege*
> *(And goes with Women, and Champagne and Bridge)*
> *Broke – and Democracy resumed her reign:*
> *(Which goes with Bridge, and Women and Champagne)*

The Party System, though making a number of good points about, for example, the sale of peerages, was also marred by what looked like an irrational obsession with their friend Charles Masterman, now held up by the two authors as a symbol of the corruption of the political system. Masterman's principal crime in their eyes was that having initially supported the Labour Party's Right to Work Bill in 1908, he voted against it after his promotion to the government. Although such U-turns are commonplace in a system of collective ministerial responsibility, whereby ministers are expected to support government policy or resign, the authors of *The Party System* accused Masterman of total abandonment of his principles.

The book contained another more unpleasant and more personal attack on Masterman in passages which, because they did not mention him by name, possibly for legal reasons, have tended to go unnoticed. Like subsequent such pieces in the *Eye-Witness* and the *New Witness* the authors drew attention to his marriage. Masterman had married Lucy Lyttelton in 1908. A woman of great character, author of an outstanding biography of her husband, she was the daughter of a general, Sir Neville Lyttelton, and the niece of Tory minister and cricketer Alfred Lyttelton, but a lifelong supporter of the Liberal Party who later stood twice as a parliamentary candidate, though unsuccessfully. Lucy was also a would-be poet who had met her husband-to-be after submitting poems to him in the hope of publication. Her family didn't think much of him. He was short of money and belonged to a different class. 'Think what would become of me,' her mother said, 'if it is known that my daughter is to marry a penniless journalist.' Fortunately she changed her tune as Masterman's star rose, and the marriage, in spite of all Masterman's subsequent setbacks, was a happy one.

Belloc and Cecil, however, seized on Lucy's Tory connections, and especially her Uncle Alfred, as proof of their thesis that the Tories and the leading Liberals were hand-in-glove, mostly interrelated and that any political conflict between them was a charade. Not only, they implied, did Masterman owe his position in the government to his wife's connections, but there was the additional suggestion that he had only married her in order to gain political preferment. In an early chapter, the authors sought to demonstrate that this was common practice. 'Is there any reason why a man should not marry a woman because her family belongs to the political party opposed to his. Not the least in the world... but when we find such things not exceptional but universal' this indicates 'a general system of government by a small, friendly and closely related clique.'[11] Masterman's name was not mentioned in this passage but it had been on the preceding page where he was credited with having married the niece of the Conservative Colonial Secretary.[12] In a later chapter, the allusion to Masterman is equally clear:

> During the late election [of December 1910] one of the younger men who had just been put upon the Front Bench by the machine, said that the 'gulf' between the two Front Benches was 'unbridgeable'; he said it to a mass of men much poorer than himself, whose votes make him what he is. *They* had no opportunity to see behind what scenes the actor moves. He deliberately deceived them. Well, this young man had his place from marrying a lady whose uncle had made many thousands in one half of the team; the same lady had a first cousin who had a much larger number of thousands in the other half of the team. One of these new-found relatives was labelled 'Opposition' the other 'Government' and the poor men who listened were told that there was an 'unbridgeable gulf' between the one relative and the other![13]

Those 'poor men' were not only being lied to, their wishes were being ignored: 'It is surely ridiculous,' the authors wrote, 'to say a man represents Bethnal Green if he is in the habit of saying "Aye" when the people of Bethnal Green would say "No".' (The mention of Bethnal Green was no accident, being yet another dig at Masterman who had stood as Liberal candidate for that constituency at a by-election in 1911.) Yet as a former MP himself Belloc knew that no member could be expected to consistently represent the views of his constituents even if it were possible to know what they were. Belloc also knew from his personal experience that Masterman was a man who owed his position not to his wife's connections but to his considerable political skill and powers of application. As Gardiner was to write after Masterman's death in 1927, 'He had a surprisingly practical mind for the details of legislation and the cut and thrust of the parliamentary encounter. He could pick his way through the mazes of a bill with a swiftness and sureness that few men in our time have equalled.'[14]

Not content with blackening Masterman in print, Belloc and Cecil Chesterton campaigned against him in the Bethnal Green by-election in person, joining forces with local Tories, the Northcliffe press and the notorious Horatio Bottomley, editor of the immensely popular scandal-sheet *John Bull*, later imprisoned for swindling. Belloc presided at a meeting of Masterman's Socialist rival telling his audience that Masterman, a man who had 'abandoned democracy for paid officialism, owed his promotion *solely* [italics added] to his relationship with its various members upon both of the two sides'.[15]

'We quoted all the names,' he boasted in the *Tablet* in answer to an attack by Gardiner's *Daily News*, 'we quoted all the ties of marriage and of blood.'[16] And that was not all he did. According to the account of Lucy Masterman, who describes being pelted with whelk shells as she drove through the streets with her husband, Belloc and Cecil issued leaflets 'on prostitution and venereal disease for which evils they appeared to regard the Liberal candidate (Masterman) as personally responsible'. As if this was not enough they also distributed a complicated family tree to show that Lucy was related to Lord Rothschild and was therefore partly Jewish (when Belloc wrote about 'the ties of blood' he was presumably referring to Lucy's supposedly Jewish ancestry) – probably a counter-productive charge, as Lucy pointed out, since a third of the electorate in Bethnal Green were Jewish. In the event, Masterman secured the seat with a small majority.

In 1914 Masterman was promoted to the Cabinet, but was required under a regulation then in force to stand again for Parliament. He therefore recontested his Bethnal Green seat in February 1914. This time all the anti-Lloyd George factions, aided by £10,000 from *Daily Express* owner Lord Beaverbrook and once again including Cecil Chesterton and Belloc, combined to defeat him. When he stood again in Ipswich in May 1914, Cecil launched a non-stop barrage of abuse in the pages of the *New Witness*. He portrayed Masterman as the willing servant of a party formed by 'the combination of [Lloyd] George and his hangers on with the Jews and their hangers on' who had been ordered by his superiors to fight the Ipswich seat. He was, Cecil wrote, a man who owed his position only to his wife and her Tory relatives. He had been 'an accomplice in a very nefarious and corrupt conspiracy' (a reference to the Marconi scandal)[17] and the electors of Ipswich should ask him whether he had ever owned any Marconi shares (a charge for which Cecil had absolutely no evidence).

In addition, Cecil travelled to Ipswich to heckle Masterman who was addressing workers outside a factory. When Masterman lost the seat, Cecil claimed to be partly responsible, while the *New Witness* wrote that Masterman 'should have been excluded not merely from Parliament but from the society of decent honourable men'. After the Ipswich defeat Masterman lost the support of the Prime Minister, Asquith, who wrote to his girlfriend Venetia Stanley that he found him 'quite clever but strangely unattractive', while mocking his failure to win the seat: 'Aren't you amused by the electoral experiences of poor Masterman?'[18] Tarred with the brush of political failure Masterman went into a protracted decline. He resigned from the Cabinet and when he stood as an independent Liberal in West Ham in 1918 he was beaten by a Tory. He returned as an MP briefly in 1923 but his health was deteriorating. All his life he had suffered from occasional bouts of deep depression, treating himself with drugs to which he became addicted. 'If his physical stamina had been greater,' his friend Frank Swinnerton remembered,

> he would have conquered everything, even the desertions to which he owed his fall from power in the government of his day. But he was too sick to deal with life and when one night Hedley le Bas gave a dinner for him, Masterman himself was the first to remark, sardonically, that

all the speeches made in his honour were in the nature of funeral orations. They were. To see him, standing plumply at the table, with his coat forcibly buttoned about him, his nose more pointed than ever, his nervous smile flitting into sadness and returning again as if it was almost a grimace, was to know that he was finished, almost to be sure that he was dying.[19]

Dubbed a 'Splendid Failure' in a series of *Daily Express* profiles by Lord Beaverbrook, now a friend, he died, virtually penniless in 1927. G. K. Chesterton was one of those he named in his will as someone to be approached after his death 'to give a small annual amount' to help his wife and children 'who would otherwise be left in poverty'.

Why did Belloc join with Cecil in such a vicious and prolonged campaign against a former friend and ally who had done him no wrong? One reason was the extent to which his own political position had changed. Previously an admirer of Lloyd George – he had described the People's Budget as 'perfectly excellent' – his views were now little different from those Tories who branded Lloyd George a dangerous revolutionary and regarded the National Insurance Act as a threat to individual liberty by making the working man dependent on the state for his pension and his medical treatment. Moreover Lloyd George's insurance plans were inspired by what had been introduced by Bismarck in Germany[20] (or Prussia as he and the Chestertons insisted on calling it), and to the Frenchman Belloc, Prussia was the arch enemy – not only of France but the whole of Christendom.

But there was more to Belloc's antagonism than a rightwards shift in his politics and animus towards Germany – underlying his vitriol lay a narcissism which predisposed him to thin-skinned resentment and envy. The ever astute Gardiner was certainly of the opinion that resentment lay behind the ferocity of Belloc's attack on the parliamentary system, and that envy lay behind his vicious attack on that system's rising star, Charles Masterman. Putting himself in Belloc's shoes he wrote:

It was the capital crime of the Liberals when they came into power in 1906 that they forgot Mr Belloc. They acted as though they were unaware that he was among them – that he, who had served in the French artillery as a conscript and knew more about war than anybody else could possibly know, who had burst upon Oxford like a tornado and swept it with the whiffs of his Gallic grapeshot, who had all the secrets of history in his private keeping, and had turned the Froudes, the Freemans and the Stubbses into discredited back numbers, who had written novels and satires and poetry and biographies and histories, who had discovered the French Revolution and put Carlyle in his place, who had invented a new mediaeval Europe after his heart's desire, who had tramped through France and Switzerland to Rome, and from Algiers to Timgad, and had written books about both, with pictures from his own hand, who could instruct you in art and explain to you the philosophy of Classicism as easily as he could sail a boat, mow a meadow, or ride a horse – they forgot, I say, that he was the Liberal member for South Salford. They formed a Ministry without him. They did not offer him even a paltry under-secretaryship when it became vacant. In a word they passed him by.

It need not be assumed that Mr Belloc would have taken office. I do not know. So turbulent a spirit could certainly not have run in harness long. But to be ignored, to be passed by for the Aclands and the Macnamaras and the Seelys – that was unforgivable. It revealed the sham of Liberalism, it disclosed the corruption of the party system, it made it clear that England was governed by a nest of rogues, chiefly Jews – probably all of them Jews...[21]

Very significantly in his devastating attack, Gardiner links this resentment of Belloc's to the anti-Masterman campaign:

Though you have been his bosom friend, yet shall old friendship not save you from scourging. When Charles Masterman, who had shared his dialectical revels in the old *Daily News* days, was given office, he turned and rent him as though he were a heathen or a Turk. He pursued him down to Bethnal Green, he told the electors he had bartered his principles for £30 a week, and, if I remember aright, even discovered some wholly illusory relationship between his wife and the Rothschilds.[22]

How did Belloc justify his attack on the parliamentary system given his participation in it as an MP? In later life he claimed that he was well aware of the degraded nature of the House of Commons when he stood as a parliamentary candidate: 'I had never thought much of Parliament in its modern decay,' he wrote in 1932, '...I had known the place to be corrupt but I had not appreciated the degree of the corruption. If I went in at all it would only be to add to my stock of experience.'[23] Yet all the evidence is that, to begin with, Belloc relished the excitement of electioneering and the House of Commons debates, telling Chesterton that his first campaign in Salford was 'huge fun'. He made a number of speeches on such issues as Catholic schools and the Prevention of Crime Bill, but made little impact due to his habit of lecturing rather than trying to persuade his listeners. His disillusionment followed only when he failed to shine, and he and Cecil, in particular, were to justify their campaign against Masterman by arguing that the only principled politician was the backbencher who spurned preferment and spoke his mind, like Belloc.

Belloc may have been uncomfortably aware that such behaviour laid him open to a charge of hypocrisy, especially in the eyes of his high-born friends like Maurice Baring: 'I detest the vulgar futility of the whole business,' he had written to Baring prior to the general election of 1910. 'So anxious are most people to get into Parliament, they will do anything to oust an opponent and I have really no desire to be mixed up with such hatreds.' Even if they were prepared to overlook the evidence that Belloc seemed to have no aversion to being mixed up with such hatreds in Bethnal Green, they will have felt increasingly uncomfortable about the persecution of Masterman when it began to look like kicking a man when he's down. At any rate Belloc was later to try and dissociate himself from the offending passages in *The Party System*, blaming Cecil as the author and claiming that he himself 'would have written it differently', adding 'I know the world, Cecil didn't'[24] – by which he meant that Cecil had little concern about upsetting the gentry or the 'swells' as he called them. For all his bravado, Belloc was aware that many of those whose opinion he valued found his anti-Jewish views offensive. Cecil had no inhibitions of this kind.

The surviving correspondence between the two makes it clear that Cecil did the bulk of the writing of *The Party System,* with Belloc playing more of an editorial role. But Cecil, by now Belloc's devoted disciple, had no objection to Belloc being billed as the principal author – *The Party System* has always been treated by critics as Belloc's book – because his famous name was bound to lead to bigger sales and both men were short of money, Belloc's claim that he would have 'written it differently', therefore, raises the question why, in his editorial role, he never asked Cecil to tone down his attacks. And if Cecil, as Belloc said, was ignorant of the ways of the world, then presumably Belloc would have had a duty to intervene. His failure to do so suggests that he actually approved of Cecil's assault on Masterman and only felt the need to backtrack later, when facing criticism that his book had grossly overstated the case and when there was widespread sympathy for Masterman.[25]

If Belloc was motivated by envy, as Gardiner states, what lay behind Cecil's attacks? Cecil knew that Masterman was an old and trusted family friend of his brother. Their friendship went back to the *Daily News* and the Christian Social Union and it embraced the wives of both men. Frances Chesterton was especially fond of Masterman, a fellow Anglo-Catholic, and was devoted to Lucy, who was not only a friend but, like her, a poet. In her diary Lucy describes a typical occasion in February 1909: 'Chestertons to dinner. A splendid evening. Gilbert in tremendous form discoursing about A. J. Balfour. "He hath a devil, I am sure of it. Charles, when you get up and speak in answer to him you ought to make the sign of the cross and say, "Leave him and come out of him." He would vanish into smoke and the rest of the House of Commons would rush down a steep place into the river.' Lucy was to remember many such occasions, the loud laughter and the writing of ballades.

Yet Cecil was prepared to taunt his brother about Masterman in the pages of the *New Witness*: 'I think it very probable,' he wrote in reply to H. G. Wells, who had criticised the anti-Masterman vendetta, 'that my brother and I should disagree to a considerable extent in our estimate of Masterman's character and motives.'[26] Cecil did not 'think it very probable', he knew perfectly well that Chesterton would not merely disagree but would be deeply offended by his description of Masterman as 'a young professional politician, once an insecure and not very successful journalist, who has intrigued and married himself into the little governing group which has the salaries and places in its gift.'[27] In making such attacks and at the same time drawing his readers' attention to Chesterton's high opinion of Masterman he seemed to be asserting his dominance over his brother, challenging him publicly to defend his friend (which he knew he was most unlikely to do). At the same time he did his best to make the anti-Masterman campaign seem like a respectable public-spirited crusade:

Mr Masterman is attacked because through him can be assailed and exposed one of the chief political evils of our time – the temptation under which young men of some ability and perhaps of originally honest intent are placed to betray their constituents for a 'career'. Mr Masterman entered politics as an avowed (and perhaps sincere) idealist because he professed and perhaps felt a passionate devotion to the cause of the poor, because he was closely associated with men of like mind [i.e. Belloc], many of whom are still working for the cause which he has abandoned; his case is an example to be continually marked and emphasised; and indeed the better you think of Masterman as he once was, the more awful will the example be to you... We have always used the name of Masterman as a warning and a scarecrow. Had his career been brilliantly successful, his example might have done incalculable evil. If I have done anything to prevent its being successful, I consider that I have done at least one public service.[28]

This specious and insincere claim concealed the fact that, in the same spirit that Cecil had lectured his brother about his writing in his anonymous book, he was now determined to wreck his friendship with Masterman and force him to declare his allegiance to his 'friends' (Cecil and Belloc) and endorse their ideas on the corruption of Parliament, the iniquity of Lloyd George, the treachery of Masterman, the Jewish threat to stability and so on. By allying himself to Belloc, and insulting Masterman in the most vicious attacks imaginable, Cecil could force his brother to change sides.

In this campaign he was to be wholly successful, as he made clear when dedicating his 1914 book *The Prussian Hath Said in His Heart* to 'My brother G. K. Chesterton in memory of many arguments *and an alliance*' [italics added]. Three years previously Chesterton had dedicated a book of his own, *What's Wrong with the World*, to Charles Masterman, concluding with the words: 'I offer it to you because there exists not only comradeship, but a very different thing called friendship; an agreement under all the arguments and a thread which, please God, will never break.' But now in early 1913 he wrote to Masterman, following the birth of his son Neville:

My dear Charles, I wish to tell you with the utmost violence that I am opposed to you in politics. About the destiny of our country I differ from you as much as my friends who have with sincerity assailed you and whom I will not abandon[29] here. The difference is that they don't know you a bit; and I do. I wonder whether I will offend you when I defend you; but I think not. I know that you and Lucy are living persons I love and admire; I know that such persons could save the situation from the inside if it could be saved; I rather think it can't. But you are not theories, but things. Excuse my calling you things – shall I say 'dear things'? – ...Well, I can't help being in the other camp – the new and mutinous camp recently built. I think they are right and I will never say no... I wonder whether this letter sounds like lunacy or insult. It is really affection. Yours G. K. Chesterton.[30]

Chesterton himself uses the word 'lunacy' and it is tempting to see in this letter the signs of his impending breakdown – the expression 'utmost violence' is bizarre. If not that, it certainly reveals the agonising difficulties that he had brought upon himself by signing up with Belloc and Cecil – going into 'the other camp', as he puts it. Chesterton has first to try to justify the brutal persecution of Masterman by his brother and Belloc in their book, in the *New Witness* and on the hustings. He knows the ferocity and malice involved, which must especially have upset Frances, yet he can write that 'they have with sincerity assailed you'. He then excuses them on the grounds that, unlike him, they do not know Masterman personally. Yet both of them not only knew him but had been his friends. Belloc (a regular contributor to the *Daily News*) and Masterman had attended all the same debates and dinner parties – often riotous occasions where Belloc would entertain his friends with jokes, songs and freshly composed ballades. Masterman greatly admired Belloc's writing, having written a very enthusiastic review of *The Path to Rome* as a result of which, according to Belloc's biographer Speaight, 'they afterwards became close friends' ('bosom friend' was Gardiner's description). As for Cecil, he had long ago referred to Masterman as 'my excellent friend' in his 1905 book *Gladstonian Ghosts* and later joined him campaigning for the Christian Social Union, both men being confirmed Anglo-Catholics.

Yet Chesterton was somehow able to shut his eyes to the facts and write 'they don't know you a bit', a sure sign of the stress and confusion that he was labouring under. Thus he assured Masterman that he would not abandon Cecil and Belloc (or 'betray' them, which had been his first thought),[31] yet he had no qualms, it seemed, about abandoning or betraying Masterman by failing to say a word in his defence or attempting to restrain his 'friends' from their vicious campaign.

Inevitably, the friendship with Masterman which he prayed would 'never break', was now broken. Chesterton's letter, Lucy Masterman wrote later, led to a breach, and although there was a rapprochement of sorts during the war, 'the days of bubbles and ballades were over'. Her refusal ever to comment publicly on her husband's treatment at the hands of Cecil Chesterton is admirable. When asked, in old age, about their relationship by Cecil's biographer Brocard Sewell she would only say that Masterman had found him 'difficult'. A more realistic assessment is contained in a letter written by Masterman to Herbert Samuel in 1912 when he too was under attack by Cecil in the *New Witness*. Here, in tones that recall Cecil's schoolfellows at St Paul's, he describes Cecil as 'a malignant and pestilential little toad who makes up for his absence of his brother's brains by such muck as this'.[32]

Being 'in the same camp' as Cecil and Belloc meant a rupture with a more significant figure in Chesterton's life: A. G. Gardiner, editor of the *Daily News* and the man who more than anyone had put the journalist Chesterton on the map. The paper was owned by the Cadbury family in the person of businessman-philanthropist George Cadbury[33] who, with his brother Richard, took over the family's cocoa factory in Birmingham and turned it into a highly profitable business. A dignified and bearded figure, a lifelong and devout Quaker like his forebears, Cadbury took an intense interest in the physical and spiritual welfare of his workforce, moving the firm's factory to Bournville, a garden village which he created in the countryside for the benefit of his workers, with whom he breakfasted every morning, listening to Bible readings and prayers. 'Mr Cadbury,' Chesterton's friend George Bernard Shaw wrote, 'stands conspicuous as a philanthropist among the whole mass of employers of labour, most of whom have no other motive apparently than to aggrandise themselves at the expense of other people.'[34]

In his memoirs, Chesterton's old schoolfriend E. C. Bentley describes a *Daily News* office outing to Bournville: 'I remember that the wearing of curling pins in the factory was prohibited and that the villagers [Cadbury's employees] enjoyed a number of advantages which I wished I could have shared in, among them a very large gymnasium, a swimming pool to match and a theatre of their own.' The only thing to complain about, particularly for a group of journalists, was the absence of drink at mealtime, and on the journey back to London on board a special saloon coach attached to the train the *Daily News* men did their best to make up for the strain of 'thirty-six hours of good behaviour and nothing stronger than lemonade... during the dinner a certain amount of bread was thrown'.

Cadbury, with little previous interest in newspapers, had bought the *Daily News* in 1901 solely in order to air his opposition to the Boer War which ironically, in view of what happened later, was based on views very similar to Belloc's, namely that the war was being fought by Great Britain on behalf of gold miners and money men. 'It is so evidently a speculators' war and no one else can derive any benefit from it,' he wrote to Labour MP John Burns. 'Just now it seems to me that speculators, trust-mongers, and owners of enormous wealth are the great curse of the world and the cause of most of its poverty.'[35] Cadbury felt so strongly about the war that he refused to tender for orders of chocolate for the British army and only agreed to cooperate when Queen Victoria personally ordered him to supply chocolate as her Christmas present for the troops. Influenced by what he had seen of conditions in industrial Birmingham, Cadbury campaigned ceaselessly for social reform, and although the Chestertons and Belloc pilloried him as the chief financial backer of the Liberals, he was just as generous in his support of the fledgling Labour party, and on intimate terms with its leaders Ramsay MacDonald and Keir Hardie.

As a result of Cadbury's influence, the *Daily News* had involved itself in a number of charitable campaigns. In the winter of 1904–5 conditions in London's dockland were so bad that famine became a reality. The *Daily News*, encouraged by Cadbury, launched a relief fund and Masterman accompanied Gardiner on a tour of the area to organise public works for the unemployed dockers. In the following year, the *Daily News*, again with Cadbury's money, organised an exhibition of sweated labour at Queen's Hall which lasted for five weeks. In the hall were workers carrying out their daily tasks such as making cardboard boxes at one shilling and three-pence for twelve hours' work, repairing sacks for two shillings a week and shirt-making at less than a penny an hour. The exhibition, similar to modern exposés of third-world exploitation, had a lasting impact, and was visited by thousands, including Mary, Princess of Wales.[36]

But to Belloc and his disciple Cecil, Cadbury was an anathema. He was a Quaker and therefore a pacifist. Cecil wrote: 'The *Daily News* and the *Star* are the property of a rich cocoa manufacturer who happens to inherit along with his wealth[37] the religious faith of a curious seventeenth-century sect, which among the madness of that age (such as that of the Adamites who went about naked to prove their innocence) developed the fantastic idea that Christianity forbade an appeal to arms.'[38]

Cadbury was not only a heretic and a pacifist, he was also a teetotaller, a pillar of the temperance movement which banned advertisements for drink in his papers and campaigned for stricter licensing laws to control the plague of drunkenness that was causing widespread poverty and crime. Cecil, however, saw any attempt to tighten the licensing laws as an intolerable interference with the Englishman's liberties and his right to drink as much beer as he wanted at any time of the day or night that suited him. He even opposed the Children's Act of 1910 banning young children from pubs, arguing that it was the thin end of the wedge and would lead to their being banned from other shops like butchers and bookshops.

In this, as so often, Cecil was merely following the lead of Belloc. As Gardiner had written in his profile: '... if there is anything more unspeakable [to Belloc] than a Jew, it is a Puritan. For to the abominable fact that he has doubts about the infallibility of the Pope, the Puritan adds an infamy that puts him outside the pale of humanity. He does not drink beer.'[39]

Cecil was particularly outraged to learn of some of the things that went on under the Cadbury regime at Bournville:

It appears that young girl workers at that industrial paradise are compelled whether they like it or not to engage in swimming daily. This is
a monstrous and disgraceful interference with the liberty of the subject
which is utterly indefensible in theory and cruel in practice. What right
have any of the egregious brothers Cadbury to insist on their work-
people taking this particular form of exercise for the gratification of

the avid eyes of the officials and the firm, and to the possible detriment of the health of the girls themselves... to us this appears <u>plain slavery</u>.[40]

Under Belloc's influence, Chesterton, whose *Daily News* column had hitherto been light-hearted and literary, had begun to write more about politics and this was bound to lead to conflict with Gardiner. The argument began in 1907 when Chesterton came to the defence of a radical backbencher H. C. Lea, but even before that there had been friction between the two men as a comic letter from Shaw to Gardiner makes clear. If Chesterton was proving difficult he wrote, it was 'because he eats too much and feels my slender figure and my vegetarianism to be a standing reproach to him. Tell him so and give him notice that you will not allow contributions from young men of more than sixteen stone after the 30th June...' H. C. Lea, the backbencher whose case Chesterton took up, no doubt with the encouragement of Belloc and Cecil, had been accused of a breach of parliamentary privilege by writing to *The Times* about the sale of peerages in exchange for donations to the party. When Chesterton submitted an article defending Lea, Gardiner, whose editorial freedom was restricted by the paper's close connection with the Liberal party, spiked it, telling Chesterton he would hold it over for a later occasion. In a long letter of protest Chesterton lectured Gardiner: 'Lea is to be humiliated and broken because he said that titles are bought, as they are; because he said that all this was hypocrisy of public life, as it is.' Further references to 'secret funds' and 'secret powers' echo the language of the Belloc/Cecil attack on the parliamentary system. 'I do not think we could quarrel,' Chesterton ended, 'even if we had to separate.'[41]

Chesterton also followed obediently in the footsteps of Belloc's newly emerged right-wing politics, writing to Gardiner, 'I think the Insurance Act not only a tyranny, but one of the historic turning points of tyranny, like Ship Money or the persecution of Wilkes. I believe our children will hold it against us.' He wanted to have the same freedom to attack Lloyd George and his National Insurance plans as those *Daily News* correspondents who sided with the suffragettes in defiance of editorial policy. He now found himself under constant pressure from Cecil, in particular, to say goodbye to the *Daily News*.

In all of Cecil's attacks on Cadbury there was an obsessive and occasionally malevolent tone. Cadbury, according to Cecil, was 'just a rich man with no brains at all distinguished by the vice of hypocrisy'. Cecil wrote in this vein well aware that Cadbury was his brother's employer. It is as if he was possessed of a fanatical, almost a manic determination to bully his elder brother, as he had done over Masterman, into abandoning his paper and his friend and adopting the Belloc creed. It is possible, of course, to excuse his behaviour on the grounds that he genuinely thought that Chesterton, in both cases, had made a grave mistake and that he Cecil, had a fraternal duty to make him see the error of his ways. But if that were the case it made no difference to the outcome, Chesterton ending up committed to causes that were quite alien to all his instincts, being a man rightly described by Shaw as 'friendly, easy-going, unaffected, gentle, magnanimous and genuinely democratic' – the very opposite of Cecil in other words.

Chesterton finally broke with Gardiner in January 1913 – about the same time as he wrote his 'utmost violence' letter to Masterman – with the publication of his poem 'A Song of Strange Drinks' in Cecil's magazine *New Witness*, the second verse of which read:

> *Tea, although an oriental,*
> *Is a gentleman at least;*
> *Cocoa is a cad and coward,*
> *Cocoa is a vulgar beast,*
> *Cocoa is a dull, disloyal,*
> *Lying, crawling cad and clown,*
> *And may very well be grateful*
> *To the fool that takes him down.* [42]

As Cadbury's papers, including the *Daily News*, were generally known as 'the Cocoa Press', it was obvious to everybody that this was an attack on him – the use of the word 'cad' as in Cadbury twice in eight lines was enough to make that clear. The viciousness of the language, so untypical of Chesterton, is a sign of the stress under which he was labouring in defecting to the Belloc camp. Applied to Cadbury the words 'Lying, crawling cad and clown' were hopelessly inept, especially as Chesterton had personal knowledge of the man and must have been aware of his record as a philanthropist, his opposition to the Boer War, his strong and sincere religious principles. He would have known too that ever since the Boer War Cadbury had been a favourite target of the Tory party and Tory newspapers, which regularly attacked the Cocoa Press, urged on by Horatio Bottomley, who dubbed Cadbury 'a serpentine and malevolent cocoa magnate'. In writing as he did, Chesterton was saying nothing original, merely adding his voice to a chorus of right-wing diehards and their friends in the press.[43]

In the tones of a pained headmaster, Gardiner, who must have been startled and shaken by the savagery of Chesterton's lines, wrote that he had 'too much respect for your sense of decency to suppose you would stoop to so gross an outrage on those with whom you have been associated in journalism for years', to which Chesterton feebly replied that he had intended nothing personal but that in the circumstances it would be better for him to resign: 'It is quite impossible for me to continue taking the money of a man who may think I have insulted him.'[44]

Gardiner's biographer Stephen Koss reports that he suffered 'considerable pain' as a result of this episode. The comings and goings of journalists, their sometimes fierce disputes and rivalries were things he was used to, but Chesterton was not that kind of journalist. He was a contributor for whom he had special affection, regarding him as his particular protégé. Well aware of this, Chesterton at least acknowledged what lay behind his departure. Claiming that he had no grounds for querying the sincerity of the Cadburys, he dissociated himself from the charges of hypocrisy 'brought by many of my friends' (again, the reference is to Belloc and Cecil), writing: 'I think my friends right about politics, but wrong about people – especially people they don't know.' The letter was very similar to the one he had written to Masterman at about the same time: 'I believe my brother and Belloc and the rest are right about the future of England and so there is nothing for me but to back them up.'[45]

As had happened with Masterman, Gardiner did his best, following the break, to maintain his friendship with Chesterton, but had only limited success. 'Their subsequent meetings were neither as frequent nor... altogether as cordial as Gardiner would have liked,' Koss records. This view is confirmed by Chesterton's very cursory – insulting even – reference to Gardiner in his autobiography.[46]

No one would have been surprised had Chesterton, when looking back at his offensive cocoa poem, admitted that in the wake of the Marconi scandal[47] he had given way to feelings of anger and resentment. But there was never any sign of this. He republished the poem from which the verse is taken in his *Collected Poems* (1927), and in his *Autobiography* some years later (1936) described the incident as 'a comic coincidence' which had occurred at the same time as he was objecting to Lloyd George and his Insurance Act. 'After all these years,' he wrote 'it can do no harm to mention that a Liberal editor wrote me a very sympathetic but rather sad letter, hoping that no personal attack was meant on some of the pillars of the party. I assured him that my unaffected physical recoil from cocoa was not an attack on Mr Cadbury.' There could be no better example of Chesterton's inability to face the facts when they involved confronting his own weakness in submitting to the will of Cecil and Belloc. After more than twenty years, he could dismiss as 'comic' an incident that caused pain and stress to both parties (himself and Gardiner); he could not even bring himself to name Gardiner or the *Daily News*, and deliberately omitted the reason for Gardiner's letter – that the attack was not on 'some of the pillars of the party' but specifically on the owner of the *Daily News*, George Cadbury, Chesterton's employer, clearly identified by the poem's two-fold reference to 'cad', thus making a nonsense of Chesterton's claim that he was merely proclaiming his distaste for cocoa as a beverage.

By the time he wrote his memoir, his antipathy to Cadbury had hardened into a fully grown conspiracy theory in line with the diktats of Belloc and Cecil and their strident campaigns against anyone showing signs of pacifism during or before the First World War. Foremost amongst them were the Jewish bankers, many of whom had links with Germany or were even themselves German. But they were not the only dangerous pacifists, according to Cecil, who referred to 'the wealthy men who finance our politicians some of whom have fancy religions' – a clear reference to Quakerism, the Quakers being linked to the Jews in Cecil's mind by their common concern with making money. Chief among powerful Quaker pacifists was 'the idealist cocoa manufacturer Cadbury' who had initially opposed the war 'on the exalted ground that if we stood by we could make money out of both sides'. As so often when making his wild claims, Cecil produced no evidence to back this up.

In obedience to the Belloc/Cecil line of attack, Chesterton's language became more hostile. Where before words like 'cad' and 'coward' had been used, now he wrote 'evil' and 'wicked'. Cadbury was even bracketed with Northcliffe, as though there was nothing to choose between them. It was as if he was trying to bolster the case against Cadbury in order to justify the cocoa poem for his own peace of mind. In 1917 he wrote:

What does the history of the Quakers really teach anybody who has his eyes open today? Simply that the attempt to refuse a priesthood, as a mere caste, ends in the worst, most worldly and more wicked of all the castes: a mere plutocracy. Those who were aghast at the vision of a country covered with poor little hard-working priests, have lived to see the reality of a country overshadowed by the mountainous accumulations of a few Quaker millionaires. Such philanthropists have more of the evil in spiritual superiority than all the priests on the planet. They are not even one caste, they are rather one firm and one family. They send a telegram: and the English coasts are nearly swept bare of their ships under the instant shadow of the Great War. They sign a cheque: and pacifist literature is sent across England like a snow storm, blinding men against blazing actualities of peril. The fear of these rich men is so heavy on our rulers that they have almost to arm the realm by stealth and warn its captives in a whisper, lest their paymasters should know they are guilty of the secret vice of patriotism. Statesmen, with a whole passionately patriotic people at their backs, are obliged to leave France in doubt, to leave Belgium almost to despair, because the gold of the Great Quakers weighs so heavily in the party funds, the Parliamentary elections and the great organs of the press. That is the manifest, materialist modern result of the Quaker attempt to abolish privilege by abolishing priests.[48]

If this had been an overblown blast of patriotic fervour inspired by the outbreak of war it might be forgiven. But the anti-Quaker obsession was to persist. In the 1930s Chesterton was still harping on the same theme, in language indistinguishable from Belloc's. Quakers in general and Cadbury in particular had somehow jeopardised the war effort:

It meant that the worst sort of traitors could and did trade with the enemy throughout the War, that the worst sort of profiteers could and did blackmail their own country for bloodsucking profits in the worst hour of her peril, that the worst sort of politicians could play any game they liked with the honour of England and the happiness of Europe, if they were backed and boomed by some vulgar monopolist millionaire; and these insolent interests nearly brought us to a crash in the supreme crisis of our history; because Parliament had come to mean only a secret government by the rich.[49]

From this lurid Bellocian picture of greedy monopolists making money out of the war, Chesterton advanced to the consideration of who had caused the war in the first place:

If I were asked who produced or precipitated the Great War... I should give an answer that would surprise nearly all sections of opinion... I should not say the Kaiser... Still less should I say the Czar of Russia or some Slavonic fanatic who committed a crime at Sarajevo. Long after the acts and attitudes of all these people were recognised, it would have been perfectly possible to avoid the war; and nearly everybody wanted to avoid it. I should say that the fire-eater who precipitated it when others might have prevented it, was some sort of worthy Quaker of the type of old Mr Cadbury, whom I knew and served in my youth.[50]

It all went back to the 'party system' as defined in Belloc and Cecil's book of that name. According to the book, both the Tory and Liberal parties were controlled not by the politicians but by their secret backers; and in the case of the Liberals, who formed the government in 1914, this meant the Jewish plutocrats and the Quaker millionaires like Cadbury. These Quakers were all pacifists in accordance with their religion, and the Liberal government was therefore unable to make public its commitment to back France if the Germans invaded.[51] Had they done so, war would have been avoided and, Chesterton concluded, 'My brother and many millions more would be walking about alive.'

Poor Cadbury – already damned as a 'lying, crawling cad and clown' he was now to be forever cursed for causing the First World War, thus being responsible for the death of Cecil Chesterton.

6

A Real Smash-Up

'I BELIEVE THAT ENGLAND IS IN DANGER OF A REAL SMASH-UP, of a great national disaster,' Chesterton said in the course of an interview with the *Jewish Chronicle* in April 1911. There was nothing specific about that belief, but it was a sign of how the mood of the country had changed. The expectations that Belloc and the Chesterton brothers had cherished at the time of the triumphant Liberal victory of 1906, 'when everything,' as Gardiner wrote, 'seemed possible and all the political earth was full of the coming of spring', had been replaced by a mood of doubt and pessimism. There were violent disputes in Parliament, a wave of strikes, the suffragette protests, and in 1912 the sinking of the *Titanic*, widely interpreted as a massive blow to the confidence of the nation. And underlying it all, the fear of a looming war with Germany.

Scandals thrive in an atmosphere of doubt and uncertainty about the future. It was almost inevitable, given the disturbing scenario, that Belloc and others, with their memories of Dreyfus, would look around for 'guilty men' to blame for the moral decline; inevitable, too, that they would find them, as the anti-Dreyfusards had done, in the shape of Jewish politicians and financiers, a sinister conspiracy infiltrating British politics to form what Belloc called an 'Anglo-Judaic plutocracy'. But the evidence was not provided – until, that is, in the spring of 1912 rumours began to circulate about a political scandal involving prominent Jews and the Marconi Wireless Telegraph Company. It was unfortunate for all those concerned that these rumours happened to coincide with Cecil Chesterton taking over from Belloc as editor of the *Eye-Witness*.

Belloc resigned in June 1912 after only a year as editor. Apart from the frustration of having to deal with petty problems, he found himself facing a financial crisis threatening the future of the *Eye-Witness*, in which he was a major shareholder, and a belated loss of confidence in his proprietor, Charles Granville.

Granville gets only very cursory coverage in the Chesterton and Belloc biographies – Keith does not even mention his name, referring only to 'one of those strange venturers who now and again break into the literary world'. He was as strange a venturer as any. His real name was Charles Hosken, son of a Cornish blacksmith, who after practising as a solicitor in his native town of Helston launched himself into business and made a fortune on the stock market. He bought a large house in the town and married Charlotte Taylor, daughter of a local councillor. They had a son, Basil, who was killed in action in 1916. In 1898 Hosken was declared bankrupt, shortly afterwards changing his name to the aristocratic-sounding Granville. He left his wife and in 1905 was in London running a language school and using the name Henry Charos James. The same year he bigamously married a wealthy surgeon's widow, Charlotte Parker, who had enrolled at the school. (He later claimed in court that he had no memory of the marriage which had taken place at Paddington Registry Office. Mrs Parker, he said, must have drugged him prior to the ceremony: 'Something must have been given me which had a peculiar effect on my brain.') Describing himself as 'litterateur and widower', Hosken/Granville then acquired yet another wife, a Mrs Fawcett, and they were married in Portobello near Edinburgh in November 1908.

With the help of funds provided by these wealthy widows Granville embarked on a literary career. He wrote novels and poetry (some of it published by A. R. Orage in the *New Age*) and launched himself as a publisher using a new pseudonym, Stephen Swift. It was thanks to this enterprise that he first came into contact with Belloc and Cecil Chesterton, publishing their book *The Party System* in 1911 and then agreeing to finance the *Eye-Witness*.

Like all such con-men Granville was plausible and convincing, as successful in wooing literary men as he was with rich widows, and Belloc was not the only writer to suffer at his hands. John Middleton Murry and his wife Katherine Mansfield relied on Granville – 'an apparently prosperous publisher' – to finance their literary magazine *Rhythm*. Granville had also launched a feminist magazine *The Freewoman* which excited a good deal of controversy and was banned by W. H. Smith. ('*The Freewoman*'s work,' Granville later boasted, 'was to cleanse the gutters of our national existence, gutters which, at present, are an offensive stench in the nostrils of God.') Another writer who came to regret his association with Granville was the young Arthur Ransome. A keen contributor to the *Eye-Witness*, later to become famous as the author of the *Swallows and Amazons* series of children's books, Ransome had been bowled over when the publisher offered to take on all his books and pay him a regular salary to write some more. 'He had a magnificent way with him,' Ransome remembered.

Belloc had likewise been taken in by the apparently wealthy businessman keen to publish his books (Stephen Swift had commissioned his verse collection *More Peers* and a series of booklets on British Battles). But his experiences after only a few months at the *Eye-Witness* were beginning to cast doubts on Granville's business acumen. Granville, who had been pestering Belloc to publish his poems, was now prevaricating about signing the contributors' cheques and on one occasion the printers threatened to down tools unless their bill was paid. Urged on by Elodie, Belloc sold his shares to Granville and took a salary, but it was clear to him that apart from being a burden on his time the paper was losing money, and Granville, his wealthy benefactor, was looking more and more like a deluded chancer unable to stem the flood. In June 1912 Belloc told everyone that he didn't have time to edit the paper along with all his other commitments and walked away from the *Eye-Witness*, handing over the editorship to his deputy, Cecil.

'So that's good riddance,' he wrote,[1] without pausing to reflect that having launched a paper to expose political corruption he was abandoning it just at the time that rumours of a major political scandal were beginning to circulate. It was left to the excitable Cecil Chesterton to cope with it, unrestrained by his proprietor, Granville, who was desperately busy trying to keep his business afloat whilst avoiding arrest by the police.

Cecil, who had been doing most of the editorial work from the start, was delighted to take charge. For the first time in his life he had the opportunity to make his mark in his own right, no longer as merely the brother of the famous G. K. Chesterton, and without Belloc sending him instructions by telegram. He showed his approach to Belloc's targets in his first issue as editor, with a ferocious attack on Charles Masterman, repeating the charge that he had married his wife Lucy for political reasons: 'He connected himself by marriage with that closely related governing group that holds English politics in its hands. He had now scores of relatives, near and remote, on each Front Bench.' Masterman had become 'the hack of the bosses, the "explainer" of the fraudulent Insurance Act, the deserter and deceiver of the poor, the associate of the Hirsches and Samuels.'[2]

The linking of Masterman to two prominent Jews, one the Baron de Hirsch, a noted philanthropist and friend of the late King Edward VII, the other Herbert Samuel the Postmaster General, two men with whom Masterman had no special connections, gave a foretaste of what was to grow into an obsession, at times of almost manic intensity.

The Marconi scandal, which seemed to confirm all of Belloc's beliefs about Jews, was to dominate the political thinking of the Chestertons for the rest of their lives. The story originated in the Imperial Conference of 1911 which, following the recent invention of wireless telegraphy by Guglielmo Marconi, recommended a chain of publicly owned wireless stations to be built throughout the British Empire. As a result the Postmaster General Herbert Samuel commissioned the Marconi Wireless Telegraph Company, whose tender had been accepted by the government, to install and manage the new system. Shortly after the acceptance of the tender but before any public announcement had been made, the managing director of Marconi, Godfrey Isaacs,[3] visited the American Marconi Company (a separate legal entity partly owned by the English company) with a view to American Marconi securing the assets of its chief rival, the

United Wireless Company of America. In order for American Marconi to achieve this objective it needed to raise capital with a fresh issue of shares, 500,000 of which were entrusted to Godfrey Isaacs for 'placing'. Prior to any public offer of the American shares he decided to offer some of them to his friends and relatives at a knock-down price knowing that the forthcoming government contract with the English company (which the public did not yet know about) would be likely to enhance the value of Marconi stock worldwide and they were bound to make a profit.[4]

One of those offered shares was Godfrey's brother, Rufus Isaacs KC, a brilliantly successful barrister who was now the Attorney General and was later made a Cabinet minister in Asquith's Liberal government. In the end another Isaacs brother, Harry, bought the shares and then sold 10,000 of them to Rufus, after assuring him that the American company was quite separate from the English company. Rufus Isaacs then sold 1,000 shares each to his colleagues the Chancellor, Lloyd George, and the Liberal Chief Whip, Alec Murray, who also bought shares for the Liberal Party, insisting later that he had done so on his own initiative without the knowledge of the party's leader and Prime Minister, Asquith.[5]

The greatest journalistic exposures are those of a single man, or team, who reveal something that has, until they reveal it, remained unknown to the public. Chesterton, in his autobiography, gives the impression that his brother was such a journalist, that until the *Eye-Witness* spoke out, Marconi was a closely guarded secret. It wasn't true. Months before the *Eye-Witness*'s first article, rumours about Marconi had been rife in the City and questions had been tabled in the House of Commons where Tory MPs in particular were eager to seize on anything that would discredit the Liberal government. The first journalist to write about the scandal was not Cecil but one Wilfred Lawson, who referred to the rumours in the Tory *Outlook* using much the same kind of anti-Semitism. When the *Eye-Witness* took up the cause it was joined by the *National Review*, edited by Leo Maxse. (Maxse, an Old Harrovian man about town and son of an admiral, was a diehard Tory, much admired by Belloc, who had once predicted that giving votes to women would be the worst thing for Britain apart from a German invasion. 'There was something eminently watchful about that dark vivid face and strong forehead,' Chesterton wrote after his death.) Maxse was acting in collusion with Tory MPs who had seized on the Marconi rumours with especial enthusiasm as one of the ministers said to be involved was the Chancellor David Lloyd George, by now regarded by the Tories as a danger to the state thanks to his land tax and Insurance Act. 'To put him out of the firing line,' Gardiner wrote, 'has become the first article of Conservative policy. Hence the extreme virulence of the Marconi campaign.'[6]

There were two streams of Marconi rumours, only one of which had any validity. Both relied on an undercurrent of anti-Semitism. The first was that the Postmaster General, Herbert Samuel, had awarded the contract to Marconi because the managing director Godfrey Isaacs was a fellow Jew and a brother of his friend the Attorney General Rufus Isaacs. The second was that ministers, including Rufus Isaacs, and possibly Samuel and Lloyd George, had profited from buying shares in Marconi prior to the signing of the government contract. There was a good deal of truth in the second rumour but none in the first. Yet it was the first that caught on because it was easier to grasp and because it seemed to justify the latent anti-Semitism then current in politics and the press. Wilfred Lawson had set the tone in his first piece in the *Outlook*, hinting at a conspiracy involving ministers 'of the same nationality'.

On 31 July 1912, a few days after Lawson's *Outlook* article was published, Belloc wrote to his faithful friend and lawyer E. S. P. (Ted) Haynes:

My dear Haynes

Have you heard the latest shameful raid on your pocket and mine, and that of the public in general? The swine Samuel has arranged with the swine Isaacs that the brother of this last who is chairman of the Marconi Co shall be given a monopoly privately and secretly thus enormously increasing the value of their shares, and condemning this country to bad machinery and antiquated methods as against their rivals. When you think of old Samuel the pawnbroker paying Asquith for his nephew's career; of the father of the two Isaacs in the dock at the Old Bailey and their uncle flying from justice in Paris after a still worse swindle it makes one sick. There is nothing for it but to peg away until the whole system is undermined.

HB[7]

Belloc's political pronouncements, of which this is typical, were made with an air of authority which impressed his followers, but his information was too often sketchy and his judgements wide of the mark. There is scarcely a single word of this letter that was true.

In all of Belloc's conspiracy theories, whether involving Jews or Freemasons, his assumption was that whatever was done, was done in secret, thereby making it difficult to prove. But there was nothing secret about the Marconi contract which for months had gone the rounds of assorted parliamentary committees. Samuel was never a shareholder in Marconi. Samuel's uncle was not a pawnbroker in Liverpool – Belloc has confused him with his great-grandfather Nathan Samuel – and the criminal charges against Rufus Isaacs's father and uncle had been dismissed by the judge.

Yet it was on the basis of this ragbag of half-baked rumours, possibly picked up by Belloc in the bar of the Reform Club, that the *Eye-Witness* (now edited by Cecil Chesterton) was to launch its reckless Marconi campaign. The opening salvo, the first of a series of articles which seemed to be inviting the ministers to sue, was published on 8 August 1912, only a few days after Belloc's letter to Haynes, and makes the same charges:

What progress is the Marconi Scandal making? We ask the question merely from curiosity and under no illusion as to the inevitable end of the affair. Everybody knows the record of Isaacs and his father, and his uncle, and in general of the whole family. Isaacs's brother is Chairman of the Marconi Company,[8] it has therefore been secretly arranged between Isaacs and Samuel that the British people shall give the Marconi Company a very large sum of money through the agency of the said Samuel, and for the benefit of the said Isaacs. Incidentally the monopoly that is to be granted to Isaacs no. 2 through the ardent charity of Isaacs no. 1 and his colleague the Postmaster-General, is a monopoly involving antiquated methods...

From all the similarities between Belloc's letter to Haynes and the subsequent *Eye-Witness* editorial it would be safe to say that Belloc wrote this article. It uses the same language as his letter – the contract being 'arranged' in secret, the 'antiquated methods' of the Marconi system, and repeats the same mistakes about Samuel and the Isaacs brothers' relatives and Godfrey Isaacs's position in Marconi. It also makes use of a favourite Belloc formula (much copied by Cecil) when advancing speculative opinions: 'everybody knows'. If everybody knew the facts already there was no necessity to repeat them, in this instance the charges that Belloc had made about the crooked career of Rufus Isaacs's father and his uncle Sir Harry. To spell out these charges would risk litigation but the 'everybody knows' formula will have left readers with the impression that the *Eye-Witness* was dealing with a disreputable family – so disreputable that their faults and failings and possibly their crookedness were common knowledge.[9]

Cecil, like Belloc, had no special information about Marconi – no 'data' as the Parliamentary Committee set up to investigate the allegations[10] liked to call it. What distinguished him from other journalists in the campaign was the virulence and outspokenness of his articles, what Maisie Ward tactfully refers to as 'Cecil Chesterton's rather fierce way of handling such matters as race questions'.[11]

With his blind faith in Belloc, a man who had served in Parliament for four years and was friends with influential politicians, Cecil convinced himself that his friend was supremely well informed. Even before he began to write about Marconi he had already attacked Rufus Isaacs, then representing the government at the tribunal investigating the *Titanic* disaster, accusing him of deliberately prolonging the hearing to enhance his fee. Writing under the pen name Junius, in the person of an imaginary barrister defending Isaacs of this and other offences, Cecil argued, in accordance with Belloc's beliefs, that Isaacs was a foreigner: 'I deny the right of an English judge to pass sentence on him... He is an alien, a nomad, an Asiatic, the heir of a religious and racial tradition wholly alien from ours. He is amongst us; he is not of us.'[12]

The facts hardly matched up to Cecil's lurid description. The Isaacs family had been living in England for over a hundred years and had established a family fruit import business in Spitalfields spanning three generations. Rufus's uncle, Sir Henry, had been Lord Mayor of London and his great-uncle was the famous Jewish boxer Daniel Mendoza, Rufus himself having been a keen boxer in his youth. He was one of nine children whose formidable mother had rejected the strict Jewish orthodoxy in which she was brought up. She presided over a happy family with a house in Hampstead. Many of their friends were Gentiles and both parents had a liking for musical evenings where everyone joined in Italian arias and Gilbert and Sullivan – a bourgeois background far removed from the 'nomad' or 'Asiatic' existence that Cecil, who showed little sign of knowing much about Isaacs, envisaged.

A boisterous, unruly child, Rufus had left school at the age of thirteen, turned his back on his father's fruit business and after a brief and disastrous episode as a stockbroker was persuaded by his mother to read for the Bar. Determined to pay off his debts, he worked hard and built up a lucrative practice thanks to his mastery of detail and brilliant courtroom technique. It was not long before he was earning £20,000 a year and living in Park Lane. Gardiner, who watched him in court, wrote, 'He talked to the jury as though he had never met twelve such luminous-minded men before; he permitted his learned friend to trip him up on the mispronunciation of a name, thanked him gaily for his correction, repeated the offence and laughingly rebuked his own forgetfulness. It was all done with a lightness of touch, a freshness and gaiety that were irresistible.'[13] A surgeon, cross-examined by Isaacs on a Friday, returned to the witness box after the weekend and told him, 'I dreamed about you last night, Mr Isaacs. You have been a nightmare to me. I have hardly slept since you let me out of the box on Friday. I dreamed you had examined me and I seemed to have nothing on except bones.'

It was this man whom Cecil now dubbed an Asiatic nomad, the shady member of an equally shady family, whose misdeeds were only too well known to his readers. It was not the best of starts for Cecil and it was to be followed by an equally ill-informed attack on the Postmaster General, Herbert Samuel, in the eyes of Belloc and the Chesterton brothers the chief villain of the Marconi scandal.

Samuel, a straight-laced, heavily moustachioed figure had none of Isaacs's charm and was not popular with his fellow ministers in the Liberal government, least of all Lloyd George who seems to have disliked him intensely. In common with Masterman he had been drawn into politics by a desire to improve the lives of the working class and in his youth had written pamphlets for the Fabian Society just as Cecil had done. On joining the Liberal Party he quickly gained promotion and in 1909 became the first non-Christianised Jew to serve as a Cabinet minister. 'There is no more industrious man in the ministry,' Gardiner wrote; 'he conveys no enthusiasm and is as free from passion as an oyster.'[14] It might have benefited Cecil if he had read Gardiner's shrewd assessment which made it clear that while Gardiner did not warm to Samuel he regarded him as being scrupulously honest: 'He will never give his leader nor his party a moment's disquiet, for he will never depart a hair's breadth from the path of strict correctitude.'[15] But to Cecil, loyally following Belloc's lead, Samuel was, like Isaacs, a foreigner, incapable of loyalty to the British Crown. Not only that, he was a puritan who in 1908 tried, unsuccessfully, to bring in a Licensing Bill, reducing the number of public houses and banning admission to children.[16] Belloc had also alleged that, just as Masterman owed his government job to his wife's Tory relations, Samuel had only been made a minister because his wealthy uncle Lord Swaythling was a generous donor to the Liberal Party – in other words, Asquith had been bribed to promote him.

Encouraged, perhaps, by the lack of any response to his diatribes, Cecil became more and more outspoken. He was soon referring to 'an appalling scandal, the like of which can hardly be paralleled of recent years in the history of any other nation', a scandal which had been 'inflicted upon our public life by a particularly low and nasty gang'. Unless they were chastised and expelled, he concluded, 'nothing in our public life is safe'. The prospect for Britain was dire: 'If our country permits the corruption to continue, it will decline. And the end of such decline is not only moral degradation but in almost all cases military defeat and national disaster.'[17]

Only another week was to pass before he decided to spell out the story of 'vice' and 'theft': 'Two men, co-opted into the administration, one called Samuel the other called Isaacs, have acted in the following fashion. Samuel, having it in his power to determine what the English people shall pay for services in connection with their postal arrangements, had arranged that a concern run by the brother of Isaacs shall have a privilege and a monopoly.'[18]

Cecil was following the Belloc line to the letter. As Belloc told the Parliamentary Committee later, he had no inside information. He simply knew, he said, along with thousands of other members of the public, 'that the Postmaster General had advantaged in enormous degree the brother of the Attorney General, and could only have done so in connivance with… the Chancellor of the Exchequer [Lloyd George]. That was the one [fact] on which I went. Beyond that I did not go.'

Belloc's momentous mistake had been to convince himself that this was a fact when it was merely idle speculation grounded in racial prejudice. In all that he and the Chesterton brothers wrote about Jews the assumption is twofold. First, that they are fiercely loyal to one another. It followed that Herbert Samuel, Rufus Isaacs and Godfrey Isaacs must be as thick as thieves. Second, that their most powerful motive in political and business life was to benefit fellow Jews. Behind such opinions lay Belloc's belief, derived from the Dreyfus affair, in a Jewish conspiracy to corrupt national institutions – and the Marconi revelations provided vivid proof that the same kind of thing was now happening in England as had happened in France. Both Belloc and Cecil believed that Jews should be barred from

G. K. Chesterton with his wife, Frances, in 1922

Cecil Chesterton
'A short stout man with round head and round red cheeks.'

Hilaire Belloc
'The direct unwavering penetrating glance of the eyes.'

Mrs Cecil Chesterton in a sleeveless ballgown

Godfrey Isaacs

Herbert Samuel

Charles Granville

Sir Edward Carson

George Cadbury

A. G. Gardiner

Rufus Isaacs, Lloyd George and C. F. G. Masterman in Wales in 1911

One of Chesterton's illustrations for E. C. Bentley's *Biography for Beginners*: George III (see page 21)

One of Chesterton's
illustrations for Belloc's
Emmanuel Burden
(see page 69)

C. F. G Masterman

participating in government because their loyalty was to their own people, not to Britain, and that regardless of Marconi, Isaacs and Samuel should never have been promoted to the Cabinet.

In October 1912, in response to the continuing campaign in the *Eye-Witness* and the Tory press, the government set up a Parliamentary Committee[19] to investigate the allegations that had been made. It was a delaying tactic: with its government majority[20] the Committee was bound to exonerate the ministers, as duly happened after seven months of hearings, involving 29,276 questions asked of sixty-six witnesses.

Masterman's friend Ford Madox Ford who was writing regularly for the *Outlook*, the paper that had originally exposed the Marconi affair, attended many of the Committee's hearings as an observer. He wrote later:

> The Marconi Commission must have been one of the most farcical bodies that ever met. There were seven Liberals and five Tories[21] who voted with the unanimity of the clockwork soldiers of the Russian ballet, each party against the other. The Tories voted that any evidence that could be helpful to the ministers concerned should not be heard, the Liberals that it should. When evidence unfavourable to the ministers was being heard, all the Liberals went to sleep in a body; when anything that could be dug up to be favourable to them all the Tories seemed to have been drugged. In addition, Lord Robert Cecil, who presumably suffered from a bad throat, continually took out an atomiser and opened his mouth extraordinarily wide. The noise of the spray and his vocal garglings would extremely disconcert any ministerial witness.[22]

As the enquiry opened Cecil Chesterton found himself facing a more personal crisis. The finances of the *Eye-Witness* had been in a parlous state for some time, and on 8 October Cecil sent a telegram to Arthur Ransome with the dramatic news that Hosken/Granville (now calling himself Godwin) had done a bunk and fled the country with a new lady friend (a novelist named Louise Heilgers) and a cheque for £1,200 stolen from a would-be business partner.

Ransome later recorded the story he was told in the Garrick Club: 'Granville had been at a dinner party where one of the guests was a well-known London magistrate who, after the ladies had left the dining-room, called Granville apart and said to him, "I never forget a face. You came up before me in such and such a year, accused of bigamy. You were given bail and absconded. I shall do nothing tonight because we are fellow-guests in this house, but I shall make it my business first thing in the morning to let the authorities know that I have seen you."'[23]

Granville was pursued by the police who brought him back to London to face a bigamy charge. In the meantime bailiffs arrived at the *Eye-Witness*'s office in John Street and removed the table so lovingly described by Desmond MacCarthy.[24] With Granville's company bankrupted,[25] the *Eye-Witness* was as good as doomed. It was saved by Cecil's father, Edward Chesterton, who was persuaded by Cecil to finance a new company with his two sons as directors. To avoid copyright problems the paper changed its title to the *New Witness* but otherwise remained the same. A new office was found in Essex Street and Cecil rushed down to Crowborough where Keith was staying to tell her the good news. 'It's all arranged,' he told her. 'I'm going to have the paper and there's only one thing left to settle. I want you...' Keith shook her head. 'I'm not asking you to marry me,' he explained. 'At the moment I want you to be my assistant.'[26]

Cecil was delighted when she agreed, other members of staff less so. Keith's abilities as a journalist were not in doubt but her powerful personality was ill suited to life in a small office. Besides which, she plainly had a hold over Cecil and felt free to throw her weight about. After she curtly rejected an article E. S. P. Haynes had submitted on patriotism – 'It is hardly in line with the policy of the paper' – Haynes, who had been a director of the *Eye-Witness*, wrote to G. K. Chesterton saying that it was pointless to complain to Cecil as he was completely under her thumb. 'She is a perfectly impossible person to have in control of a paper,' he wrote.[27]

As for Marconi, Keith was fully in support of the campaign and was later to show that she could hold her own when it came to attacking Jews. There was to be no let-up in Cecil's attacks and he had even been looking for Jewish members of the Parliamentary Committee to scrutinise, singling out Mr Neil Primrose 'who has indeed a certain measure of racial affinity with the chief actors in the drama which may enable him to understand their actions better than a pure European could'.[28]

In February 1913 the Marconi affair took off, but it was Leo Maxse not Cecil Chesterton who brought about the change in tempo. Appearing before the Parliamentary Committee Maxse proclaimed that the ministers under fire should have assured the Committee at the outset 'in the most categorical and emphatic manner' that they had had no shares in *any* Marconi company throughout the negotiations with the government. The implication, namely that Maxse must have information that the ministers had dealt in American, not English, shares was not lost on the ministers in question.

Two days later the French newspaper *Le Matin* published an account of Maxse's evidence in which it was inaccurately claimed that the ministers had been dealing in English Marconi shares. Herbert Samuel and Rufus Isaacs now took a decision to sue *Le Matin* for libel, provoking Chesterton to write a satirical poem[29] and later to comment, 'Some fool who has got the facts wrong is always prosecuted, instead of the serious critics who have got the facts right' (unaware of how aptly those words could later have been applied to Cecil). The motive for suing was partly for the ministers via their lawyer, Carson, to admit publicly that they had purchased and dealt in American Marconi shares. This let the cat out of the bag – the Tories and their allies in the press now seized on the fact that the ministers had, when previously denying their purchase of English shares, kept mum about the American ones. This looked horribly like an attempt to cover up their misdeeds and to deceive Parliament and the British public – a clear admission that they were aware of the impropriety of their actions.

The Tories now redoubled their attacks on Asquith's government, and while the Committee ploughed on with its interviews of politicians and journalists, Cecil Chesterton, writing in the *New Witness*, turned his attention from Rufus Isaacs to his brother Godfrey, cataloguing the various hopeless business ventures, including gold mines and taxi cabs, which he had fronted prior to being appointed managing director of Marconi. All this was perfectly true, but for Cecil it was not enough that Godfrey Isaacs should be incompetent. He was also, quite obviously, a crook: 'The files of Somerset House of the Isaacs companies,' he wrote, 'cry out for vengeance on the man who created them...'[30] And brother Rufus was hand in glove: 'This is not the first time in the Marconi affair that we find these two gentleman [Godfrey and Rufus] swindling.'[31] Godfrey Isaacs, he considered, should and would have been prosecuted had it not been for the fact that his brother was the Attorney General.

Seemingly desperate to provoke a libel action, Cecil or his wife-to-be, Keith, then hired sandwich-board men to parade outside the Marconi offices bearing placards advertising the *New Witness* with the slogan GODFREY ISAACS' GHASTLY RECORD. For Godfrey Isaacs it was the last straw. He now applied to bring an action for criminal libel. Cecil was unperturbed, even pleased, claiming to welcome the writ, which he framed and hung on the office wall.

The law of criminal libel had long been a useful weapon in the government's armoury to deal with troublesome journalists like Wilkes or Cobbett, particularly as it could justify a prison sentence. Since Regency days however it had rarely been used, with one famous exception in the case of Oscar Wilde, who brought a criminal libel action against the Marquess of Queensberry after he was accused of posing as a 'Somdomite'[32] only to find himself in the dock, his case falling apart after Queensberry rounded up a gang of witnesses to support his charge.

It has always been difficult if not impossible to uncover legal secrets so we cannot be sure what, if any, role was played by the Attorney General, Rufus Isaacs, in the decision to prosecute. It is known that he had previously tried to dissuade his brother, a compulsive litigant, from suing, but that was before he himself had been subjected to a libellous barrage by Cecil. Whether he was actively involved or not, Rufus Isaacs must have seen the advantage of Godfrey taking action rather than himself. The case would therefore centre on Godfrey's business record and the allegation of a conspiracy in the awarding of the Marconi contract, while the share dealing (the real meat of the scandal) which Cecil, in any case, had largely ignored, would be a side issue if it was thought to be relevant at all.

The trial, which opened at the Old Bailey on 27 May 1913, attracted widespread press attention, mainly because of the Chesterton name. The court was crowded with journalists who noted the presence not only of G. K. Chesterton but also of J. M. Barrie, the creator of Peter Pan, who sat in court throughout the hearing. Cecil himself was cocksure and cheery, but his very respectable parents, who can never have expected to see their son on trial in the Central Criminal Court, could not share his high spirits and, in keeping with Edward Chesterton's distaste for unpleasant reality, sat outside in the foyer leaving it to Gilbert to bring them news of what was happening within.

The prosecution was in the hands of two leading Tory lawyers, both of whom had acted for Herbert Samuel and Rufus Isaacs in the *Le Matin* libel action: the Ulsterman Edward Carson, who had famously prosecuted Oscar Wilde in 1895, and F. E. Smith (later Lord Birkenhead), who in his youth had vied with Belloc to be the best speaker in the Oxford Union – 'Slim and clean shaven,' Gardiner described him, 'with long hatchet face, scornful lip, defiant eye and hair oiled and smooth.' At the time of Cecil's trial both lawyers were engaged in fomenting a Protestant rebellion in Ulster to sabotage the Liberal government's policy of Home Rule for a united Ireland. They were fiercely attacked by fellow Tories for defending the reputations of Liberal ministers, but at a perilous time for them both, when they were being widely accused of treason, they may have thought it advisable to keep on the right side of the Attorney General, Isaacs.[33]

In any event, as Owen Dudley Edwards has pointed out,[34] both Carson and his colleague F. E. Smith had bones to pick with the Chesterton brothers, which may have helped persuade them to take on a case which was bound to land them in trouble with their Tory colleagues. In one of a series of profiles in the *Eye-Witness*, using the pseudonym 'Junius', Cecil had accused Carson – 'a dangerous and desperate lawmaker stirring people up to Civil War' – of taking up the cause of the Ulster Unionists in order to make money (a typical Cecil allegation, for which there was no evidence). Smith's quarrel was with Gilbert, who had ridiculed him, also in the *Eye-Witness*, after Smith had stated in a parliamentary debate that the Liberal Government's Bill to disestablish the Anglican Church in Wales had 'shocked the conscience of every Christian community in Europe'. The rebuke took the form of a poem, 'Antichrist, or the Reunion of Christendom: An Ode'.[35] The poem, which belied Belloc's opinion that Gilbert was incapable of savagery and therefore ineffectual, was devastating. With its punchline 'Chuck it, Smith', it immortalised Smith in the last way he would have wanted, and was omitted entirely from the official biography written by his son, the second Lord Birkenhead.[36]

Smith, playing second fiddle, cross-examined Herbert Samuel who, like Rufus Isaacs, gave evidence about the Marconi contract. The major interrogation was left to Carson. 'There is something in the mere presence of the man that is shattering and masterful,' Gardiner had written of Carson in one of his long, revealing profiles which managed not to refer to Oscar Wilde, a sign, perhaps, that like drink and gambling Wilde was a subject that could not be mentioned in the *Daily News*. 'The retreating forehead, with the black, well-oiled hair brushed close to the crown, the long, hatchet face, the heavy-lidded eyes, at once dreamy and merciless, the droop of the mouth, the challenging thrust of the under-lip, the heavy jaw...'[37] Having crossed swords with Oscar Wilde and failed to unsettle him, Carson had an easier opponent in Cecil, a man who had a brain as sharp as Wilde's and the same kind of urge to make himself a martyr, but who lacked his gift for dazzling repartee. Cecil also seemed to find it difficult to grasp the principles of libel law, and reacted with unappealing conceit when the bona fides of the *New Witness* was queried by Godfrey Isaacs's counsel R. D. Muir: 'If any man acquainted with letters were to make out a list of say the twenty best-known literary men in England today I will undertake to find twelve of them among the contributors to my paper. It is perfectly absurd to represent that paper, as Mr Muir has tried to do, as a sort of gutter rag trying to get into notoriety by throwing dirt.'

Cecil did not tell lies, as Wilde did, but he had no evidence to support his claim that the Marconi contract was the outcome of a criminal conspiracy, and Carson, after getting him to make the ridiculous excuse that he had used the word fraud 'rhetorically', forced him, after a good deal of posturing, to withdraw the charge of criminality against Herbert Samuel and the Isaacs brothers:

Carson: Do you accuse the Postmaster General [Herbert Samuel] of anything dishonest or dishonourable?

Chesterton: After the Postmaster General's denials on oath I must leave the question. I will not accuse him of perjury.

Judge: I think you must answer the question a little more precisely.

Chesterton: I think the natural interpretation of the Postmaster General's conduct would be that he was unduly influenced in his public capacity by private considerations, but as he has denied it upon oath, if it is a question of accusing him of perjury, and I do not know that I can take the responsibility of doing so.

Judge: That is a very argumentative answer.

Carson: Could you not answer Yes or No?

Judge: Do you or do you not accuse the Postmaster General of corruption?

Chesterton: That is the only answer I can give.

Judge: We do not want to know your motives – We want to know what you say now.

Chesterton: I say I do not accuse him on the ground that I have given.

Judge: That is evasive. Do you or do you not accuse him?

Chesterton: I have said No.

The judge, Mr Justice Phillimore, summed up, asking along the way how the charge of corruption could be upheld when the defence had admitted that Mr Samuel had not been guilty of corruption. After a retirement of only forty minutes the jury pronounced Cecil guilty and he was fined £100 which was paid, along with Cecil's legal costs, by a group of Tory MPs – a fact that the Chestertonians tended not to emphasise in their subsequent accounts in which Cecil featured as a lone, independent crusader.

Cecil had been fully expecting a prison sentence and the £100 fine was greeted by him, his family and supporters almost as a victory. 'A more or less nominal fine,' Gilbert later described it. To the surprise of many there was applause and cheering in court. 'Cecil shook innumerable hands,' his widow Keith recalled, 'and as a final thrill – just in time for the shouting, Belloc, travel-worn and dusty, pushed his way to his friend.'[38]

Cecil and Keith were perhaps thrilled by Belloc's arrival in court. Others may have been wondering why he had left it to the very last minute to put in an appearance. 'I shall do everything I can for Cecil Chesterton,' he had told his great friend Maurice Baring, 'whose position I support and whose attitude is largely due to my action.' (Belloc was perhaps thinking of his 'What progress is the Marconi Scandal making?' piece which had sparked the *Eye-Witness* campaign.) But there were strict limits to what he was prepared to do. Though he was to boast later that together they had taken 'the heavy and perilous task of exposing the whole Marconi affair', at the time he had been very anxious to keep Cecil at arm's length and distance himself from the *Eye-/New Witness*. His difficulty was that he was still thought to be the editor, an assumption made by the Postmaster General Herbert Samuel, who referred to 'Belloc's paper' when writing to Rufus Isaacs about a possible libel action. In October 1912 the society magazine *Throne and Country*, a right-wing weekly crusading for Edward Carson's anti-Home Rule rebellion in Northern Ireland, began to take an interest in Marconi, referring to 'specific charges made by Mr Hilaire Belloc in the *Eye-Witness*' and quoting the latest diatribe about 'the trio of adventurers, Isaacs, Samuel and George, all three belonging to a very unpleasing and hitherto almost unknown type in English politics. It is quite on the cards that the indignation which their careless ignorance of the English temper has aroused may rid us of their power to work any further negotiation of the kind.' Although *Throne and Country* was writing in support of Belloc and had only a limited circulation, the suggestion that he was responsible for the attack so alarmed him that he instructed his faithful lawyer E. S. P. Haynes to send a letter of protest to its editor as a matter of great urgency, telling Haynes, 'I gave up the *Eye-Witness* in June with a public announcement and it will never do if I am saddled with a responsibility which I deliberately abandoned long ago because it was impossible with the rest of my work. Would you therefore write professionally to the *Throne and Country* rubbing this well in... It would relieve my mind if you could let me know *by return* [italics added] that such a letter has been written.'

Haynes obliged, writing:

Dear Sir,

Our client Mr Belloc has instructed us to write to you in reference to your remarks about him on page 139 of your current issue. He wishes us to point out that he resigned the editorship of the *Eye-Witness* in June last, and that the paper cannot be called 'Mr Belloc's organ' to use your own words. About the same time Mr Belloc sold out his shares in the *Eye-Witness* company and his connection with the paper is neither editorial nor proprietary. In these circumstances we rely upon your publishing these facts in your next issue, and shall be glad to hear that this will be done.

Yours faithfully,

Hunter and Haynes

Throne and Country published the letter a few days later, adding, 'We were under the impression that Mr Hilaire Belloc was the author of the article referred to but we gladly publish the above correction.' This careful wording corrected the statement that he was the editor and proprietor of the *Eye-Witness* but left open the possibility that he had written the article they quoted, a suggestion the paper had not previously made (in fact, that article bears all the marks of Cecil Chesterton's manic style). It is clear that Belloc was in a jittery state: he was still faced with the prospect of answering questions about Marconi from the Committee who were bound to ask about the authorship of various *Eye-Witness* articles, almost all of which in the 'Notes of the Week' section were anonymous, and some of which he had written. If pressed, Belloc would have to admit not only that he was responsible for these pieces, including the opening attack, but that he was not in agreement with some of Cecil's diatribes, even if this meant saying, as he did with Masterman: 'I would have written it differently.' The question would then arise – had he expressed his objections to Cecil, and if so when?

Faced with these difficulties, it seems that Belloc reached an agreement with Cecil that the latter would take responsibility for all the published pieces about Marconi, leaving Belloc in the clear. We can assume that as the older and dominant partner, Belloc would have insisted on this arrangement, though it is possible, given Cecil's gung-ho approach to his prosecution, that he would have put up little resistance to the idea. All this is, however, speculation as there is a mysterious gap in the correspondence between Belloc and Cecil from 5 May 1912 to September 1913, the period covering the Marconi articles and Cecil's subsequent trial. Considering that Belloc, according to his biographer, kept all his business correspondence 'carefully filed', the omission is suggestive.

Belloc finally appeared before the Committee on 24 April 1913. Only a few days previously Bernard Shaw had mocked him in the *New Statesman* (12 April 1913), recording his amusement that the proprietor of the paper that had led the attack 'on the Jews and on Cabinet Ministers [i.e., Charles Granville] was the first to retire from the fray at the hands of the police.' It was easy, perhaps, to brush aside Shaw and his little joke, but more difficult to do the same with Granville who had given evidence to the Committee the previous day. He had been escorted to the hearing by two prison wardens as he was under arrest awaiting separate trials for embezzlement and bigamy[39] and it was hardly surprising that he was not at his best, and at times evasive or incoherent. But he had been insistent on one particular point: asked by the leader of the Tory group of MPs Lord Robert Cecil, 'Can you tell us what are the real motives of the articles and the instigation of them?' Granville replied, 'The real motives are an attack upon Jews as Jews... The instigators are Messrs Belloc and Chesterton.' Insisting that there was no 'data' (i.e. evidence) to support the attack, Granville repeated over and over again that it was 'an attitude of mind' that lay behind the paper's campaign – 'to down Jews as Jews'.

Belloc was well aware that Granville was right about this and that it was potentially a very damaging charge. 'Now it will be obvious to the Committee,' he pointed out in a prepared statement,

> that if it could be suggested that what, in my case at least [in other words he cannot speak for Cecil Chesterton], was honest indignation and an honest desire to criticise thoroughly – and I would go further and say, to expose – what I thought a dangerous piece of public policy; if it could be proved that this was but the result of a crazy piece of prejudice, such as some ill-balanced men entertain against Jews as Jews, then late in the day as it is for such a manoeuvre, that trick might score a point or two in favour of what I will call, by your leave, the other side.

Amid the flow of florid phrases, Max Beerbohm might well have spotted a 'dead cat' in the use of the word 'trick' to describe a powerful argument which Belloc himself had advanced privately in a letter to Maurice Baring. There is no doubt at all that Belloc agreed with Cecil about the Jewish conspiracy in general, and the Marconi scandal as clear proof of the conspiracy at work. But as someone who, unlike Cecil, 'knew the world', he was well aware that the attack on the Isaacs brothers and Herbert Samuel could be discredited if it could be shown to be motivated by racist prejudice.[40]

Belloc therefore felt obliged to defend himself against the charges which Granville had made, so he began by reminding the MPs of the low standing and general unreliability of the man who had accused him of being motivated, principally, by his attitude towards Jews. Poor Granville, he was someone for whom Belloc professed 'a profound sympathy... an unfortunate man I do not desire to say a word against, a man in a position so difficult and tragic'. This desire on Belloc's part was not apparently strong enough to stop him saying the word 'falsehood' in response to Granville's charges of race hatred. But when it came to defending his position Belloc could only fall back on the time-honoured response of those accused of anti-Semitism: 'some of my best friends are Jews':

> I have in my life enjoyed the friendship, and I hope still enjoy the friendship, of Jews. From my college days when two of my fellow colleagues at Balliol, with whom I had close relations of friendship, were of that race, to the present, I have never to my knowledge so lost either my judgement or my sense of humour as to permit myself to do anything unjust to a fellow man because he was of a nationality or race different from mine. My life is open. I have written very many books and innumerable articles. Everybody knows [that expression again] who cares to consult my works, and all who have heard my conversation, what I feel in this matter.[41]

The Committee did not press Belloc further on the subject but did succeed in extracting an admission from him that he had had no inside information about the scandal, thus conceding the weakness of the *Eye-Witness* case. Both he and Cecil had persistently harped on the corrupt nature of the government's contract with Marconi (for which there was no evidence), ignoring the ministers' share dealings (for which there was plenty). As for the contract, when put on the spot, Belloc could merely argue that you only had to put two and two together.

Asked by the Committee member Handel Booth MP what 'definite data' he had, he replied that there was only a single 'datum' – 'There is not more than one.' He had discovered, he said, 'in common with thousands of other members of the public, that the Postmaster General had advantaged in an enormous degree the brother of the Attorney General and could only have done so by connivance with or by the permission of, if you prefer the word, the Chancellor of the Exchequer.' 'Had you any information at all,' Mr Booth asked, 'other than what is read generally in the newspaper?' 'None whatsoever,' Belloc answered.

In accordance with his agreement with Cecil, Belloc repeatedly refused to answer questions as to whether he had or had not written certain pieces in the *Eye-Witness* – one of which referred to the Marconi contract as 'a fraud', another as 'a swindle' and a third which said of Herbert Samuel (commended by Gardiner for his intellect), 'Mentally he is decidedly below the average of his countrymen' (in other words, fellow Jews). Belloc insisted that Cecil was the responsible editor and that the questions should be put to him when his turn came to be cross-examined.

The chairman, Sir Albert Spicer, asked him, 'Are you going to refuse to answer the question, yes or no, whether you wrote certain statements that have appeared in the *Eye-Witness*?' Belloc insisted, over and over again, that such questions had to be put to Cecil. 'You must ask Mr Chesterton, the editor of the paper, under what circumstances things appeared in the paper – and why – whether he altered them, changed them, added to them or what, or who wrote them.'

It was hardly surprising that the impression was given that Belloc was passing the buck. 'By referring continually to your late or present colleague,' Mr Booth suggested, 'do you not realise that you are really putting all the responsibility from your shoulders on to his?' To which Belloc could only make the feeble reply, 'I do not agree that I am doing anything of the kind.'

To anyone following the case it must have looked as if Belloc was leaving Cecil to carry the can for a crisis which he himself had originated. Plainly Cecil seems to have felt obliged publicly to defend Belloc from this line of criticism, as he inserted a disclaimer in the *New Witness*: 'In refusing information which could not properly be asked of anyone but the editor, Mr Belloc took a loyal and courageous course which we need hardly say we thoroughly approve.'[42] G. K. Chesterton himself was keen, at a later date, to stamp on any suggestion of a falling out between Belloc and his brother – 'there was never a word of truth in this supposed division or desertion' – insisting that Belloc's refusal to own up to the authorship of any of his pieces quoted was done by mutual agreement with Cecil. In his autobiography he writes: 'The policy of my brother, claiming to answer all questions himself, may have been wise or unwise; I myself had my doubts about its wisdom. But such as it was it was adopted by him in consultation with Mr Belloc, as part of their common policy... The result was simple and significant. The Commission [Committee] never dared to call him at all.'

Chesterton's argument was nonsensical. If Belloc insisted and went on insisting that all the Committee's questions should be put to Cecil, why should the Committee be fearful to call him? In fact the Committee made several attempts to call Cecil, who at one stage seemed willing to attend but later declined on the perfectly reasonable grounds that his lawyers advised him that it could prejudice his trial.

In his memoir of Belloc his devoted son-in-law Reginald Jebb writes a lengthy account of the Marconi affair which skates over Belloc's evidence to the Parliamentary Committee and manages to avoid any mention of the words 'Jew' or 'Jewish'. He does however assert that Belloc 'ran grave personal risks' in conducting his Marconi campaign: 'At least two of his closest friends,' he writes, 'who were in a position to know what was going on, were so worried by the risks he was running that they did everything they could to dissuade him from persisting in his attack.'[43]

Belloc himself was to refer later to 'the old threats of ruin and imprisonment against us in the worst days of Marconi', and this same expression, 'ruin and imprisonment', was echoed by Chesterton in two separate contexts, suggesting that both men were remembering a specific warning that had been made, possibly by the same two unnamed friends of Belloc.

Jebb's suggestion that it was Belloc who was running risks is puzzling considering that it was under Cecil's editorship that the attacks on ministers were published. Belloc had lit the fuse with his introductory piece but he had sold his shares, given up the editorship and gone to considerable lengths to make it clear that he was in no way responsible for what was being published in the *New Witness*. It was still possible, though unlikely, that he could be sued for libel. A more probable consequence was that he might be compelled, by subpoena, to be a witness at Cecil's trial, in which case he would be in the same difficult situation that he had been in with the Parliamentary Committee, only this time giving evidence on oath and facing cross-examination from two formidable lawyers, including his old rival from Oxford days, F. E. Smith. Belloc could be asked not only which Marconi articles he had written, but whether he agreed with Cecil's more outrageous remarks – his talk of crooks and swindlers, of nomads and aliens.

In the circumstances it is likely that Belloc was advised by those two friends of his, and possibly his own lawyer E. S. P. Haynes, to go abroad, which he did. However, this must remain speculation as Belloc was extremely evasive about his movements throughout the period of the Old Bailey trial, leaving Keith, for example, to explain his absence with the unsatisfactory formula that he had been 'called to the Continent on literary business'.[44]

In a letter to his friend Wilfrid Blunt written on 7 June 1913 Belloc says he came back to England from Spain 'immediately' to attend Cecil's trial 'when I first saw notice of it in a paper'. This wasn't true, as Blunt must have suspected. Was it, after all, likely that Belloc would not have known when the trial was due, or that he could only have become aware of it when he happened to see it mentioned in a newspaper in Spain? In fact Belloc knew perfectly well the date on which the trial was due to start. Originally set down for 29 April it was postponed for a month after Cecil, via his counsel Ernest Wild, pleaded that he was suffering from laryngitis. Belloc claimed to be annoyed by the postponement but it gave him a good excuse for telling his wife Elodie, the only person who knew of his movements at this time, that he was not going to alter a plan, already made, to go walking in Spain and France where he would later be joined by Elodie and their two young daughters. At the same time he persuaded Elodie that he was suffering from a minor breakdown or panic attack and needed to get away to recuperate. It was most unusual for Belloc, with his iron constitution, to register such symptoms and Elodie was alarmed – as Belloc clearly intended her to be – not only about his health but by his frequently expressed fears that as a result of his illness he would not be able to earn the necessary money to support his family.

Once safely in France it did not take long for Belloc to recover. Only two days after arriving he was telling Elodie, 'Already the fear has gone and sleep has come.' For the next ten days he made his way slowly to Spain on foot and by train keeping in touch with his wife via frequent letters and telegrams. She in turn kept him informed about Cecil's trial. Contrary to what he told Blunt, Belloc had no intention of returning. Thanks to Elodie he was well aware that the trial had opened on 27 May, by which time he was back in France and heading for Paris where he was expecting to meet up with Elodie and the girls. They were hoping to have a little holiday, touring round France and possibly visiting Lourdes. In the meantime Belloc looked forward to the arrival in Paris of his great friend, the wealthy Tory MP George Wyndham.

Wyndham arrived on 2 June and the two men went walking in the woods at Bougival and later dined at a restaurant in St Germain where they took exception to the presence of a number of Jews, Belloc later referring to the restaurant as a 'ghetto'. He was meanwhile eagerly expecting Elodie's arrival, telling her, 'You must rest a little in Paris if you like for as many days as you like... I think it may be as well to bring my letters along. I can see if there is anything pressing... it is possible that some publisher or editor wants an answer.'[45] He must have been surprised when Elodie cabled him the following day: 'Things going badly mitt [*sic*] Cecil. I think you should return immediately.' It is unlikely that Elodie had been in court, but she may have heard from Cecil himself, who had always been expecting a prison sentence, that he was now especially despondent as to the outcome. Belloc immediately complied with her summons, making his apologies to Wyndham who, while regretting Belloc's decision, acknowledged that 'showing a front' was something that sometimes had to be done. Belloc took his leave and never saw Wyndham again, as he died suddenly only a few days later.

Perhaps 'showing a front' was all that Elodie was expecting from Belloc. If Cecil was to be given a prison sentence, he ought at least to be in court to lend moral support. Belloc, however, was in no hurry to go to the Old Bailey. Arriving back in London on 4 June he went straight home to King's Land where he spent the next day (the day on which Cecil was crushed by Edward Carson) dealing with his correspondence – though he later claimed to his friend Blunt that he had been travelling all that day. The following day he was in court to hear Cecil's friends giving evidence of his good character. Three men appeared as character witnesses – Revd Conrad Noel, who had helped bring him into the Anglo-Catholic Church, Chesterton himself, who announced to the court that he envied his brother his position – a claim that was greeted with laughter as so often happened when Chesterton made a serious pronouncement – and Maurice Baring.

Baring's loyalty on this occasion was admirable as he strongly disapproved of Cecil's journalism and later complained to Belloc about what he called his 'bullying shriek... almost anyone who reads the *New Witness* for a spell either flies into a passion of rage or freezes into contempt. He has no judgement... and he ruins a case by insisting on some irrelevant detail.'[46] Belloc had agreed with Baring previously when he wrote that Cecil had put himself in a bad position over his Marconi articles and in particular his attacks on Jews: 'I told him repeatedly that I thought the things he allowed O'Donnell[47] to publish were unwise and deplorable,' he told Baring. (The order in which those two words appear is significant. Belloc agreed with Cecil's basic attack on the Marconi ministers as fellow Jews doing one another favours, but he considered he was unwise to spell it out in such lurid and provocative terms as it was likely to offend many of his cultured aristocratic friends. But then he thinks that 'unwise', a tactical rather than a moral error, may be inadequate from Baring's point of view, so he adds the word 'deplorable', which by rights should have come first.)

As a Catholic convert, Baring's principal concern was the damage Cecil might be doing to the Catholic community, since many people still regarded Belloc as the best known Catholic in England, prior to Chesterton's conversion. 'What annoys me,' Baring wrote, 'is that some people treat the *New Witness* as the official utterance of Catholic England and I can imagine people saying when they read the reckless statements and wildly intemperate and intolerant diatribes, "If this is Catholicism, give me Protestantism, Nonconformity or anything else."'[48]

The belligerent Catholic crusader Belloc would most probably have remained unmoved by his friend's argument as he had little interest in appeasing Protestants and others he considered to be heretics. Nor does he ever seem to have been aware how similar were the fears of Jews and Catholics in the England of his day, both communities being victims of ignorance and prejudice, both anxious not to provoke further animosity. In this respect Maurice Baring and Herbert Samuel were strikingly similar in their response to the *New Witness* and Cecil Chesterton.

As a consequence of the reluctance of Samuel and the Isaacs brothers to raise the issue of anti-Semitism, it was scarcely mentioned in the course of the trial.[49] Had the prosecution pursued the issue they could have called Granville to repeat what he had told the Parliamentary Committee. But poor Granville was himself on trial for bigamy in an adjoining court at the Old Bailey and no doubt had other things on his mind. All the same, Cecil's counsel Ernest Wild felt obliged to dispel any suggestion of racist bigotry, and had asked Cecil what he meant by 'the power of Jewish finance', to which Cecil replied that he had strong views on the subject, whilst adding, 'I have not the slightest prejudice against the Jews as a people.' It would have been very easy for Carson or Smith to demolish that statement with a few choice quotations from Cecil's articles, or those of his contributor Frank Hugh O'Donnell, which would have proved very damaging to him. Belloc himself was well aware of this, having written earlier to Baring: 'There is nothing easier than to make out to an English jury that your adversary is fantastic... when, therefore, an opponent can be pointed at as quite irrational about something, and as having brought in utterly extraneous matter, it does him more harm in England than anywhere else.'

Despite the obvious advantage, it seems that Godfrey Isaacs, possibly advised by his brother, had no wish for the Jewish issue to be raised. That conclusion accords with a letter Herbert Samuel wrote earlier to Rufus Isaacs following Belloc's 'What progress is the Marconi Scandal making?' opening salvo in the *Eye-Witness* campaign. Cecil had previously attacked Samuel, repeating Belloc's assertion that he only owed his position to his wealthy uncle, Samuel Montagu (Lord Swaythling), who had bribed the Liberal Party to give him office. Samuel now told Isaacs that he was tempted to sue the *Eye-Witness* but realised that this would only give more publicity to an article which had only a small circulation, adding, 'Secondly, it would not be a good thing for the Jewish community for the first two Jews who have ever entered a British cabinet to be enmeshed in an affair of this kind.'[50] It is a sign of Samuel's extreme sensitivity on this point that when he was being questioned by the Committee he read out his letter but omitted this sentence, telling them, 'There is one sentence in it which is not strictly relevant and which I would rather not read, but I will hand it to the Committee and I will mark it for them to see and I think they will understand the reason why I do not wish to read it. It does not cast any reflection on anybody in any way.' As for Carson and Smith, they no doubt felt it was easy enough to discredit Cecil without raising the issue.

Thus the principal motive which lay behind Cecil's diatribes, which included attacks not only on Samuel and the Isaacs brothers but also their close relatives, was scarcely ever mentioned in the proceedings, no doubt to their relief, but also to the benefit of Cecil, who under cross-examination would have quickly revealed himself as someone, in Belloc's words, 'quite irrational about something'. As it was, Cecil and Keith may well have walked away from the Old Bailey convinced not only that the £100 fine was a victory of sorts but that anti-Semitism, which had loomed so large in the *New Witness* attacks, was a minor issue, one that had rightly been dismissed by both sides as having little bearing on the Marconi story. Certainly Cecil showed no regrets for his actions, and in his first post-trial editorial boasted that he would now restate his case: 'When we began our attack, we were striking at something very powerful and very dangerous... but we were striking at it in the dark. If we had not ventured to strike in the dark, we and the people of England should be in the dark still.'[51]

As for Belloc, he continued to hark back to the Marconi scandal whenever possible.[52] Later, as the Great War thundered on with no end in sight, he warned of the dangers of a premature peace due to the fact that 'the Marconi men' – he did not mention the ministers by name – who in the old days 'would have been done for' had survived the scandal. 'The

Marconi men remained in public life, and not only so remained, but were regarded by their colleagues as peculiarly suitable to further and graver responsibilities as a consolation for their recent sad experience.' If the country were to fail and patch up a peace with Germany 'the crime will proceed from just such secret powers as gave us Marconi, and the weakness and the folly will lie at the door of just those professional politicians who permitted what followed and obeyed their private masters. There is no logical connection between swindling and inefficiency, but there is an organic connection. God is not mocked.'[53]

Marconi had become, like Dreyfus, an *idée fixe* for Belloc (and consequently for Chesterton). Neither man acknowledged that it was partly thanks to their mistaken charges about the contract and Cecil's overtly racist attacks that 'the Marconi men' had been able to weather the storm and even to attract a great deal of sympathy from their parliamentary colleagues. Belloc continued to insist that Marconi had been an event of major importance, and in his 1922 book *The Jews*[54] he linked it to the catastrophic Panama scandal[55] which had rocked France in the 1880s, paving the way for Dreyfus: 'The similarity was of universal comment,' he wrote. But the only similarity was the involvement of Jews in both cases – the Marconi scandal was a very trivial affair compared with Panama, which brought down the French government and caused thousands of small investors to lose their savings while over a hundred government ministers and officials were convicted of bribery.

It was Belloc's hero Paul Déroulède who had led the attack on the French government over Panama, denouncing the future Prime Minister Clemenceau as a British spy in the process, and Belloc now seemed to see himself as the Déroulède of the Marconi affair. In 1926, when rumours were reported in the French press that Rufus Isaacs was to be appointed British Ambassador in Paris, Belloc wrote in an open letter to the Prime Minister Stanley Baldwin: 'The whole world knows of the Marconi scandal: the whole world remembers it. It does not diminish, it becomes classic with the passage of time. It was I who with the late Cecil Chesterton took on the heavy and perilous task of exposing the Marconi affair.'[56] 'We,' he wrote later, 'went at it hammer and tongs… the Marconi scandal would never have been the magnificent thing it was but for our paper. We hammered at it every day. We took every risk.'[57] He had apparently forgotten that he had given up editing the *Eye-Witness* after only a year and before the Marconi affair became a public issue. As Chesterton was to do, he ignored completely those other journalists like Maxse who helped to expose the scandal, and the Tory MPs who paid Cecil's fine and legal expenses. As for fighting alongside Cecil through thick and thin, he ought to have recalled that he had instructed his lawyer to correct any suggestion in the press that he was responsible for the *New Witness*, had refused to acknowledge any responsibility when summoned to the Parliamentary Committee, and had privately expressed serious misgivings about Cecil's anti-Semitism while keeping his head well down when the Old Bailey trial started. Far from taking 'every risk', Belloc had done his best to avoid anything of the kind.

With this amnesia came a typically Bellocian note of self-pity – 'the suggestion of a personal grievance' which Hugh Kingsmill noted as something that marred so much of Belloc's journalism and satire.[58] 'I alone have nothing to lose,' Belloc wrote, 'I have paid the price.'[59] It was exactly the same expression he had used about his hero Déroulède with whom he now seemed to be identifying himself. Déroulède had challenged the corruption of the French Republic, had denounced Clemenceau as a British spy and had been imprisoned for his half-hearted military coup. He had 'paid the price'.

Coincidentally Gardiner, in his very perceptive *Daily News* profile of Belloc, also used this same expression, portraying him not as the heir of Déroulède but as one of the heroes of the French Revolution:

What a figure he would have made on that tremendous stage! What deeds he would have done! I see him thundering at the Palais Royal and in the Assembly, the square, pugnacious face red with internal storm, his foes redder under the lash of his terrible tongue. I see him at the head of the mob wherever the mob surges, his head bare, his voice rising shrill above the storm. I see him bearding the mighty Danton and hurling hot bolts against the supple Robespierre. I see him at last, standing erect and defiant in the tumbril as it lumbers along the Rue St Honoré to the Place de la Révolution. He has had his day and is content to pay the price.[60]

It was in almost identical terms that looking back at his career, by which time, as his sister Marie had noted, his star had waned, Belloc consoled himself with the thought that he had exposed Marconi and thereby made a gallant attempt to rid the system of corruption. But, in keeping with his Déroulède-like role, he had failed. 'That battle was lost. I have since that date refused to take any further part in any attempt to cleanse what I think is beyond cleansing. Public life now stinks with the stench of a mortal disease; it can no longer be cured.'[61]

Thus Belloc conveniently absolved himself from any commitment to political reform, comforted by the thought that, along with Cecil, he had fought the good fight and *paid the price*.

There is no evidence that either he or Cecil ever gave a moment's thought to the one person who had paid the price for Marconi – G. K. Chesterton.

7

THE ART OF STIRRING MUD

MRS MEREDITH, A FRIEND OF CHESTERTON'S BEACONSFIELD neighbours the Solomons, had been engaged as his secretary despite her admission that she couldn't spell and that only the Post Office could read her writing. She had many vivid memories of Chesterton – the way that he was able to write one article whilst dictating a different one, and more mundane details, for instance his dislike of jelly: 'I don't like a food that's afraid of me,' he had said. She especially admired Frances Chesterton who, she said, 'would never speak of herself... she worried *dreadfully* over Cecil's libel action while G. K. would only joke over it and say funny things.'

That recollection suggests not that Chesterton was taking the trial lightly, but that he was unable to cope with his emotions, seeking refuge in flippancy. This must only have added to his wife's concerns. Some indication of Chesterton's turbulent state of mind at the time can be gleaned from his *Daily Herald* columns. For example, on 24 May 1913 (three days before the Old Bailey trial opened), he wrote, 'There is no Liberal Party; there is no Unionist Party; there is no Labour Party. There is no such thing as Individualism; there is no such thing as Socialism; there is no such thing as Anti-Semitism. There is honesty, and there is roguery; there is fact and there is the official statement; there is death and there is deliverance... There is nothing but a trumpet at midnight, calling for volunteers.'[1]

The Marconi story and Cecil's trial affected Chesterton deeply, and the resulting stress, coinciding with overwork and the outbreak of war in August 1914, was to bring about a major breakdown later in the same year. Like Keith and Cecil, Chesterton seems never to have accepted that

Cecil had withdrawn the charge of corruption against Herbert Samuel, and he continued to revile him along with Rufus Isaacs. Writing in the 1930s[2] when the Marconi affair was long forgotten, Chesterton could still include Samuel in a trio of political villains who had brought disgrace and ruin on their respective countries, the other two being Joseph Caillaux[3] and the 'Mad Monk' Rasputin. Compared with either man Samuel had had little or no political influence, but Chesterton could hardly nominate Lloyd George (who unlike Samuel was at least guilty of dealing in Marconi shares) as he had since been widely acclaimed as 'the man who won the war'.

The perceptive critic Hugh Kingsmill once wrote of Chesterton that 'Whatever his theme, he simplified it into a conflict between an evil oppression and a crusading champion.'[4] Never was this more true than with his reaction to Marconi. If Cecil was to be newly created in Chesterton's mind as a 'crusading champion', the 'evil oppression' which he had opposed had, in turn, to be blown up to suitable proportions. As so often taking his cue from Belloc, with his wild talk of the whole world being 'cognisant' of Marconi, Chesterton was to speak of the affair in equally extravagant terms. In his 1936 autobiography he wrote:

> It is the fashion to divide recent history into Pre-War and Post-War conditions. I believe it is almost as essential to divide them into the Pre-Marconi and Post-Marconi days. It was during the agitations upon that affair that the ordinary English citizen lost his invincible ignorance; or, in ordinary language, his innocence. And as I happened to play a part, secondary indeed, but definite, in the quarrel about this affair, and as in any case anything that my brother did was of considerable importance to me and my affairs, it will be well to pause for a moment upon this peculiar business; which was at the time, of course, systematically misrepresented and which is still very widely misunderstood. I think it probable that centuries will pass before it is seen clearly and in its right perspective; and that then it will be seen as one of the turning-points in the whole history of England and the world.

It is a sign of the uncritical benevolence with which his biographers have written about Chesterton that this passage has been quoted with approval or without comment, when it is patently inaccurate and, as a prophecy, ridiculous. No evidence of a conspiracy had been provided and Rufus Isaacs had convincingly denied any knowledge of the contract until it had been agreed. As for the shares, the investment had been, for all the ministers, more in the nature of a 'flutter' than a carefully thought-out plan to amass a fortune. From his knowledge of political history, which was considerable, Chesterton was well aware that political corruption on a far greater scale had existed long before the days of Marconi and was endemic in all governments.[5] He nevertheless was to invest the Marconi scandal with unique status in the annals of political chicanery.

In his determination to elevate Cecil to the status of a crusading champion Chesterton had also to shut his mind to the charge of anti-Semitism which, by the time he wrote his memoirs in the 1930s, had become an issue of major controversy. 'That is another of the legends of the Marconi Case; that it was an attack on Jews,' he wrote, at the same time absolving Cecil of the charge. 'He always spoke of the brothers Isaacs and their set in private conversation with perfect good humour and charity... though it is extremely typical of the real attitude of our group... that he was always more ready to excuse the Jews than the Gentiles.'[6] Chesterton shamelessly omits the reason for this magnanimity, though Cecil had stated the matter very clearly: 'We do not attack them for being Jews, indeed we rather excuse them on that ground, thinking them less morally guilty than an Englishman would be if he acted in the same fashion.'[7] In other words we should not be too hard on the Jews if they behaved badly because that was how Jews tended to behave, whereas decent upright Englishmen were judged by very different standards and should be justly vilified if they failed to live up to them. It is hard to see much good humour or charity in such a poisonous viewpoint.

Sometimes, driven by his compulsion to defend Cecil from the charge of anti-Semitism – a charge which he must have known was perfectly justified – Chesterton was reduced to writing nonsense. He had been especially disturbed by Charles Granville's evidence to the Marconi Committee accusing Cecil and Belloc of being motivated solely by a desire to attack Jews.[8] Granville, who was awaiting trial on a number of charges, and who was brought to the Committee by two prison wardens, ought to have evoked some sympathy from Chesterton, considering that, whatever his faults, he had published *The Party System* and financed the *Eye-Witness*. But instead, Chesterton poked fun at him, suggesting that he had been coerced by the authorities, brought out in chains to make his horrible revelations about Belloc and Cecil Chesterton – 'Fresh from the torture chamber so to speak... Mr Granville was inside the *New Witness* and could find nothing worse than anti-semitism. I do not know what anti-semitism is.'[9]

From this bizarre admission Chesterton moved into the realms of lunacy: 'But, as I say, we must not depend too long on this stupendous stupidity. If once fear is universal, even mud will begin to move. We must be prepared for swamps ebbing like seas and men as trees walking. We must be ready for weeds beginning to whisk themselves off like birds and clay beginning to crawl...'[10]

Chesterton's growing confusion might have been averted if following the Old Bailey trial Cecil had reined in his obsessions. This meant acknowledging his failure to substantiate the charge of corruption. It also meant accepting the criticism of fellow journalists, some of which had been damning in the extreme, such as this leader in the *Manchester Guardian*:

> There is much to criticise in the story of the Marconi contract. There was a way of criticising which might have done good; and another way – which Mr Chesterton chose – which could only do harm. A man who writes on business affairs with no knowledge of business, who brings grave charges with no sense of evidence, whose chief equipment for discussing a very difficult question of finance and politics is a bitter racial prejudice and a turn for epigram, ought not to expect commiseration if he is punished. If every journalist wrote like Mr Cecil Chesterton the press of this country would lose its character; if everyone in private life made charges as recklessly as he did, the police force would have to be

trebled; and if all public controversy were conducted as he conducts it politics would cease to be a reasoned argument to advance the general well-being and would become a public nuisance, a thing like a bad smell, not to be argued with or about but only to be stopped or avoided.[11]

Perhaps if the punishment had been more severe, Cecil might have taken such criticism to heart. But the £100 fine was transformed by Cecil and Keith into 'a victory for clean government'.[12] Belloc was no wiser. Even though he had correctly predicted to his friend Blunt that 'a nominal sentence would be welcomed by the authorities', when it actually happened he changed his tune and decreed that the £100 fine was a great success for Cecil, one which showed that a rift had opened between the politicians and the judiciary in the person of Mr Justice Phillimore, whom he accused of 'outrageous partiality', ridiculing 'his silly little finnicky way of speaking'.[13] On the basis of what little he had witnessed of the trial he decreed that the outcome was a success for Cecil – 'altogether it was most excellent,' he assured his friend Blunt.

Bolstered by Belloc's interpretation of the verdict, Cecil convinced himself that he had been vindicated, and decided he now had a patriotic duty to fight the corruption, of which Marconi was a flagrant example. With Keith urging him on, he launched a national League for Clean Government, the aims of which were set out in *The New Witness*. Some of these – publishing party donors' names, state funding of election expenses – still have a topical relevance. Others could be traced back to the Marconi case – banning ministers from speculating in shares, publishing the conditions of government contracts and so on.

'The idea caught on immediately,' Keith writes, 'for it appealed to people of the most divergent opinions, centralising all kinds of warring factions in a common cause. Tories, Socialists, Atheists, Liberals, Catholics and Jews eagerly joined...'[14] The suggestion that Jews signed up is far-fetched as there was little attempt to conceal the anti-Semitism which underlay the Clean Government campaign. What gave the game away was the choice of chairman in the person of Frank Hugh O'Donnell, a former Home Rule MP for Galway once described by his fellow Irishman W. B. Yeats as 'a mad rogue – half genius half sewer-rat'.[15] Considering that O'Donnell referred to Jews in one of his *New Witness* articles as 'locusts' and 'weevils' that description seems appropriate. Chesterton was cajoled by his brother into presiding at the inaugural conference of the League, at which 'dear old Hugh O'Donnell', as Keith describes him, attacked Rufus Isaacs as a disgraced stockbroker and rounded on the Jews for claiming to be victims of religious prejudice: 'When you catch an English pickpocket he does not quote his Church membership. When you catch a Jewish pickpocket what right has he to scream out, "You are attacking my holy religion"?' Cecil followed him on to the platform, repeating his charge against Herbert Samuel for fixing a corrupt contract as if the Old Bailey trial had never happened. The League, he made clear, would campaign against MPs like Masterman of whom they disapproved. Later in the year an opportunity arose to renew his attack on Rufus Isaacs when, following his appointment as Lord Chief Justice, a by-election was held in his Reading constituency. While O'Donnell complained about 'Liberal rowdies' making trouble at meetings led by 'the undesirable alien', the local press noted that G. K. Chesterton who in the 1910 election had supported the Liberal candidate Philip Morrell was now supporting the Tories.

None of these events can have done much to restore Chesterton's peace of mind. If he was uncomfortable about presiding at the inaugural meeting of the League, he must also have felt some anxiety at the possibility of a fresh prosecution being brought against the *New Witness*, particularly as Cecil was continuing his campaign ever more vehemently, even challenging Rufus Isaacs and Lloyd George to sue him for libel.

Belloc, for all his brave talk about Cecil's victory in the courts, was equally concerned about this possibility of further trouble and was keen to keep the *New Witness* at arm's length. He even confided in his friend Maurice Baring that he was doubtful whether the paper could survive. No one was taking any trouble to make it broad or witty, he said, or 'even moderately business-like'. In any case he added, he had no time to work for it unrewarded. 'More important still is the fact that if I dabbled in it people would make me responsible for its enormities.'[16] Cecil himself was not worried by such concerns any more than his trusted contributor 'dear old Hugh O'Donnell', who wrote:

> Beyond all possibility of a doubt Rufus Isaacs – of a notorious Jew financial family, insolvent member of the Stock Exchange, skilful commercial lawyer, knowing every turn of company law practice – was the planning brain and the crafty will in the whole transaction. The mean treachery of the Isaacs person is of course manifest. But that is of less moment. Isaacs had it in his blood and tribe... Israel, like the leopard, changes its habitat but not its spots.[17]

Such opinions were more extreme than any that had preceded Cecil's trial, a fact of which Chesterton (and Belloc) must have been aware.

Some of Chesterton's own journalism in the post-Marconi period affirms his odd mental state at the time. On breaking with the *Daily News* he had signed up as a columnist for the socialist *Daily Herald*. Founded in 1911 during a print-workers' strike, the *Daily Herald* was a lively, radical paper with a satirical edge and outstanding cartoons by Will Dyson – 'There was a cheery truculence about the rag,' W. R. Titterton, a leader writer, wrote. The paper staunchly defended Cecil over Marconi, though it was at odds with Belloc's orthodoxy, being anti-war (thanks to the influence of the pacifist Christian, George Lansbury) and in favour of 'votes for women'. Chesterton was considered a prize catch for the paper and a selection of his columns was later published in America in a book titled *Utopia of Usurers* (i.e. Jews). There is little evidence here of the high spirits that could be found in *Tremendous Trifles*, and A. L. Maycock, in his selection of Chesterton's writings *The Man Who Was Orthodox*, detects signs of a disturbed mind quoting, as an example, 'Men in England are ruled, at this minute, by brutes who refuse them bread, by liars who refuse them news, and by fools who cannot govern, and therefore wish to enslave.'[18]

Chesterton was also drinking heavily. In an unusually candid paragraph Maisie Ward relates that during the post-Marconi period he was breaking his own rule that you should drink because you are happy, never because you are miserable: 'Before his own severe illness,' she writes, 'intimate friends have told me that they had seen him unlike himself, that they felt he had come to depend, "almost absent-mindedly" one said, on the stimulus of wine for the sheer physical power to pour forth so much.'

Keith, who was well aware of these upsets, writes: 'We all knew he was heading for a smash – he was due for a breakdown.' Typically, though, she blamed this, when it happened, on the unhealthy, sedentary life he had lived since moving from London to Beaconsfield. More perceptively, Maisie Ward writes of his being 'mentally oppressed by the strain of the Marconi case... To him the Marconi case was a heavier burden than the war.'[19] She will have had good grounds for making this rather startling statement as she was a family friend of the Chestertons and her mother, Josephine Ward, was a close friend of she in whom Frances confided all the details of Chesterton's later illness. But where Maisie Ward erred was to infer that Marconi had 'oppressed' Chesterton both because he feared Cecil being sent to prison (an anxiety immediately lifted by the imposition of a fine which Chesterton himself was to dismiss as 'nominal') and because of the political corruption exposed by Marconi. But men do not generally suffer mental collapse from worrying about a decline in political standards. The explanation had to lie elsewhere.

Chesterton was a very scrupulous man of great intelligence, blessed with a gift of insight into human motives. He had sat in the Old Bailey for ten days and witnessed his dearly loved brother being brutally exposed as a liar and a racist and finally being humiliated, forced to withdraw the charge of a corrupt contract, and condemned by the judge for his 'invincible ignorance of business and prejudice'.[20] He had not read about this in the newspapers – he had seen and heard it all with his own eyes and ears. He had now not only to reject and banish from his mind all the evidence of Cecil's folly but to substitute an alternative picture of his brother as a brave crusader for truth and justice who had been unjustly prosecuted by the state. (The picture was a little compromised by the 'nominal' fine which did not quite measure up to the theory of savage revenge by the

Establishment.) To a man of Chesterton's integrity, this feat helped to create a degree of stress which was to result in heavy drinking and later a major breakdown.

Towards the end of 1913, a few months after Cecil's conviction at the Old Bailey, Frances was writing to her great friend, the Roman Catholic priest Father John O'Connor, that Gilbert was suffering from bronchitis and a stiff neck. The bronchitis continued to trouble him. In April 1914 he missed three weeks at the *Daily Herald* due to illness. On 16 October 1914, following the outbreak of war, Frances wrote to Father O'Connor: 'Appallingly busy, no time for anything. Doing a lot of government stuff which is most wearing and difficult. *The New Witness* must keep its end up whilst Cecil is in the trenches.'[21] This last sentence is curious as at the time Cecil was not in the trenches – if indeed he ever was. He was not even in the army. Why then should Frances Chesterton think otherwise? It is hard to resist the conclusion that Frances had been told this by Chesterton himself. If so, it is a sign that he was suffering from delusions at the time.

The following month she told the priest that Chesterton was seriously ill: 'It is mostly heart trouble but there are complications.' Chesterton had collapsed on his bed with such force that it broke under his great weight. He showed no inclination to extricate himself from a grotesquely awkward position and when the doctor remarked to him, 'You must be horribly uncomfortable,' he replied, 'Why, now you mention it, I suppose I am.' Two nurses were later engaged to take care of him.

Accounts of Chesterton's long illness are vague. Frances told friends that his heart was the problem. Father O'Connor wrote of him suffering from gout all over: 'He was for weeks unconscious and had to be kept so.' Cecil told Shaw that his brother had 'a complication of troubles' which had grown worse and included 'something wrong with his kidneys'. Maisie Ward says he had 'sunk into a coma' but there is no evidence that he was ever unconscious – had he been he would have been hospitalised. One possibility is that he was suffering from a prolonged episode of catatonic depression which left him unable to think or communicate clearly: 'If you come he would not know you,' Frances told Father O'Connor.

Vincent McNabb writes that when Chesterton finally recovered he said he thought he had been captured by pirates. As he slowly recuperated, he found himself in a very different world – one in which the Marconi affair had been forgotten, and the war, which contrary to first impressions now looked as if it would last a long time and involve a massive amount of casualties, was dominating the thoughts and actions of almost everyone in the country. It meant an end to the world the Chestertons had thrived in – the debates, the political protests, the poetry writing and literary pageants. There was pressure on all men to respond to the call of Kitchener and Lloyd George and enlist, but Chesterton, grossly overweight and short-sighted, was obviously unfit to serve. Cecil volunteered but was rejected owing, he said, to varicose veins.

The alternative to active service was the propaganda campaign that both brothers were keen to promote. Cecil, who in the pages of the *New Witness* had been deploring the moral decay of England in vivid images of squalor and corruption, greeted the outbreak of war as possibly a hopeful event. 'Worse things than the war now at our doors, the world has never seen,' he wrote; 'better things than the world has ever known may result from it.'[22] On the military side, the propaganda agenda was to be determined by Belloc. At the outbreak of war he had volunteered his services as a liaison officer, confident that his knowledge of the French language and his brief career in the French army would be of value. So confident was he that he even prepared his kit for travelling to the Front. But all his attempts to enlist were rebuffed, and much to his disappointment he was told he could not leave the country. It seemed like another deliberate slight by the authorities, similar to his rejection by All Souls and his failure to be offered ministerial office in the Liberal government – a slight made even harder to bear when his attempt to enlist was also rejected by the French army. It served to increase his overall sense of grievance and his contempt for politicians.

Belloc's view of the war was predictable. Following the lead of his hero Déroulède, he had long believed that a war between France and Germany was inevitable and indeed necessary if *revanche* was to be achieved and the honour of France restored. From a wider perspective, to justify British involvement, Belloc interpreted the war as a simple struggle between Christendom and barbarism (Prussia).

As a former private in the French army and a historian who had vividly described famous battles like Blenheim and Waterloo in many books and lectures, Belloc now launched himself as an expert commentator on warfare, with a regular weekly column in *Land and Water*, a paper founded by a wealthy Australian Murray Allison which achieved a huge circulation. Paid the almost unheard of sum of £40 per article, Belloc pontificated on the progress of the war with his usual air of confident omniscience. But he was more concerned with propaganda than reporting, his patriotic aim being to foster civilian and military morale by consistently maintaining that all was going well for the Allies. Thus in 1917 when General Nivelle launched his disastrous offensive which resulted in 100,000 French casualties and led to widespread mutinies in his army, Belloc was telling his *New Witness* readers that there had been a 'sweeping and triumphant advance' and an 'increasing loss of enemy morale'.[23]

Historians have since, quite rightly, blamed British and French Generals like Haig and Nivelle for their conduct of the war and the resulting casualties, but Belloc had a high regard for them, particularly the French,[24] and put all the blame for any setbacks on the despicable meddling politicians, the 'ridiculous parliamentarians of France, Italy and England', the 'little twisting clots of politicians' who interfered with the brave soldiers and sailors until the very end. To a great extent Belloc was forced into this position by his long-held contempt for Lloyd George, the one outstanding politician who had inspired countless volunteers with his patriotic speeches in 1914 and later, as Prime Minister, was to take masterful control of the war effort – yet who remained in Belloc's eyes, the uneducated, untravelled Welsh solicitor, Marconi man, and creator of the National Insurance plan.

Though Belloc eventually made a number of trips to France and met members of the High Command, including Pétain and Foch, his military opinions were widely ridiculed by the army, and posters appeared on the streets of London during the war listing all his howlers. Later a spoof book was published entitled *What I Know About the War* by 'Blare Hilloc' consisting only of blank pages. The writer Richard Aldington, an admirer of Belloc who fought in the war, wrote later that he damaged his reputation with his 'too often chimerical analyses of war strategy in *Land and Water*'.[25] Chesterton, however, followed Belloc's war commentaries religiously, recording that the first thing he asked for when he recovered from his illness was a copy of the latest *Land and Water*. He himself wrote two short books – *The Crimes of England* (1915) and *The Barbarism of Berlin* (1914) – in support of the government's propaganda campaign. He also wrote a pamphlet in praise of Kitchener following his death in 1916. Though Kitchener had been one of the villains of the Boer War and the proponent of concentration camps, Chesterton now hailed him as a great Englishman (he was in fact Irish) whom he compared to St Paul, with 'the power of being a great convert as well as a great crusader'.

Cecil wrote two books to assist the war propaganda. The second of these, *The Perils of Peace*, published in 1916, had a long preface by Belloc and was dedicated to his old Oxford friend and *Eye-Witness* contributor F. Y. Eccles with some lines of Paul Déroulède: '*La France et les Français n'aient qu'un seul but: détruire La Prusse et les Prussiens!*' (France and the French have only one aim: to destroy Prussia and the Prussians.) Like Belloc, Cecil took his cue from Déroulède and decreed that the war aim was a simple one: the destruction of Prussia. According to Cecil's forecast this would have two benefits for England. First, it would put an end to Prussian-style policies like Lloyd George's Insurance Act; and second, it would ensure that in future 'the English governing class shall at least be English... We have seen how our national action has been embarrassed, both before and since the outbreak of war, by the presence in positions of great political influence of men who were not of our blood and could not be expected to share our national feeling.' As for the Germans, the fact is,' he wrote (in tones that anticipated the ideology of the Nazis), 'that there is no country in Europe – not even this one – where the Jews are more pre-dominant in all directions. They have in their hands finance to a considerable extent, journalism to an unprecedented extent and, as everywhere else in Europe, pornography to the extent of a virtual monopoly.'[26]

Much of Cecil's book was devoted to an attack on the anti-war movement, which had been growing in influence as the casualties mounted and the prospect of victory receded. Meanwhile, Belloc harked back to Marconi and *The Party System*. 'Mr Chesterton and I worked side by side for months in making public the nature of Parliamentary decline' but the 'Marconi men', who by rights should have been imprisoned, 'remained in public life'. Belloc now sounded a new and openly reactionary note, pouring scorn on jumped-up, ill-educated parvenus like the Marconi man Lloyd George and his ally, the powerful press baron Lord Northcliffe. To redeem the situation Parliament needed 'a good stiffening of aristocrats',[27] as the present lot had failed to come up to scratch. The country had made 'a marvellous effort' only to be sadly let down by the aristocracy: 'Now the organism of a nation thus politically threatened is, perhaps, better defended by an aristocracy than by any other form of government. An aristocracy is vividly alive to the national interests, and is prompt, ruthless and exhaustive in the pursuit of them.' But, to Belloc's regret, the aristocracy had sold out to the Jews: 'The aristocrats are dining with the Samuels and sneering at their hosts.' And meanwhile 'low-born men' had taken over, and behind such 'scum in office' there were the newspaper owners – 'men of similar origins, similar morals, similar immunity from the law, and yet masters of our political life'.[28]

Chesterton, who was to echo Belloc's lament for the aristocracy, maintained later that *The New Witness*, with Cecil still in charge, was 'passionately patriotic and Pro-Ally but as emphatically opposed to the Jingoism of the *Daily Mail*'.[29] Like so many of the things Chesterton said about his brother this wasn't true. The *New Witness* joined wholeheartedly in the hysteria fanned by the *Mail* against expatriate Germans, identifying all hotel owners on the south coast with German or Jewish surnames as potential spies who might well assist the enemy if and when the Germans invaded.

Cecil now turned his attention to the radical socialist E. D. Morel, pursuing him with the same viciousness with which he had hounded poor Masterman. Morel, a man of shining integrity, had, with Sir Roger Casement, exposed the appalling atrocities being perpetrated in the Congo which was then under the absolute rule of the King of Belgium, Leopold II.[30] With the support of writers such as Mark Twain, Joseph Conrad and Arthur Conan Doyle, Morel founded the Congo Reform Association further to raise public awareness. In attacking Morel, Cecil, just as he had with Dreyfus, was following the lead of Belloc who, as Gardiner noted in his profile, was one of the very few who had publicly defended Leopold,[31] accusing the Congo Reform Association of 'cant and hypocrisy', and informing the House of Commons: 'It is an elementary fact that wherever Europeans come into contact with races so inferior as the races in the Congo basin there must necessarily be acts of cruelty and tyranny.'[32] Belloc's attitude to the atrocities may also have been influenced by the involvement in the Congo campaign of his *bête noire*, Herbert Samuel, who was the first MP to raise the issue in the Commons. Belloc later refused to join with Chesterton and other writers petitioning for a reprieve for Morel's fellow Congo campaigner Roger Casement, who was hanged for treason in 1916.

Cecil based his attack on Morel solely on his insistence, shared by many socialists, that Germany did not bear sole responsibility for the outbreak of war in 1914. He ignored Morel's Anglo-French parentage and was convinced that his name was false (hence his continual use of inverted commas when referring to 'Morel') and that he was almost certainly a German agent, all of whose actions (including his Congo campaign) being done to support the aims of the German government.

In fact Morel's family history was almost identical to Belloc's, he being the son of an English mother and a French father who died when he was only four, having suffered in the Franco-Prussian War. 'The general air of mystery and concealment which surrounds the story,' Cecil concluded after a brief and inaccurate account of Morel's early career, 'suggests the type of man who *might* be a foreign agent or spy. Of course they are not direct evidence.'[33] Cecil's suspicions hardened when he challenged Morel at a public meeting to sue him for libel. Morel did nothing, leaving

Cecil confident enough to suggest, in his book, that Morel had acted as a go-between, passing money from the German government to Labour Party leader Keir Hardie. There was no evidence to support this fantasy.

As with Marconi, Cecil was not acting alone, being one of a jingoistic pack baying for Morel's blood, and he was no doubt delighted when Morel was arrested on a trumped-up charge in 1917 and imprisoned for six months, which he spent knitting mail bags with a burglar on one side and 'a violator of little girls' on the other.[34] By now *New Witness* readers had grown used to continual references to 'Morel', and also to Rufus Isaacs's German chauffeur, almost certainly another agent. They were warned of the alarming number of German barbers, particularly well placed for gathering information helpful to the enemy. German–Jewish bankers like Sir Edgar Speyer, all with German contacts, were especially suspect and Cecil proposed, with apparent seriousness, that they should be sent to concentration camps and put to useful work like wood-chopping. Cecil had earlier protested when Speyer, along with his fellow Jew, Harry Levy-Lawson MP, had helped to raise a fund for a memorial to Speyer's friend Captain Scott, whose Antarctic expedition had ended tragically with his death in 1912. Speyer, Chairman of the London Underground railway, was a Privy Counsellor, a friend of the Prime Minister Asquith and the close friend and patron of prominent musicians, including Edward Elgar, but in Cecil's eyes, being Jewish, he was incapable of patriotic emotions. Neither he nor Levy-Lawson, Cecil wrote, 'know anything about the country whose memorial they are directing'. Frank Hugh O'Donnell had previously written in the *New Witness* of his admiration for Captain Scott's heroism 'at a time when so many of the old traditions of England are tainted by alien evils'.

The *New Witness* even protested about the presence of two Jewish ladies on the board of a charity set up to help refugees who had poured into the country from war-torn Belgium: 'The Belgians are an Ancient European people,' Cecil wrote, 'Catholic in religion. We should all desire to make them feel as strongly as possible that in coming to England they had come to a friendly country where their traditions would be respected, their religion held sacred and where their race might find, during evil times, a secure, a peaceful and an honourable home.' And all the time the same old targets – Lloyd George, Cadbury and Co – were relentlessly attacked, and there was never any danger that readers would be allowed to forget about Marconi.

It was all too much for one important *New Witness* reader and occasional contributor in the shape of H. G. Wells. The son of a lady's maid and her husband who combined the life of a cricketer with keeping a chinaware shop in Bromley, Kent, Wells was a self-taught man who had triumphed over a background of poverty and ignorance to become an acclaimed writer of realistic novels and early science fiction. Despite their differences, especially over religion – 'Wells cannot ever come across the name of Catholic Christianity without losing control of himself' – he and Chesterton remained lifelong friends. A. G. Gardiner's view of Wells could equally well have been written of Chesterton – a man with 'an intense curiosity about life' and 'an infinite capacity for being interested. There is nothing in the heavens above or in the earth beneath that he does not want to know about.'[35] Wells's attitude to his work was also very similar to his friend's. He liked to be thought of as a journalist, despite the success of his novels. 'What I write goes now,' he claimed, 'and will presently die.' It was the same attitude, in Chesterton, that had so exasperated Cecil. But Chesterton approved. 'What I have always liked about Wells,' he wrote, 'is his vigorous and unaffected readiness for a lark.'[36]

Chesterton's new-found loyalties were bound to put a strain on his friendship with Wells, just as had happened with Gardiner and Masterman. Like Gardiner, Wells had been saddened by the way, as he saw it, in which his friend Chesterton had been led astray by Belloc and Cecil. In August 1916 he provoked a controversy with a critical article about the *New Witness* in Chesterton's old paper the *Daily News*. Its thinking, he said, had 'the simplicity of the taproom and its sub-title should be "The Art of Stirring Mud".'

It was not the first time Wells had criticised the *New Witness*, but when Chesterton attempted a reply, Wells retaliated with a crushing retort. It was all the more embarrassing to Chesterton as it raised his brother's persecution of his old friend Masterman:

> Let me pass to what I may call your staple victims. I come to judgement in these matters with no particular bias: or if I have a bias, it is rather against the people you attack; and after years of it – how many years has the *New Witness* run? – I have to record that so far as Mr Lloyd George, or Lord Northcliffe, or the Cadburys, or Mr Herbert Samuel, or Lord Reading go, I remain not simply unconvinced of the scoundrelly and plottesque character of these people, but persuaded that on the whole they intend well and are doing well in spite of many drawbacks and much opposition. I can write this all the more cheerfully because for certain of the personalities you assail I have a very hearty but quite personal dislike. You say the English parliament 'almost unanimously passes laws almost unanimously detested'. I say to that 'Stuff!' You say 'it obeys a small group dealing with huge funds collected in the dark, distributed in the dark' and so on. I answer 'Rubbish!' I have heard of that 'group' ever since I read Eugène Sue's *Wandering Jew,* but in those days it was called 'Jesuits'. I get warnings about its variegated activities from time to time in letters from lunatics. I believe that this idea may be a fruitful seed of *mental disorder*...[37]

Wells, correctly, saw that there was a note of insanity in Cecil's attacks, if not in his brother's attempts to defend him:

> Take for example your question 'Are we to forgive Lloyd George for buying shares from Isaacs because he has sold the poor to Rothschild and Sassoon?' Now *nobody really sane* [italics added] believes that Lloyd George has sold the poor to Rothschild and Sassoon. You just get out of your noisy little group for a bit and ask any ordinary people, and you will find that what I am telling you is true. Nobody. And also you have persuaded yourself that the Insurance Act is a highly unpopular measure. It is nothing of the sort. The mass of intelligent people think quite rightly

that the Insurance Act was a well-conceived attempt to lift the sick and unemployed wages-serf out of the pit of private charity and to begin the socialisation of the medical profession. It was a blow struck at the parochial domination of the wealthy. The great rage into which the rich old women of this country flew is its best testimonial. Mr Belloc or Mr Bottomley could not address a meeting against the Insurance Act anywhere without a titled harridan or so upon the platform... Mr George very unwisely did not consult the medical profession... but he had all the rich Toryism of the country against him, vast interests to square, the bitter jealousy of every 'expert' who wasn't in complete control of the new development... He wasn't working in clean air: he was toiling through mud, as everyone, my dear Chesterton, has to do who tries to do something real in social organisation rather than follow *our* serene method of comment, inactivity, and airy mockery from our rose gardens and sunlit lawns. On the whole I envy Mr George his Insurance Act.[38]

Though at the time of writing (August 1916) Lloyd George was not yet Prime Minister, Wells highlighted the difficulty facing Belloc and the Chesterton brothers, who had conducted a vehement and occasionally vicious campaign against the one man who, for all his many faults, was capable of heading the war effort:

And I have watched him through this war, watched the dissensions, the intrigues, the threats and fits of temper the outbreaks of silly rhetoric – he is a man with long hair and a Welsh dissenter, and I don't like statesmen with long hair and I hate Welsh Dissent, especially the hymn-singing most violently – and when I have set all that aside for condemnation, there remains something in Mr Lloyd George that extorts my gratitude and respect. I think it would be difficult to overrate the debt the country owes him. The British system is the system of the slacker and the dignified obstructive: the real evil thing in it is not the plotter – that is your *insanity* – it is the deadly absence of creative purpose; and I am convinced that the Cecils, the Barnacles, the Tennants and Asquiths, the beaming foolish Birrells, the influential easy-going place-fillers and way-blockers, would certainly in the most gentlemanly way, have lost us this war last year if it had not been for the undignified energy of Mr Lloyd George and Lord Northcliffe...You pose as the antagonists of a general corruption, but the reality is a personal pursuit and an individual spite... I want very much that you should understand clearly, my dear Chesterton, that the *New Witness* has totally failed to convince me of the reality of its general indignation... I consider the *New Witness* exposure – I choose deliberately a word that I know will stick like a thorn in your mind – *Cant*, a Cant of Exposure.[39]

And there was more in the same vein, a ferocious critique that drew no distinction between Chesterton and his brother, whilst making the kind of points about Lloyd George and Co that the old pre-Belloc Chesterton might well have made himself – in particular the suggestion that the personalities that the *New Witness* attacked were all of them acting patriotically and effectively (had not Chesterton written in this vein about Lloyd George's colleague Lord Kitchener?).

Chesterton had shown his total inability to break ranks with Cecil on a previous occasion, when Wells had protested about a book review in the *New Witness* written by Cecil's wife-to-be Keith, under her pen name J. K. Prothero. The book in question, *Zeppelin Nights*, was the work of Ford Madox Ford (then writing under his former name of Ford Madox Hueffer). Ford was the son of Francis Hueffer, the German-born music critic of *The Times* and an authority on Wagner. His mother was the daughter of the Pre-Raphaelite artist Ford Madox Brown. Ford was by now an established novelist and briefly editor of the *English Review* – according to Graham Greene 'the best literary editor England has ever had'.[40] He had lived for a time near Rye, was a close friend of Joseph Conrad, Henry James and John Galsworthy, and had launched many young writers, most notably D. H. Lawrence who described him as 'everybody's blessed Uncle and headmaster.' 'A large blond confident man', according to Arthur Ransome, he was active in wartime anti-German propaganda on behalf of the French and British governments. He was commissioned in the Welsh Regiment in 1915, and was gassed in the fighting in France.

Ford was a prolific writer of plays, novels and journalism and his book *Zeppelin Nights*, written in collaboration with his mistress Violet Hunt, was a pot boiler, dashed off, perhaps, to please the propaganda chief, his great friend Charles Masterman.[41] It consisted of a series of stories told to one another by a group of friends in London to pass the time while sheltering from the Zeppelin bombing raids. Each story was related by the imaginary eye-witness of a famous historical event, and the book ended with a vivid description of George V's coronation in Westminster Abbey in 1911, which as a piece of fine patriotic writing could not be bettered.

There is nothing in Keith's review to suggest that she had read Ford's book or that she knew anything much about its well-known author. She claims that it was plainly written 'for German consumption', portraying Londoners 'cowering in their cellars, apart of course from the non-Europeans' (in other words the Jews) 'in Whitechapel' (there is nothing in the book to this effect). It looked as if in attacking Hueffer/Ford, Keith was loyally following Cecil in singling out anyone with a German name as a traitor and probably a Jew to boot: 'It is generally supposed,' she wrote, 'that Mr Hueffer is not exactly of pure European extraction and this book is certain to confirm such an impression.'[42]

The readers of the *New Witness* were normally slow to take issue with its editor's excesses but on this occasion there were a number of letters of protest which at least were printed in the paper's correspondence column. But Keith refused to give an inch, and when one reader pointed out that Ford was a Catholic, who though over forty had secured a commission in the army, she replied that none of this meant that 'he ceases to be a Jew'. She added for good measure that Ford had written a novel (*The Good Soldier*) about 'a particularly brutal type of sensualist'.[43] Not only a Jew, a German and a traitor, but a pornographer, in other words.

It was all too much for Wells who wrote to his friend Chesterton:

...the business of the Hueffer book in the *New Witness* makes me sick. Some disgusting little greaser called Prothero has been allowed to insult old FMH in a series of letters that makes me ashamed of my species. Hueffer has many faults no doubt but firstly he's poor, secondly he's notoriously unhappy and in a most miserable position, thirdly he's a better writer than any of your little crowd and fourthly, instead of pleading his age and his fat, and taking refuge from service in greasy obesity as your brother has done, he is serving his country. His book is a great book and Prothero just lies about it – I guess he's a dirty minded priest or some such unclean thing. I will never let the *New Witness* into the house again.[44]

In replying to Wells, Chesterton decided to go along with his mistaken belief that J. K. Prothero was a man, if not, as Wells implied, 'a dirty minded priest':

Most certainly you have always been a good friend to me and I have always tried to express my pride in the fact. I know enough of your good qualities in other ways to put down everything in your last letter to an emotion of loyalty to another friend. Any quarrel between us will not come from me; and I confess I am puzzled as to why it should come from you, merely because somebody else who is not I dislikes a book by somebody else who is not you, and says so in an article for which neither of us is even remotely responsible... I cannot help being entertained by your vision of Prothero who is not a priest, but a poor journalist, and I believe a Free-Thinker. But whoever he may be... he has a right to justice: and you must surely see that even if it were my paper, I could not either tell a man to find a book good when he had found it bad, or sack him for a point of taste which has nothing to do with the principles of the paper.[45]

Chesterton thus by-passes Wells's protest, which was not about the quality of the book but the personal, and, incidentally, highly libellous, attack on Ford. It was another sign of the way in which his uncritical support of Cecil and Belloc was forcing him to be evasive and dishonest. He concluded:

> By all means drop any paper you dislike, though if you do it for every book review you think unfair, I fear your admirable range of modern knowledge will be narrowed. Of the paper in question I will merely say this. My brother and in some degree the few who have worked with him have undertaken a task of public criticism for the sake of which they stand in permanent danger of imprisonment and personal ruin. We are incessantly reminded of this danger and no one has ever dared to suggest that we have any motive but the best. If you should ever think it right to undertake such a venture, you will find that the number of those who will commit their journalistic fortunes to it is singularly small: and includes some who have more courage and honesty than acquaintance with the hierarchy of art.[46]

So Keith, in falsely attacking Ford as a cowardly Jewish traitor, is to be defended for 'courage and honesty' whilst 'he' and her colleagues, in particular Cecil, should be given the benefit of the doubt as they are undertaking 'a task of public criticism' whilst being in permanent danger of 'imprisonment and personal ruin'. (Chesterton repeats this dramatic phrase in his autobiography.) It was always a feeble argument, as the Marconi ministers, Rufus Isaacs especially, were only too keen for the scandal to be forgotten, as was in any case likely to happen now that the war had taken precedence over the whole political scene. Chesterton was grasping at any argument, however feeble, to avoid all criticism on his part of either Keith or Cecil. (It appears that he did not even tell Keith of Wells's protest as she writes in her memoir that he had complained not to Chesterton but to the lawyer E. S. P. Haynes, and dismisses the whole incident as a bit of a joke.)

It may seem irrelevant to devote so much attention to a forgotten review of a forgotten book, yet the episode is significant as showing

Chesterton's manic determination not to break ranks with Keith (and therefore Cecil) even when the case against her is unanswerable and even when siding with her means jeopardising his relationship with one of his greatest friends, H. G. Wells.

Luckily for Chesterton, Wells was magnanimous enough not to pursue the quarrel – he was well aware of the extent to which Chesterton was in thrall to Belloc and Cecil, and equally well aware that it was humbug on Chesterton's part to claim that no one had ever queried Cecil's motives, when several critics, in politics and the press, had deplored his racist attitudes, as had Mr Justice Phillimore.

It was just a pity that H. G. Wells, when railing against personal attacks, should, rather typically, make just such an attack himself against Cecil, accusing him of dodging the column and skulking about 'in greasy obesity' while others volunteered for army service. In fact, Cecil had been to a recruiting office just after the declaration of war but had been rejected on health grounds. He was eventually called up two months after Wells's letter to the *New Witness* was published, following the introduction of conscription earlier in the year. He was classified 'B2', fit for home service only, and drafted to the East Surrey Regiment and their base at Westgate-on-Sea.

Cecil took his leave, helped on his way with an emotional tribute from the Dominican priest Father Vincent McNabb, the man who, with Elodie Belloc's help, had converted him to Roman Catholicism four years previously: 'Au revoir,' he wrote to the *New Witness*, 'until we see you again and see you more drilled and vigorous than before. May your hand, your pen-hand, never lose its cunning, no matter how weary it becomes under the weight of your rifle. May your eye never lose its sight, its insight, no matter how many winter mists chill and swell its lid. May your heart never flag or droop, no matter along how many miles of bleak sodden road you have to plod. God love you. Au revoir.'[47]

Cecil had asked his brother to take over the editorship of the *New Witness* in his absence, knowing that he would agree, despite the inevitable opposition of Frances. It was an insensitive thing to do, given all of

Chesterton's other commitments and his obvious unsuitability for the job of editor. From a practical point of view the appointment was bound to lead to problems as Chesterton lived outside London in Beaconsfield and, unless he changed his routine, could be only an occasional visitor to the office, just as Belloc had been.

Cecil had little concern with such matters and, in any case, seems to have been more interested in the value of his brother's name than his editorial abilities. In a round robin appealing for funds he announced that Chesterton was taking over – 'His name will in future appear on the paper.' He had every confidence, he wrote, that it would soon be self-supporting 'with my brother's name upon it'. It was the same attitude that had led him to appoint his brother as chairman of the inaugural meeting of the League for Clean Government – his name was all he needed to draw in members. More importantly, the name lent respectability to both the League and the paper, its appearance on the cover seeming to guarantee the quality of the inside pages. Yet this, as Cecil must have known, posed a risk for Chesterton when he was not a full-time editor, particularly when he was relying on the erratic and volatile Keith to hold the fort for him. She had already shown her unreliability in the treatment of Ford Madox Ford's book and was later to cause Chesterton acute embarrassment with another, more violently anti-Semitic, contribution.

Ignoring such possibilities, Cecil now assured readers that his brother's name was 'a guarantee of continuity in principles, a guarantee that the national attitude of the paper will show no weakening, that any suggestion of an inconclusive peace with Prussia will be strenuously resisted, that the attack on all forms of political corruption and unnatural plutocracy will be hotly pressed'.[48]

It was not an agenda ideally suited to Chesterton's temperament, though in obedience to Cecil he was to do his best to live up to it, whilst insisting that he was the worst editor in the world: 'I no more expected to be an editor than to be the policeman in the Strand,' he wrote.

An editor is required to make all kinds of decisions, often as a matter of urgency. But Chesterton was incapable of this. In a way it was a repeat of his experience when canvassing in an election campaign with Masterman, who having been down one side of a street looked back to see Chesterton still talking to the first householder on his side:

> I am bound to do the work badly, because I find it so interesting in that it is like life itself: nearly the chief trouble of life is that there is nothing dull in it: it is not a waste of monotony but a jungle of distractions. We are told of the editor yawning over heaps of merely tiresome trash: but I am not sure it would affect me like that, even if I had more of it than I do. There are cartloads, of course, of things that are not in the practical sense worth printing: but I hardly admit that they are not worth reading... It is because I am so enthusiastically, so utterly editorial that I cannot be an editor. I never saw a letter to this paper, published or unpublished, to which I did not want to add a note as long as an essay. If I seem oblivious of a book sent last week, it is because I am still occupied on one or two articles suggested by a postcard received last month. I have often had to explain this in private life. Even the communications which it is most impossible to publish are among the most delightful to read: so delightful that it seems a pity that they cannot be published and therefore more widely read. In the writings of those whom I may respectfully describe as lunatics there is often something livelier than literature... I received yesterday a letter from a lady closely associated with the glorified spirit of Lord Kitchener[49] who (I was earnestly assured) is no longer called Horatio but only 'Herbert – God's precious Herb'.[50]

Quite apart from his editorial shortcomings, Chesterton was expected to cope with the paper's shaky finances which belied Cecil's confident assurances of improving circulation when appealing to potential backers. The outbreak of war had affected advertising, which had never been plentiful, but even before that in January 1914 there had been a threat of bankruptcy. On 4 June 1915 Cecil sent out an appeal to shareholders asking them to help save the paper: 'We urgently need £2000,' he wrote, stressing the fact that he himself had contributed over £280 – practically the whole proceeds of a recent lecture tour in America. 'I think it is due to show to you,' he wrote, 'that I have been and am prepared to make very considerable sacrifices myself.' He did not point out that such sacrifices had enabled him to do what he wanted to do, namely edit the *New Witness*, and furthermore that he was living as a bachelor with his wealthy parents and so had very limited expenses.

Like its successor *GK's Weekly*, the *New Witness* survived – but only for a time – thanks to the help of millionaire benefactors, the most generous of whom was the orchestral conductor Sir Thomas Beecham, famous, among other things, for his championing of the music of Frederick Delius. A very rich man due to his family connection with Beecham's Pills, Beecham, like others, had, on first acquaintance, been disconcerted by Cecil's appearance[51] but he came to admire him, calling him a born fighter and 'the finest journalist of his day'.[52] Beecham regularly attended the weekly editorial meetings where, in accordance with Belloc's wishes, each person present was provided with a glass and a bottle of Burgundy. 'At the end of half an hour the next week's issue was wholly planned.'[53]

Apart from Beecham the paper had another more mysterious benefactor who, according to Keith's account, arrived without warning one day in the Essex Street office – 'a tall, grey-haired old gentleman wearing a top hat and shabby frock coat'. He came several times afterwards, ostensibly to look through the back numbers, and agreed to provide financial support for the paper. His name is not mentioned by Keith, she and Cecil referring to him as 'Godfather', but she writes that he invited Cecil to dinner in 'a fine old house in an opulent square' and persuaded him to stand as an Independent candidate for Clean Government. Cecil took the suggestion seriously, and the year before his death was proposing to stand in Masterman's old constituency of West Ham, promising would-be backers that he would stand for 'a vigorous prosecution of the war till complete victory is achieved... the elimination of corrupt influences (especially when there are also enemy influences on policies), the restoration of Trade Union rights… opposition to fussy and tyrannical interference with personal liberty and especially with the family.'

When it came to the *New Witness* finances, Gilbert Chesterton was even less qualified than Cecil. Beecham's support was short-lived as he was already, by 1917, having to finance the London Symphony Orchestra out of his own funds, leaving it to Chesterton to spend the very considerable monthly sum of £200 to meet the printing bill and contributors' fees. Apart from money, there was also the problem of Keith, whom he had now to rely on to deputise for him in the Essex Street office. She writes scornfully of Chesterton's editorship, comparing him adversely to Cecil and complaining about his rare visits to London when he would spend most of the time in the office dictating his own articles. 'Somehow Gilbert did not inspire the same enthusiasm for the *New Witness* that his brother had.' All this was unfair, when Chesterton himself admitted that he was no good as an editor – something that could have been perfectly well foreseen by Cecil when he pressured him into taking his place in the hope that, whatever his shortcomings, his famous name on the front cover would be enough to keep sales up.

Reading between the lines – something one has to do quite a lot of when unravelling the Chesterton story – it is clear that Chesterton's relationship with the woman who was to become his sister-in-law was strained. But now he would have to rely on her to hold the *New Witness* fort for him and, being Cecil's girl and a very forceful character, he could do little to stand in her way. As he explained to Belloc after Cecil's death: 'She is not and has never been a person I could treat like an ordinary subordinate.' He could have added that as a Free Thinker and a Communist (if not a party member then a fellow traveller) Keith was not in sympathy with the *New Witness*'s Bellocian stance. She was, however, keen to show that when it came to harrying Jews she could hold her own with Cecil. By far the most objectionable article printed in the *New Witness* was an account by Keith in October 1917 of Jews sheltering on the London Underground during a German bombing raid, which would not have been out of place in *Der Stürmer*.

The press, she began, had previously referred to 'scenes of depraving cowardice' on the London Underground, 'the dehumanised herds who at the first hint of danger run screaming like hares to shelter, but only the *New Witness* had the courage to say that they were Jews... These people in many cases take up their positions early in the day... when not content with having secured a place of safety they exhibit symptoms of fear so abject that they adopt ape-like attitudes slavering at the mouth and uttering animal cries of dread.'

It was as if Keith was determined to show her solidarity with Belloc and Cecil and even to go beyond them in her outspokenness and racist scorn – it was not enough for her to describe the horrific scenes on the Underground, she had to make it the basis for a generalised attack on Jews. So just as Cecil had excused Isaacs and Samuel on the ground that being Jewish it was inevitable that they would indulge in chicanery, so the Whitechapel Jews were simply behaving in accordance with their racial stereotype:

> Individually there are of course courageous members of the race, but in the mass they always have been and always will be unable to face the prospect of violent death with anything akin to human dignity, being possessed by a craven terror which it is almost indecent to gaze upon... I contend that such sights are not desirable and that these Jews should be afforded shelter from the exhibition of their shame. We have admitted them to this country as our guests. We have given them our hospitality and as their hosts we are under an obligation to provide them with protection. As, however, they are congenitally incapable of behaving in a decent fashion, I suggest that they should be cleared from the cities and made welcome in a bomb-proof ghetto in the Midlands where they can exhibit the cowardice of their race in decent privacy. I should like to make clear that I do not blame these people that in the face of danger they are unable to stand upright – but I do blame the authorities that they have not arranged suitable seclusion for these suffering Hebrews...'[54]

In any charge sheet against Chesterton for overt anti-Semitism the fact that as editor of the *New Witness* he printed this article by Keith would have to rate as the most damning piece of evidence. Given his rather tenuous hold on the editorship he could have been excused for letting it into the paper due to a failure properly to check the content. But the fact is that he went out of his way to commend Keith's article in the following issue: 'An able colleague has described with a vividness approaching ferocity a Jew with a gold watch-chain grovelling on the floor of the tube.'[55]

Even assuming that Keith had written an accurate report of what she had seen, there was nothing to excuse her absolute lack of sympathy for the Whitechapel Jews, let alone the way she compared them to animals. It would be an insult to Chesterton to say that he was indifferent to her obnoxious abuse – his reference to the 'ferocity' of the article is, perhaps, a feeble attempt on his part to register some faint concern – yet his response shows in the most vivid form his preparedness to sacrifice his own reputation to feed an overwhelming compulsion to support Cecil, and now, by proxy, Cecil's appointed deputy and soon-to-be wife.

'When my brother went to the Front,' Chesterton wrote, 'he left the paper in my hands.' Like most of his statements about Cecil this wasn't strictly true, as Cecil was not to make it to the Front, if he ever did, for another six months. In the meantime the nearest he got to France was Westgate-on-Sea, headquarters of the East Surrey Regiment to which he had been drafted. 'Work has been found for me,' he wrote. ' If I have little hope of killing any Germans, I may set better men free for that just, happy and necessary task.' In the meantime Cecil had plenty of spare time to continue writing regularly for the *New Witness*, contributing a number of long features on mostly literary topics.

Cecil approached military service in the same boisterous spirit as he had faced his libel trial. But he was ill suited to army life. Shaw, whom he visited in uniform, describes him as 'a hopelessly unsoldierlike figure' and even Keith writes 'it was impossible to visualise him in battle'. A comrade in the East Surreys confirms the picture, calling him 'a man naturally unsuited to the military life… some of us still gleefully remember the sensation he caused at reveille when he commenced his toilet by spreading a waterproof sheet in the mud and then putting on his boots and puttees only to find he had first omitted to don his trousers.'

'There is little or no information about Cecil's military service,' his biographer Brocard Sewell writes, and his own account only adds to the mystery. Thus he refers to Cecil's vivid letters from the trenches, having previously informed us that all his wartime letters were destroyed in the Blitz. It is safe to assume that during the course of the fourteen months that Cecil was in France he wrote a number of letters home, not only to Keith but to his brother, his parents, Belloc and other friends. If so, not a single one has come to light.

The person best qualified to describe Cecil's military career was his widow Keith, who played a crucial role in the story. Unfortunately her account of how he came to volunteer was rendered, once again, as a scene from a Mills & Boon-style romance.

As she tells the tale, the two of them are on the French coast where Keith has gone to write a report on military hospitals:

We walked to Wimereux in the afternoon – the sun suddenly shining, lit up the cliffs, the blue paint of the cafe, the white walls of the Casino… 'You know I want to join up, kiddy… I shan't rest until I'm passed A1.' 'You'd be doing more important work on the *New Witness*,' I protested. 'There's nothing so important as fighting today,' said he. 'It'll take a devil of a lot of doing but I mean to get there all the same. And then' – he paused – 'when I'm passed for the front do you think you could marry me?' It was the old story, but this time there was a difference. He was so wistful, so indomitable that somehow I could not refuse. It was impossible to visualise him in battle, and in a rush of feeling for what seemed to me an inevitable heartbreak, I promised. But when I said 'yes' there came into his eyes a look of such adoration, such unfathomable joy that I felt suddenly, strangely humbled.[56]

So Keith was in the compromising position of a woman who didn't want her man to go to war whilst at the same time giving him the strongest possible incentive to make himself fit to do so.

Quite how Cecil, initially marked down as C3, the lowest medical grade, managed to be passed as A1 after a few months in the army is a matter only for speculation. The feat would almost certainly have involved giving up, or drastically reducing, his intake of drink. But the motive, according to Keith, was more personal than patriotic – she describes how, once he had been passed as A1, he rushed up to London arriving at her flat well after midnight and seized her with excitement: 'I'm through. I'm A1 and I'm going to the front and I've three days' leave. You'll marry me, kiddy – now?'[57]

Keith gave her consent and in her account of the subsequent wedding night seemed determined to show that it had been altogether a more successful affair than her brother-in-law's: 'I was all ready when he emerged from his bedroom, astonishingly well groomed. He looked at me from the door, and his face lit up, almost ecstatically, as though it had glimpsed some sort of vision. "For mine is the kingdom, the power and the glory, sweetheart," he said softly, and I wondered at the worship in his eyes.'[58]

When it came to writing her book in 1941 she was confronted by a serious difficulty. Chesterton had published his autobiography five years earlier, shortly before his death, and had stated that Cecil had died a hero 'in a dark hour of doom', or, in another context, 'of the effects of exposure in the last fierce fighting that broke the Prussian power over Christendom, fighting for which he had volunteered after being invalided home'. Likewise, in his open letter to Lord Reading published in the *New Witness*[59] he says: 'Cecil Chesterton found death in the trenches to which he had freely gone.' Such was the extraordinary respect Chesterton was able to command both in his lifetime and subsequently that his false account of Cecil's death has been generally repeated, though the true facts are easily verifiable. Several books – A. N. Wilson's *Hilaire Belloc*, Denis Judd's *The Life of Lord Reading* and *The Letters of Maurice Baring* edited by Jocelyn Hillgarth and Julian Jeffs – claim that Cecil was killed in action. Other reports are equally inaccurate. His biographer Brocard Sewell writes in his own memoir *My Dear Time's Waste* (1966) that Cecil 'endured two years active service in atrocious conditions in Flanders'. 'He immersed himself in the fighting,' Frank Harris wrote in 1920, 'and died with the colours in France.' In *The Marconi Scandal*, Frances Donaldson states that he was 'wounded in action' while 'serving his country with gallantry'. *The Dictionary of National Biography: Missing Persons* (1993) states that Cecil was wounded *three times*. Michael Ffinch claims that 'he had been brought back from France wounded' and W. R. Titterton writes that Cecil 'died at the front'.[60]

All these statements are false. Keith knew the more prosaic truth – that Cecil had died in a French hospital of complications from chronic nephritis after a long march in the rain three weeks after the declaration of the Armistice in November 1918. Thanks to Maurice Baring, who intervened with the military authorities, she had been with him at the military hospital in Wimereux when he died on 6 December. It was a tragic anti-climax and proof of the fact that he should never have been passed A1. But she could scarcely say as much without making it clear that Chesterton had lied when stating that his brother was killed in action, or as the result of fighting 'in the last glory of the great war'.

Her own account is therefore deliberately vague, referring to 'rat-ridden trenches, waist deep in water, verminous dugouts, all the foulness and the stench of slaughter' without specifying how precisely Cecil related to this nightmarish scene, and at no point referring to his taking part in actual combat. Instead she writes: 'Cecil wallowing in mud at Ypres, had been given a liaison job as his French was fluent.' This 'liaison job' cannot have included liaising with the French military as that work was entrusted only to commissioned officers. The likelihood is that Cecil was involved with the huge army working behind the lines liaising with French tradesmen and transport workers in supporting the fighting units at the front. The fact that Cecil was not at the frontline in 1917 is confirmed by his note in a *New Witness* article referring to 'this remote backwater behind the Front to which fate for the moment has confined me'.[61] In her sketchy account of the final months of the war Keith describes Cecil as being provided with a daily bottle of wine 'for extra duty' as well as cashing innumerable cheques. More significantly, both Keith and Chesterton write that Cecil completed his book on the history of America while he was in France – 'in the intervals of bitter warfare', according to Chesterton – a difficult if not impossible feat for a solider serving in the frontline. Given his record of poor health, so poor that he had been declared unfit for service a few months previously, it seems highly improbable that Cecil ever took part in active service.[62]

Information about Cecil's health and the cause of his death is as hard to come by as any military data about him. George Bernard Shaw writes that he died of trench fever, frivolously noting his failure to follow a vegetarian diet. Trench fever is repeated by Belloc's biographer Robert Speaight, though deaths from trench fever are known to have been exceptionally rare, and again by Joseph Pearce in *Old Thunder*, his 2002 biography of Belloc. Thomas Beecham blames influenza, as does Frances Donaldson in *The Marconi Scandal*. The only specific evidence about Cecil's condition is to be found in the short memoir by the journalist Bill Titterton, a devoted follower of both Chesterton brothers who took over from Keith as assistant editor of the *New Witness* and later worked on Chesterton's paper *GK's Weekly*. He writes: 'A fine old fellow James Stephens said to me, "Cecil ought to go [to France]; he's been telling others to go. He can't stay at home"... I said to him, "You silly old fool – don't you realise that Cecil has been running from recruiting office to recruiting office trying to be accepted. No sane medical officer would pass him. He has Bright's Disease."'[63]

This account tallies with Cecil's premature death from nephritis brought on by a long route march in the cold and wet – fatal to a man already suffering from chronic kidney disease and, according to Keith, drinking a bottle of wine a day – something that would have aggravated his condition.

Chesterton, well known for his aversion to anything to do with illness, makes no mention of it at all, though Cecil's anonymous comrade from the East Surreys begins his obituary tribute in the *New Witness* with the words: 'Cecil Chesterton's career in the army was one long cheerful fight against physical disabilities.'[64] Keith was keen not to stress this aspect of the story, perhaps because it too conflicted with Chesterton's false account of a heroic brother killed in action. So her version refers almost casually to the fact that Cecil was sent home twice from France (once with a septic hand) and mentions that at one stage he spent 'a few weeks in hospital' without specifying the cause.

There is scarcely any documentary evidence of Chesterton's reaction to the news of Cecil's death. He must have received scores of letters from friends – Belloc, Baring, Vincent McNabb, etc. – but none have surfaced. Only the faithful Titterton, then holding the fort at the *New Witness* office in Little Essex Street, records, 'Of course he never exhibited his grief... Throughout the bad time that followed the death of Cecil, GKC was always courteous and kind and he was jolly...'[65] But it is not difficult to imagine the shock, coming so soon after the Armistice, when Chesterton must have experienced a feeling of intense relief that Cecil had been spared and would soon be coming home. Relief, too, that he himself would now be freed from the strain and worries of editing the *New Witness,* a job he had never wanted and felt himself ill-equipped to do, and which created tension with his beloved wife Frances.

Only the neglected chronicler Keith records that Gilbert could not face his brother's death and was unwilling even to phone their mother, asking Frances to do it. 'Can't I speak to my son, even now?' she pleaded, and eventually Chesterton broke the tragic news to her.

Almost as hard to bear was the sense of anti-climax. After all the bravado, the talk of killing Germans, Cecil had died in hospital as a result of his chronic illness, *after the war was over.* Chesterton was quite incapable of accepting that mundane version of events, so just as he had created a false picture of Cecil as the man who had single-handedly exposed the Marconi scandal, he now convinced himself of a second Cecil, a soldier who had died a hero's death on the battlefield. This was not a deliberate deception on his part. It was a fantasy, a delusion so powerful that he persisted with it for the rest of his life, making it his primary duty to honour the memory of a mythical hero whose courage in the courts and on the battlefield he said he could never hope to emulate.

Apparently incapable of expressing his grief or even accepting the truth about Cecil's death, Chesterton reacted in a startling and bizarre way by writing and publishing in the *New Witness* of 13 December 1918 (a week after his brother died) a long and hateful open letter to Rufus Isaacs (now Lord Reading), whom he appeared, by inference, to blame for Cecil's death:

The Sign of the World's End: An Open Letter to Lord Reading

My Lord – I address to you a public letter as it is upon a public question: it is unlikely that I should ever trouble you with any private letter on any private question: and least of all on the private question that now fills my mind. It would be impossible altogether to ignore the irony that has in the last few days brought to an end the great Marconi duel in which you and I in some sense played the part of seconds; that personal part of the matter ended when Cecil Chesterton found death in the trenches to which he had freely gone; and Godfrey Isaacs found dismissal in those very Courts to which he once successfully appealed. But believe me I do not write on any personal matter; nor do I write, strangely enough perhaps, with any personal acrimony. On the contrary, there is something in these tragedies that almost unnaturally clarifies and enlarges the mind; and I think I write partly because I may never feel so magnanimous again. It would be irrational to ask you for sympathy; but I am sincerely moved to offer it. You are far more unhappy; for your brother is still alive.

If I turn my mind to you and your type of politics it is not wholly and solely through that trick of abstraction by which in moments of sorrow a man finds himself staring at a blot on the tablecloth or an insect on the ground. I do, of course, realise, with that sort of dull clarity, that you are in practice a blot on the English landscape, and that the political men who made you are the creeping things of the earth. But I am, in all sincerity, less in a mood to mock at the sham virtues they parade than to try to imagine the more real virtues which they successfully conceal.

In your own case there is the less difficulty, at least in one matter. I am very willing to believe that it was the mutual dependence of the members of your family that has necessitated the sacrifice of the dignity and independence of my country; and that if it be decreed that the English nation is to lose its public honour, it will be partly because certain men of the tribe of Isaacs kept their own strange private loyalty. I am willing to count this to you for a virtue as your own code may interpret virtue; but the fact would alone be enough to make me protest against any man professing your code and administering our law. And it is upon this point of your public position, and not upon any private feelings, that I address you today.

Not only is there no question of disliking any race, but there is not here even any question of disliking any individual. It does not raise the question of hating you; rather it would raise, in some strange fashion, the question of loving you. Has it ever occurred to you how much a good citizen would have to love you in order to tolerate you? Have you ever considered how warm, indeed how wild, must be our affection for the particular stray stockbroker who has somehow turned into a Lord Chief Justice, to be strong enough to make us accept him as Lord Chief Justice? It is not a question of how much we dislike you, but of how much we like you; of whether we like you more than England, more than Europe, more than Poland the pillar of Europe, more than honour, more than freedom, more than facts. It is not, in short, a question of how much we dislike you, but of how far we can be expected to adore you, to die for you, to decay and degenerate for you; for your sake to be despised, for your sake to be despicable. Have you ever considered, in a moment of meditation, how curiously valuable you would really have to be, that Englishmen should in comparison be careless of all the things you have corrupted, and indifferent to all the things that you may yet destroy? Are we to lose the War which we have already won? That and nothing else is involved in losing the full satisfaction of the national claim of Poland. Is there any man who doubts that the Jewish International is unsympathetic with that full national demand? And is there any man who doubts that you will be sympathetic with the Jewish International? No man who knows anything of the interior facts of modern Europe has the faintest doubt on either point. No man doubts when he knows, whether or no he cares. Do you seriously imagine that those who know, that those who care, are so idolatrously infatuated with Rufus Daniel Isaacs as to tolerate such risk, let alone such ruin? Are we to set up as the standing representative of England a man who is a standing joke against England? That and nothing else is involved in setting up the chief Marconi Minister as our chief Foreign Minister. It is precisely in those foreign countries with which such a minister would have to deal, that his name would be, and has been, a sort of pantomime proverb like Panama or the South Sea Bubble. Foreigners were not threatened with fine and imprisonment for calling a spade a spade and a speculation a speculation; foreigners were not punished with a perfectly lawless law of libel for saying about public men what those very men had afterwards to admit in public. Foreigners were lookers-on who were really allowed to see most of the game, when our public saw nothing of the game; and they made not a little game of it. Are they henceforth to make game of everything that is said and done in the name of England in the affairs of Europe? Have you the serious impertinence to call us Anti-Semites because we are not so extravagantly fond of one particular Jew as to endure this for him alone? No, my lord; the beauties of your character shall not so blind us to all elements of reason and self-preservation; we can still control our affections; if we are fond of you, we are not quite so fond of you as that. If we are anything but Anti-Semite we are not Pro-Semite in that peculiar and personal fashion; if we are lovers, we will not kill ourselves for love. After weighing and valuing all your virtues, the qualities of our own country take their due and proportional part in our esteem. Because of you she shall not die.

We cannot tell in what fashion you yourself feel your strange position, and how much you know it is a false position. I have sometimes thought I saw in the faces of such men as you that you felt the whole experience as unreal, a mere masquerade; as I myself might feel it if, by some fantastic luck in the old fantastic civilisation of China, I were raised from the Yellow Button to the Coral Button, or from the Coral Button to the Peacock's Feather. Precisely because these things would be grotesque, I might hardly feel them as incongruous. Precisely because they meant nothing to me I might be satisfied with them, I might enjoy them without any shame at my own impudence as an alien adventurer. Precisely because I could not feel them as dignified, I should not know what I had degraded. My fancy may be quite wrong; it is but one of many attempts I have made to imagine and allow for an alien psychology in this matter; and if you, and Jews far worthier than you, are wise they will not dismiss as Anti-Semitism what may well prove the last serious attempt to sympathise with Semitism. I allow for your position more than most men allow for it; more, most assuredly, than most men <u>will</u> allow for it in the darker days that yet may come. It is utterly false to suggest that either I or a better man than I, whose work I now inherit, desired this disaster for you and yours. I wish you no such ghastly retribution. Daniel son of Isaac, Go in peace; but go.

> Yours,
>
> G. K. Chesterton

From a logical point of view Chesterton would have done better to write his open letter to Herbert Samuel. He, after all, was, in the eyes of Belloc and Cecil, the chief villain of the Marconi scandal. The two of them had falsely maintained from the beginning that as Postmaster General Samuel had secretly awarded the contract to Marconi as a favour to a fellow Jew (Godfrey Isaacs) who was also the brother of the Attorney General, Rufus Isaacs. Even after Cecil had been forced to withdraw the charge in the witness box, both men persisted in their belief, which was based on nothing more than a conviction derived from Belloc that this was the kind of thing Jews did.

As for Rufus Isaacs, there was never anything to connect him with the awarding of the contract. His offence was that he had dabbled in Marconi shares and had subsequently tried to cover his tracks along with his friend Lloyd George. But Belloc and Cecil had never focused on this aspect of the story, even though that was what the Marconi scandal was all about.

The reason why Chesterton, following Cecil's death, unleashed a volley of abuse against Rufus Isaacs rather than Samuel was that he had created in his powerful imagination a false picture of two sets of brothers, both bound by strong family ties, with himself defending a noble courageous brother, Cecil, and the other, Rufus, defending a debased disreputable brother, Godfrey.

To sustain this fantasy Chesterton had to ignore the complex web of characters involved in the Marconi story and reduce it to a duel – duels being something of a Chestertonian obsession – the duelists being Cecil and Godfrey Isaacs, with himself and Rufus cast as seconds, holding the cloaks and spare pistols. This scenario might have inspired the plot of a Father Brown story but it bore no relation to the facts. Unlike Chesterton, with his blind devotion to his brother, Rufus Isaacs had no special affection for Godfrey, seven years his junior, and had had no prior knowledge of the Marconi contract. When, before the contract was signed, Godfrey had offered him shares over lunch at the Savoy he had refused, only buying them later from another brother, Harry, to whom he was much closer than Godfrey.

Chesterton was equally dishonest in his depiction of Isaacs's role at the historic post-war peace conference in Paris, where he had accompanied Lloyd George as British representative on the Supreme Council of Supply and Relief with the task of deciding whether or not to continue the blockade of Germany, which by now had resulted in the near starvation of the civilians. Far from appeasing the Germans, as Chesterton had persuaded himself, Isaacs was keen to continue the blockade and at the same time do everything he could to support Lloyd George, the man who had gone to Paris promising to put the Kaiser on trial for war crimes. But once the Council started work, Isaacs, frustrated with all the inconclusive meetings, wrote to Lloyd George, 'I have come to the conclusion that I should return to my judicial duties.'

This was a far cry from the picture painted by Chesterton, of Isaacs elevated to 'Chief Foreign Minister' posing a real threat to world order. Even if he had been involved in promoting a private agenda, any Jewish influence at the Paris Peace Conference was focused on the need to implement the recent Balfour Declaration and secure the Jewish homeland in Palestine. Paradoxically, this was something that, in common with many antisemites, Chesterton was very keen on. But Isaacs was not. Chesterton saw the creation of a Jewish homeland as a solution to the so-called 'Jewish problem', ignoring the wishes of those countless Jews who considered themselves British citizens and had no wish to make a new home in the Middle East. Rufus Isaacs was typical of those Jews. Although, as British Ambassador to the United States, he had been obliged to speak in favour of the Balfour Declaration, he did so reluctantly: 'I have no great personal sympathy for Zionism,' he told a correspondent of *The Times*. 'Why should I have? Here I am Ambassador, Lord Chief Justice, Peer – and I started from nothing. I owe it all to England. I am English. How can I help it if I do not feel strongly about the national home for the Jews?'[66] Such were Isaacs's strongly patriotic feelings that he left instructions in his will that 'I Vow to Thee My Country' was to be sung at his Jewish funeral.

In contrast to Chesterton's fanciful picture in his open letter of Isaacs scheming to do down the Poles[67] at the Paris conference, a first-hand description was later provided by the famous economist John Maynard Keynes, then a Treasury advisor working side by side with Isaacs. He was, Keynes says, 'terrified of identifying himself with anything controversial'. That description is consistent with Isaacs's general lack of confidence following the Marconi scandal, which at one stage he thought might bring an end to his career – 'All the gaiety, the boyish high spirits that had been so characteristic of him had gone,' his son Gerald writes of his father during the weeks of waiting for the Committee's report.[68]

Chesterton never regretted his open letter or acknowledged that his feelings had been distorted by grief. However, when he wrote his memoirs seventeen years later he made what for him was a most unusual admission, revealing a faint awareness that his behaviour had been irrational.

The letter, written, he bizarrely claimed, 'with all due restraint... was an odd reaction which I cannot altogether explain'. The reason he could not explain it was that he was incapable of delving any deeper into his motivation because it would mean confronting the false image of Cecil that he had created, suppressing all the evidence that belied it – the overt racism, the humdrum death from natural causes. He had to maintain Cecil's status as a hero, the one man in all England who, as he wrote in his autobiography at the end of his life, 'possessed the two kinds of courage that have nourished the nation – the courage of the forum and the courage of the field'. Quite apart from the fact that there is no evidence that Cecil took part in actual combat, the remark is insulting to many other men who better fitted his description. As for 'the courage of the forum', referring to the Marconi campaign, Chesterton again distorts the facts by claiming that Cecil was punished for 'saying about public men what those very men had afterwards to admit in public'. In fact, he knew perfectly well that Cecil's prosecution had nothing to do with the speculation in shares – which was what they had denied but later admitted to in public – but related to Godfrey Isaacs's business record and his contract with the government.

In a damning verdict, Professor Dudley Edwards writes that 'Chesterton during the Marconi crisis and his own breakdown and again after the death of his brother Cecil emitted sentiments disgraceful to himself and detestable to humankind.' But such was her uncritical devotion that Maisie Ward could reprint the full text of the open letter in her biography without a word of adverse comment. Equally remarkable is her account of Cecil's death which consists of a single sentence: 'On December 6 1918, Cecil Chesterton died in hospital in France', thus avoiding any reference to the cause of death, let alone Chesterton's false claims that his brother had died in battle. By going on to quote Belloc – 'His courage was heroic...' Ward deliberately leaves her reader with the impression that she is referring to his courage on the battlefield. She goes on to propose her own fantasy of Rufus Isaacs going to Paris to protect the Germans, and of Chesterton vividly aware of all the terrible consequences of his presence at the Peace

Conference – 'the peril to Poland; the danger of a Prussia kept at the head of the Germanies for the sake of international finance [the Jews]; an abasement of England before these countries that had not forgotten Marconi...' She then commends Chesterton for his prophetic powers as though his warnings of the 'Jewish problem' had been ignored, thus paving the way for Hitler to impose his own solution. Yet it was the Chesterton brothers and Belloc who had constantly insisted on a Jewish problem, arguing that Jews were aliens belonging to a different nation, while Chesterton himself had proposed that Jews should proclaim themselves as such, and if necessary be instantly identifiable by wearing Arab dress,[69] an idea that anticipated Hitler's decree making Jews wear yellow stars.

So far from condemning past pogroms or future persecution, Chesterton and Belloc (both highly respected proponents of Christianity) helped to promote a conception of Jews as foreigners and aliens (or worse), thus fostering, in Britain, a more tolerant attitude towards Nazi barbarities than might otherwise have prevailed.

8

THE DEATH OF THE NEW WITNESS

I N THE FINAL SENTENCE OF HER 564-PAGE BIOGRAPHY OF
Chesterton, Maisie Ward makes an astonishing claim. After dismissing Keith's suggestion that Frances Chesterton had sacrificed Gilbert and
herself on the altars of her family, she writes: 'But the heaviest cost they
paid lay in the years of toil that was *literally killing Gilbert* [italics added]
while Frances watched him growing old too soon and straining his heart
with work crushingly heavy: and if there was a single altar for that supreme
sacrifice it was no other than the altar of Cecil's memory.'[1] The passage is
all the more remarkable in that in the preceding narrative there is nothing,
apart from a rather wistful sentence in which she is 'tempted to wish' that
things had been otherwise, to suggest anything quite so dramatic as she
describes. Given her close relationship with Frances Chesterton and the
description of her watching her husband growing prematurely old before
her eyes, it is safe to assume that Maisie Ward was repeating something
that Frances herself had said, and probably more than just once.

Frances Chesterton, who never warmed to Cecil but was aware of
Gilbert's uncritical devotion to him, had no doubt hoped that following
his death her husband would be able to 'move on', as we nowadays say,
and devote his time to his writing. But it was not to be. Armed with his
false convictions about Cecil's heroism, Chesterton was more determined
than ever to do all he could not just to preserve Cecil's memory but to go
on fighting for all the causes he himself had championed.

But what were they? As Chesterton resumed the editorship of the
New Witness, it was clear to others, if not to him, that the paper's role
was ill-defined if not non-existent. The war was won, thanks in part to

the dynamic leadership of the Chesterbelloc's[2] despised Mr George, the pacifists had been confounded, Marconi was forgotten, Masterman discredited – all that remained was the dark conspiracy of 'cosmopolitan finance' and the pledge to expose political corruption, which went hand in hand with Belloc's 'Anglo-Judaic plutocracy'. But who would do the exposing? The *Tablet*'s verdict, written by Douglas Woodruff in 1953 following Belloc's death, was painfully true:

> What was wrong with the *Eye-Witness* was that there was not enough witness... Belloc was the last person to forgo all the other things he wanted to do for the absorbing and often quite unrewarding enquiries, the close attention to the political scene, which would have been required to make the *Eye-Witness*, soon the *New Witness*, achieve what they intended... and the continued harping on the Marconi case for the next twenty-five years was not a source of strength. It suggested all too plainly that there was a great dearth of scandal, or else that these journals were missing what they believed to be happening but lacked the patience or resources to expose.[3]

The events leading to the closure of the *New Witness* in 1923 and the launch of *GK's Weekly* two years later are obscure. Of those most closely involved only Keith wrote an account, and not a very convincing one. Bill Titterton, who served as Chesterton's deputy on both papers, is reticent on the subject and Maisie Ward, who must have heard the story from Frances, is likewise uninformative. However Ian Ker's recent biography, quoting correspondence between Belloc and Chesterton, has helped to clarify the episode.

Following Cecil's death, which Chesterton had transformed into a matter of heroic sacrifice and courage, he issued a solemn pledge to readers of the *New Witness*: 'I must now either accept this duty [the editorship] entirely or abandon it entirely. I will not abandon it; for every instinct and nerve of intelligence I have tells me that this is a time when it must not be abandoned. I must accept a comparison that must be a contrast and a crushing contrast; but though I can never be so good as my brother, I will see if I can be better than myself.'[4]

These were brave if delusory words which Chesterton must have come to regret. He knew, in calmer moments, and had said more than once, that he was no good as an editor and that political journalism was not his forte. But a more serious obstacle was Keith, whom he had inherited as his deputy along with the paper and whom he was now reliant upon to deputise for him.

Chesterton never defined in writing his objection to his sister-in-law. His biographer Maisie Ward says that the problem was politics: 'Her political outlook was gradually approximating more and more closely to Russian Communism and she wrote disparagingly of Belloc's Distributism ideas.' This was no doubt true – as was the lawyer E. S. P. Haynes's verdict that she was 'a perfectly impossible person to have in charge of a paper'.

At the same time it has to be recognised that Chesterton's attitude to women was decidedly old-fashioned. He believed that their role was primarily a domestic one and so may well have felt uncomfortable about Keith doing a man's job on a paper, something which at the time was highly unusual. Whatever his reasons, Chesterton seems to have decided, early on, that if he was to continue as editor he would have to get rid of Keith. But as always, he shied away from confrontation. Unable to inform her in so many words that her services were no longer required he conceived an improbable plan, telling her that Belloc, with whom he had already discussed the idea, was going to secure financial backing for the *New Witness* and that in exchange he was expecting to 'manage' the paper and might not want to continue with her as deputy editor. Whether she swallowed this unlikely story or not, Keith, who had already received an offer to travel to Poland on behalf of the *Daily Express,* agreed to take a year off, leaving Chesterton free to try to persuade Belloc to intervene and so save the *New Witness.*

Chesterton seems to have convinced himself that Belloc was going to be the man not only to save the paper but also to relieve him of the problem of what to do about his sister-in-law. Possibly egged on by Frances, he now resolved that he would give up the editorship altogether and that Belloc would take over. In order to prepare the ground he suggested to Belloc that he should contribute a number of pieces on foreign affairs as this would make his task of sacking Keith easier: 'I think I should be more in a position to say, "I want this vein to be worked thoroughly; and nobody but Belloc can work it."'[5] At the same time he urged Belloc to raise some money from his wealthy friends, 'which would make it possible to use something of the same argument as before',[6] namely that Belloc as chief fund-raiser was entitled to 'manage' the paper as he saw fit.

There was one rather basic obstacle to Chesterton's plan, namely that Belloc had no intention whatever of editing the *New Witness* let alone managing it. It is a sign of Chesterton's loss of contact with reality in the period following Cecil's death that he could persuade himself otherwise – he seems to have banished from his mind the history of the *Eye-Witness*, when Belloc abandoned the editorship after only a year and handed it over to Cecil. Like Chesterton, Belloc lived out of London and, like him, had found it impossible to write books while editing a weekly journal. As always, Belloc was short of money (he borrowed £300 from Chesterton at this time) and he was in no mood for taking up editing again. But at the same time he was very keen that the *New Witness* should survive – cold-shouldered by the national press, he was convinced that, as one of 'the travelled and educated' who, unlike his fellow Englishmen, had extensive knowledge of the political situation, particularly in continental Europe, he should have a platform to give the public the benefit of his opinions. At no stage therefore did he reject Chesterton's suggestion – rather, he continued to encourage him to keep the *New Witness* going while avoiding any commitment to step in either as editor or manager. He wrote to Chesterton:

> My dear Gilbert, yes I still think an arrangement ought to be come to. I find that an organ really is needed. Nothing can take its place and the attempt to get things said in other papers is hopeless. Meanwhile, there is one absolutely essential condition and that is someone should

be present always in the office who could see that not only the tone of the paper but – what is absolutely essential – the *details* should never go wrong... The peculiarity of the situation is that neither you nor I could exercise that function. That is certainly the crab of the whole concern. Normally – in old days in England, and to this day in France and Ireland – the editing of the paper by a man like you or me would be a thing taken for granted. That is because under normal conditions a paper edited by a man like you or me would have a sound economic basis. It would not be boycotted. It would be widely read and supported by advertisements and circulation. The highly abnormal condition of our present society makes that impossible. We both have to earn our livings outside the paper and the paper could not possibly support its editor. Therefore neither you nor I could be present with sufficient regularity to make certain that it did not go wrong... The trouble is that with a paper of this kind a single sentence, even a single adjective, may have one or two almost equally disastrous consequences. It may ruin the paper by giving enemies the opportunity for a false issue in a law court which might make the public, and even friends, quite misunderstand it. Or it might cause a very wide circle of readers to be disgusted by either the lack of knowledge or the lack of sympathy – the lack of harmony with the general tone of the paper – [and feel] betrayed. You know this as well as I do and I only emphasise it because it is the key – the only really important point of the affair... Now I can think of no-one who would be permanently present thus and who would have the right negative judgement (to know what ought to be in) except Miss Townsend. If she was there permanently every day, or such days as were necessary to the paper every week, we should only have to send in our contributions and ask other people to write and so forth. The person you mention [Keith] could perfectly well continue dramatic criticism, which she does excellently, but she would have to work with Miss Townsend in the chair... I want to see you about this as soon as possible. I am particularly anxious that the *New Witness* should now have a series of articles on foreign politics from me, for the moment is critical and there are a great many things that ought to be said.[7]

As usual Belloc was obsessed with his travel arrangements, oblivious to Chesterton's notorious indifference towards such matters:

> I am going to Oxford to lecture next Monday and I could take the 2.40 from Oxford reaching you at 4.11 on that day April 26th if it suited you. Or I could meet you any time you like on the morning or early afternoon of Friday April 30th in town, as I shall be sleeping in town on Thursday night and not leaving again till the evening of the Friday. I will telephone you the day after tomorrow, Sunday evening, from London to your house and find out which is the most convenient for you.[8]

Belloc lectures Chesterton as a man of the world explaining things to an eager but inexperienced apprentice – 'opening his eyes to reality'. He ignores Chesterton's main concern – what to do about Keith (whose name he cannot even bring himself to mention) – and he ignores the dire financial situation the *New Witness* is in. His egoism is such that he assumes that in a just world someone of his talents would be able to make a living out of a paper which all good men and true would want to read. He shows no awareness of the need for an editor to recruit and inspire his contributors. The sole purpose of the paper is to be a vehicle for his own, or Chesterton's, views. And all that is needed is a reliable assistant like the admirable Miss Townsend to do all the work, leaving him and Chesterton free to write their important books.

To use Max Beerbohm's phrase, there were plenty of 'dead cats' here. But, Miss Townsend or no, Chesterton still clung to his hope of Belloc taking over the editorship, thus relieving him of responsibility for the paper whilst remaining true to Cecil and ridding him of his controversial sister-in-law.

Keith returned from Poland in July 1920, and encouraged by all the contacts she had made on her travels launched an East European News Agency with an office in Mitre Court off Fleet Street. She resumed her theatre criticism at the *New Witness*, where Titterton was still acting as Chesterton's assistant. Whatever Chesterton told her, she must have agreed to Titterton's continuing until anything definite was decided – something she was happy to do as it left her free to concentrate on her News Agency, which was proving a success.

A few weeks later a curious letter was printed in the paper's correspondence column signed by a number of *New Witness* contributors including Vincent McNabb, Charles Scott Moncrieff and W. R. Titterton:

> We, the undersigned contributors to the *New Witness*, would like to draw attention to the work done by Mrs Cecil Chesterton for the paper. It is common knowledge to us that under your editorial guidance Mrs Cecil Chesterton has kept the *New Witness* going for years past. It is not only that she has, like us, written without fee, but she has put in the best part of each week at the office, which, to a journalist who has to earn a living, means a considerable pecuniary sacrifice. We think, therefore, that the devotion which she has so ungrudgingly shown should be acknowledged in your columns. We feel sure that your sympathisers and supporters will join with us in appreciating what Cecil's widow has accomplished.[9]

Even more curious, considering the recent correspondence with Belloc, was the editor's reply which followed:

> I need not say how warmly I welcome and how emphatically I endorse the tribute paid by so many of my colleagues to my principal colleague on this paper. In some respects I have even better reason to know the truth of it than they; though for other reasons it may come with more authority from the many than the one. Most certainly for a long time past there could never have been a single number or a single item in the *New Witness* in existence without Mrs Cecil Chesterton; and while I owe much to all those journalists, friends of mine who have signed the tribute, neither they nor I will have any doubt about where my first gratitude is due.[10]

It is most unusual, if not extraordinary, for a paper to publish a letter from a group of its contributors in support of the assistant editor, and for the editor to reply, also in public, pledging his full support for the latter. This exchange strongly suggests some kind of crisis in the affairs of the *New Witness*. What may have happened is that on her return Keith had quickly grasped that Chesterton's plan to give way to Belloc was a sham and a smokescreen in order to get rid of her, and had then rallied the contributors behind her and forced Chesterton publicly to declare his abiding confidence in her abilities. She herself says nothing about this incident in her memoir, while Titterton, writing of the period following Cecil's death, says that he 'needn't go into details'.[11] He will have known the facts, but as Chesterton's most devoted admirer, he would not have wished to tell a story that showed the great man in a very bad light.

The issue was in any case irrelevant in view of the ever-worsening state of the *New Witness* finances. Alongside his glowing tribute to Keith, Chesterton listed the results of the appeal to readers with an apocalyptic message in the best Bellocian style:

> Meanwhile everything at home and abroad tends increasingly to a crisis and even a dissolution in which all the essentials of social sanity may be finally lost – or may perhaps be fully rediscovered. An aristocracy that has lost its aristocrats without producing democrats is a society whose foreign policy is a servile riot... We should be very glad if other people would compete with us in the task of building on permanent foundations, of the land and the family and the permanent rights of man, instead of drifting with dead fashions of bureaucracy and big business.[12]

This idealistic programme of campaigning for land and the family was to inspire *GK'S Weekly*, which eventually replaced the *New Witness*. But in the meantime, despite prophesying doom, Chesterton was doing everything possible to keep the paper going. 'I can't let my brother's paper, that stands for all he believed in, go without doing all I can,' he wrote to Ronald Knox, 'and I am trying to get it started again, with Belloc to run it if possible.'[13]

If all else failed, he himself would meanwhile try to raise the necessary funds even though this meant absenting himself from the office for long periods, thereby lessening the effect of any benefit that might accrue from his presence. In December 1919 he had accepted a lucrative offer from the *Daily Telegraph* to visit Jerusalem and the Holy Land. Denying, as he regularly did, any charges of anti-Semitism, Chesterton maintains that 'my friends and I' – by which he means Belloc and Cecil – had always desired 'to give the Jews the dignity and status of a separate nation... we desired that in some fashion, and so far as possible, Jews should be represented by Jews, should live in a society of Jews...'[14] It never seems to have occurred to Chesterton or his 'friends' that a great many, possibly the majority of, British Jews (including Sir Rufus Isaacs, described by Chesterton as an 'intelligent Israelite') were very happy living in the United Kingdom and had no wish to live in 'a society of Jews'. Were they then to be forced to do so? With the creation of Palestine as a Jewish home made possible by the Balfour Declaration of 1917 this was now a possibility. But on his travels, Chesterton discovered to his dismay that the Jews in Palestine were not at all popular with their Arab neighbours, making it less likely that British Jews would wish to emigrate. He therefore proposed a ridiculous scheme whereby British Jews should be made to identify themselves as such by wearing Arab clothes. Unable to resist the opportunity to take another dig at Rufus Isaacs, who had resigned as Lord Chief Justice immediately following the publication of his vicious open letter, Chesterton wrote:

Let a Jew be the Lord Chief Justice if his exceptional veracity and reliability have clearly marked him out for that post... But let there be one single-clause bill; one sweeping law about Jews, and no other. Be it enacted... that every Jew must be dressed like an Arab... If my image is quaint my intention is quite serious; and the point of it is not personal to any particular Jew. The point applies to any Jew, and to our own recovery of healthier relations with him. The point is that we should know where we are; and know where he is, which is in a foreign land.[15]

The jokey way in which Chesterton outlined his suggestion, which, as he says, was advanced in all seriousness, made it seem doubly offensive. At any rate it was too much even for the conservative *Daily Telegraph*, who refused to publish it, to the distress of Chesterton who took the ban as yet another sign of England's failure to face up to the 'Jewish problem' – a problem of which the great majority of the population seemed to be completely unaware.

It is strange that Chesterton never argued that there was a 'Jewish problem' in America, where there were many more Jews than in Britain. He first went there with Frances in 1920 and was given a hero's welcome by the American press, fascinated by this 'voluminous figure' with his 'cascades of grey hair above a pinkly beaming face, a rather straggly blond moustache and eyes that seem frequently to be taking up infinity in a serious way'.[16] Like many British writers before and since, Chesterton had responded to the lure of the American lecture tour as a means of raising much-needed funds, in his case to keep the *New Witness* alive. Wherever he and Frances went they were besieged by journalists seeking interviews, which must have reminded Chesterton of the scenes he had described in his book about Dickens and his visit to America in 1842. But Chesterton could not avoid the inevitable controversy about his alleged anti-Semitism.

Cecil had run into difficulties during his own lecture tour in 1915 when he was challenged in a public debate in New York about his attacks on Jewish bankers. Now Chesterton, whose book *The New Jerusalem* had just been published, found himself publicly denounced by a New York rabbi, Dr Nathan Krass, particularly for his Bellocian belief that Jews were aliens: 'The American Jew protests against any, even the mildest, insinuation that he is an alien in this great country,' Rabbi Krass proclaimed in a sermon at New York's Central Synagogue. 'The American Jew has given and always will give of his wealth, of his power, of his possession, yes, of his life, for his country. Religiously the American Jew is loyal to the Torah, which is the symbol of Judaism. Traditionally he is faithful to his family... politically and nationally he claims the Stars and Stripes as his flag for which he is willing to die, with which he is proud to live.'[17]

Overwhelmed by the warmth of their reception, unlike anything they had experienced in England, the Chestertons travelled by train from New York to Boston, where Chesterton lectured on 'The Ignorance of the Educated' and where, once again, they were mobbed by a crowd of journalists, much to the distress of Frances who noted in her diary, 'So far my feelings for this country are entirely hostile.' As so often she was plagued by ill health, but managed in spite of it to accompany her husband to Philadelphia, Washington and then to Canada before returning to America and more lectures in Chicago, Oklahoma and St Louis. But Chesterton never lost his sense of alienation: 'Nowhere in the world,' he wrote, 'does an Englishman feel so much a stranger as in America.'[18] As for the American, he lives in an 'airless furnace in the middle of which he sits and eats lumps of ice'.[19]

The Chestertons returned to England in April 1921 – Frances vowing 'Never again' – to find the *New Witness* situation unchanged. Belloc was still prevaricating – not dismissing Chesterton's proposal whilst simultaneously hoping that something better might turn up. The following year it did when he received a tempting offer from Major Crosthwaite-Eyre, a former Indian Army officer, now head of the publishers Eyre & Spottiswoode, to edit a new Catholic monthly to be called, rather prosaically, the *Illustrated Review*. Lured by the prospect of what looked like easy money – Crosthwaite-Eyre was investing £5,000 in the project – Belloc agreed to be editor, shareholder and director and signed a seven-year contract. The launch was scheduled for June 1923 but prior to that date Belloc was due in America for a five-month lecture tour leaving him only the month of May to work on the first issues. With the indispensable Miss Townsend not available to do all the work, Belloc enlisted as his assistant a *New Witness* regular, Michael Pope (according to Beachcomber, 'one of those self-effacing meek men who seem to be helpless in the face of the world'), and before leaving for America wrote to Chesterton asking him to help out by getting in touch with Crosthwaite-Eyre and commissioning some pieces for the *Review*: 'We want them about 2,000 to 4,000 words long and illustrated.' Chesterton himself would be expected to contribute a 3,000-word piece every month – 'What we want is an article of the most general kind and precisely as you choose such as you habitually write... The copy must be in by May the 20th for the first number and on a corresponding date monthly but there is no reason why you should not stack up articles for us since the topical character is quite unnecessary.' In the meantime Chesterton should fix up his fee: 'The amounts must be negotiated between you and them, they being Major Crosthwaite and our mutual friend Pope.'[20] Not a word of thanks to Chesterton for helping him out. No apology for his own absence in the USA. No apparent awareness of any burden imposed on Chesterton by expecting him to recruit contributors and write a series of 3,000-word articles to be 'stacked up' for future use.

However, even if Chesterton had agreed, his efforts would have been in vain. When the first issue eventually appeared Belloc expressed himself dissatisfied with the quality of the *Illustrated Review* and asked Crosthwaite-Eyre to remove his name from the cover which, generously, he agreed to do. Thus, as A. N. Wilson records in his account of this affair, 'Belloc had now forced them into the position where they paid him a full editorial salary for work done by Michael Pope, and were not even allowed to use his name.' The paper closed after only four issues, Belloc blaming Crosthwaite-Eyre for 'thoroughly mismanaging the whole affair', but it was relaunched as *English Life* under a young Catholic Irishman recruited by Crosthwaite-Eyre. His name was Brendan Bracken, subsequently Viscount Bracken and the right-hand man and devoted companion of Winston Churchill – as close to him as Charles Masterman once had been.

The failure of the *Illustrated Review* and the fact that Belloc had since taken on a well-paid job as European correspondent of the *Philadelphia Public Ledger* must finally have convinced Chesterton that there was no hope of his friend coming to the rescue of the *New Witness*. He now had to face the fact that the paper could not continue and that he had failed in his sacred duty to carry on the work of Cecil. There remained only the task of breaking the sad news to Keith, who had resumed her former role as deputy editor – a task that filled him with apprehension. But Frances was adamant that it had to be done and agreed to support him by sitting at his side for the fateful showdown. Keith recounts how she was invited to Beaconsfield to discuss the future of the paper. 'We got together after dinner,' she writes,

> Frances sat in her fireside chair, her pale delicate face set in the curious graven expression it wore for questions of finance. For it was finance. There was, Gilbert intimated, very little money in the *New Witness* and he could see no possibility of raising more. This meant that there would be no salary available for an editorial assistant, and no fees for contributors... the *New Witness* must close down. It was a possibility that I had never visualised. I simply could not believe that the paper which had won through so many and such gallant fights was to end. I went straight to the main point. 'The sales ought to pay the printers?' I suggested. Gilbert agreed. 'And the rent,' I found myself arguing, 'the rent is not due for another three months.' My brother-in-law looked uncomfortable, and suggested that the manager felt the paper should not go on. 'But we must go on,' I protested. 'The paper *can't* stop.' Frances looked up. 'It's impossible for Gilbert to find the money to continue,' she said, and her voice had a finality I recognised.[21]

For Frances, who normally kept well out of Chesterton's business affairs, to involve herself in this instance was a sign of her anxiety about Gilbert's wellbeing – his state of health, not to mention his finances, which she knew more about than he did. Where he had a tendency to prevarication she could be firm and make it clear to Keith that the *New Witness* could not continue.

Yet she failed. 'I finally won the day,' Keith records,[22] without saying how she had managed to overcome Chesterton's own inclinations and Frances's determination to wean him away from the burden of editorship. The explanation has to lie, once again, with the power of Cecil over his brother, a power in some ways even stronger in death than in life. Chesterton had pledged himself to take up Cecil's crusade and now only two years later he was proposing to surrender. Keith may not have spelled it out like that but it is fair to assume that Chesterton must have felt very uneasy about his situation, while Frances knew from long experience how impossible it was to go against Cecil's wishes, now represented by his forceful and determined widow.

Keith now proposed to soldier on at the *New Witness* and spearhead a drive to save the paper, despite having what she called 'a faint foreboding' that all her efforts would be in vain: 'I felt that the virtue had gone out of the *New Witness*; that minus its creator it could not flourish. The mainspring had broken.'[23]

There were several reasons for this. The post-war situation, the irrelevance, now, of all Cecil's campaigns – against Lloyd George and the other Marconi ministers, against the Insurance Act (now passed), the German agents and Prussian power. But, most crucial of all, Chesterton's incapacity as an editor – a failing he had acknowledged from the beginning.

Keith was well aware of this and makes frequent references to Cecil's superiority when it came to editorship. Yet in spite of everything she was determined to keep Chesterton at it. It was Keith who conceived the idea of what would now be called a relaunch of the paper, using Chesterton's name as its main selling point: 'I came to the conclusion that a weekly review called after him would enlist enough financial support to enable us to start on a sound financial basis.'[24] Chesterton, she writes, found the idea attractive and 'even Frances was not too discouraging'. An appeal was launched in the *New Witness*, the response was favourable and it was eventually decided to call the new-look paper *GK's Weekly*.

The resurrection of the paper was a posthumous triumph for Cecil, obliging Chesterton to continue editing, which he was to do until his death in 1936, while struggling to earn sufficient funds to keep the paper in business. But he was still faced with the problem of what to do about Keith, who was no doubt assuming that once the new paper was launched she would continue in her old role of assistant editor.

A year went by and nothing happened, while Chesterton dithered and worked on his book *The Everlasting Man*. And then one day Keith went to see him at Essex Street. 'After a while Gilbert explained that even yet he was not quite sure when he was starting the paper and, in those lovely verbal undulations which flowed so easily, conveyed the impression that he was going to run *GK's Weekly* by himself... As, fascinated, I watched him trace the curves of a French cavalier on the blotting pad before him he murmured: "I think, do you know, that one Chesterton on the paper is enough."'[25]

Not surprisingly this news came as a bitter blow to Keith who had just spent weeks drumming up financial support for *GK's Weekly* and was now told that her services would no longer be required. But Chesterton did not elaborate, dismissing her with 'a fraternal pat'.

Chesterton's biography contains no reference whatever to this scene and ignores completely Keith's claim to have been the leading force behind the creation of *GK's Weekly*. Brocard Sewell, who wrote a brief history of *GK's Weekly*, likewise has nothing at all to say about her involvement in the launching of the project. Either he and Maisie Ward dismissed Keith's account completely or, what is more likely, neither wished to invite any adverse reflections on Chesterton for sacking Keith when she had done more than anyone to get the new paper off the ground. Both writers shied away from drawing attention to Chesterton's inability to disentangle himself from the complex situation he had created in order to do honour to, and preserve the legacy of, Cecil and provide Belloc with his 'platform'. This involved ignoring his own lack of editorial abilities – which he acknowledged continually – and also the wishes of his beloved wife. It also meant taking on work, going on overseas trips and writing more Father Brown stories in order to keep the new paper in the black. Most problematic of all for him was a situation in which he proposed to continue his brother's work in spite of having sacked his widow, the only person on the staff who shared Cecil's aggressive political instincts and who showed, by her subsequent career, that she had a great many useful contacts and the energy and flair to get things done, qualities that were otherwise in short supply. 'It seemed incredible,' Keith wrote, 'that Gilbert, ignoring the years I had worked with him for mutual ideals, should have no further use for me.'[26] Yet it is a sign of her strength of character that she writes of the rebuff without any special resentment and, looking back at it, concludes that Chesterton, though intensely committed to his brother's memory, 'perhaps felt that if I still worked side by side with him, Cecil's ideals rather than his own must inevitably have been pushed to the front in the policy of *GK's Weekly*'.[27]

On the other hand it is possible that once again Keith put the blame for her rejection on the influence of Frances, and that this in turn helps to explain the spiteful tone in which she writes about her sister-in-law in her memoir. Whatever the reason, Keith soon recovered from the unexpected blow. She was a resilient woman with many friends in Fleet Street and the theatrical world. With her niece Ada she rented a flat above a tobacconist at Number Three, Fleet Street, directly opposite the Law Courts. 'Our great joy was the loft, reached by a ship's ladder, fastened by grappling hooks to a trap door... It was the scene of many unforgettable "rags"' (her word for parties, then all the rage among the 'Bright Young Things' of the 1920s).[28] One such 'rag' was recorded in his diary[29] by the young Evelyn Waugh: 'In the evening Keith Chesterton was giving a party at her garret at 3 Fleet Street. There were a comic collection of all the Caves of Harmony[30] set – pansies, prostitutes and journalists and struggling actors all quite, quite drunk and in patches lusty. Peter Pusey with whom Hugh Lygon[31] sodomises was there and Elsa but these were practically the only people I knew so I contented myself with climbing the roofs. Alec [Evelyn's brother] turned up late and a little drunk and after his fashion fixed upon the ugliest woman in the room, bore her off and lechered with her... I got home in broad daylight at 5 and this morning feel more than a little weary.' Keith confirms that Waugh was in the habit of leaving her roof garden and climbing across the roofs of Fleet Street 'frightening timorous women *en route* by tapping at their windows'.

Given her tough upbringing and despite her summary dismissal, Keith never fell out with Chesterton and remained a particular friend of his mother Marie-Louise with whom she had always had a close relationship. She continued to write a regular theatre review for *GK's Weekly* and during the General Strike of 1926 helped Bill Titterton produce a six-page roneoed edition of the paper strongly supporting the striking miners and the compositors at the *Daily Mail* who had refused to print a government advertisement appealing for volunteers to break the strike. 'The small band of printers at Carmelite House,' she wrote, 'were acting in the interests of law and of the constitution when they downed tools.'[32]

In 1927 she wrote a series of articles for the *Sunday Express* after proposing to the editor that she would live on the streets of London for a fortnight wearing shabby clothes, without any money apart from what she could earn or beg. 'It is a queer feeling,' she wrote subsequently, 'to shed your habits, identity, clothes, customs, and without protective social covering emerge in the raw. During that fortnight I went right to the depths of penury and hunger, sampled filthy beds, met thieves and prostitutes, hard-working and respectable women, courageous women whose only crime was poverty... I had to walk the streets when I could not get a bed, for I found there were too few beds for the destitute, and I tramped and tramped, until I was drugged with tramping and my sodden clothes clung to my tired body.'[33]

Her articles, which were later published in a book, *In Darkest London*, were widely read and donations poured in, including a cheque from Queen Mary. So much money was raised that a committee was set up to create hostels for homeless women 'where any woman, no matter how lonely, how unfriended, could get a clean bed with plenty of hot water for baths, tea and biscuits for 1s. a night'. There was only one rule: that no questions should be asked of the women applying for help. Called 'Cecil Houses' in memory of Keith's husband, the first hostel opened on 28 March 1927. By March 1929 there were two more, accommodating 160 women and 34 babies.

Shunned by the Chestertonians following the publication of her memoir in 1941, Keith devoted herself more and more to her Cecil Houses. After the war she opened 'Cecil Residential Clubs' for low-paid working women and female pensioners (which are still in existence). An expert fund-raiser who was awarded the OBE in 1928, Keith was never a mere figurehead and took a personal interest in the welfare of her residents, who treated their 'Mrs Cecil' with affection and respect. She died aged ninety-three in 1962 having become a Catholic in 1942, thus joining a long list of converts, including both Chesterton brothers, Frances Chesterton, J. B. Morton, Reginald Jebb, Maurice Baring and even Godfrey Isaacs.

9

'CHESTERTON'S POTTY LITTLE PAPER'

A FTER MONTHS OF UNCERTAINTY AND DELAYS *GK's WEEKLY* finally appeared on 21 March 1925. Its format was identical to that of the *Eye-/New Witness* – a long leader, 'Notes of the Week' consisting of short anonymous items mostly on political matters, Chesterton's weekly essay under the title 'Straws in the Wind', a number of articles by contributors, reviews and poems. Bill Titterton, the veteran of the *Daily News* and the two *Witnesses*, was thrilled to be reappointed as assistant editor, replacing Keith, at a weekly salary of £5. 'When do you think you can begin work?' Chesterton asked, 'there's no hurry of course.' 'I said that I could begin at once,' Titterton recorded, 'and great peace blossomed in his face. I think that he was very tired.'[1]

Freed from Keith and the need to continue the vendettas of Cecil and Belloc, Chesterton felt confident about the new paper, though disapproving of its title. Titterton's hope was to produce a magazine with more general appeal than the *New Witness*. He included humorous items and even cartoons, some by Chesterton himself, though, to his great regret, there were insufficient funds to take up an offer from David Low, the greatest political cartoonist of the time, to do a regular cartoon for a token fee. Despite the lack of funds the early issues had stories by Walter de la Mare and humorous pieces by Ronald Knox. The issue of 29 December 1928 included the first piece of printed journalism by a certain E. A. Blair, later to become better known as George Orwell. And there was the occasional contribution from Beachcomber, for example his 'Ballade of Spirit Voices'.[2]

The outstanding sculptor and engraver Eric Gill, whose reputation has since been tarnished by revelations of his perverse sexual habits,

volunteered at an early stage to be the paper's art critic. A Catholic convert since 1913, he had become a Dominican tertiary, presiding over a
small religious and artistic community at Ditchling in Sussex and later in
Wales, where he pursued his career with a group of apprentices. In 1928
he moved to a village near High Wycombe and so became a neighbour of
Chesterton, whom he had always revered. Gill agreed to write about art
for the paper, but on his own terms. Chesterton and Belloc would have to
accept his views on art as those of *GK's Weekly*, and he would accept theirs
on other matters. 'I don't intend to write for you as an outsider (have I
not put almost my last quid into your blooming company?...) God forbid
that you should have an art critic who'll go round the picture shows for
you and write bilge about this painter and that...'[3] As it turned out, Gill's
contributions were infrequent, though he later addressed a gathering of
Distributists telling them, 'We wear clothes that are altogether unreason-
able if not positively obscene. What excuse is there for collars and ties?' Gill
also managed to offend Chesterton by writing a letter running to about
a thousand words taking issue with Vincent McNabb and his hatred of
machinery. 'Why should he waste his valuable time,' Chesterton riposted,
'how splendidly might he not have been cutting stone or cutting wood in
his spirited woodcuts in the time he has spent splitting hairs.'

Chesterton himself resumed the editorial role he had previously
played at the *New Witness*, making only occasional visits to the office
but writing a disproportionate amount of the copy – in addition to his
weekly essay, he wrote a double-feature page called 'Top and Tail' as
well as anonymous items for Notes of the Week. All this put a heavy
burden on him at a time when he was continuing to write books, but
lacking any business sense he never succeeded in making the venture
profitable. Money was to remain a constant problem from the start, and
it soon became clear that insufficient funds had been raised to support
the relaunch. The most generous contribution, ironically in view of
Chesterton's attitude towards millionaire landlords, came from Lord
Howard de Walden, owner by inheritance of great swathes of property
in Central London. De Walden was a remarkable character – a sportsman

and former army officer who had fought in the Boer War and later at Gallipoli and in France. When not editing a history of the Peerage on his Scottish estate he might be practising as a member of the British Olympic fencing team or speedboat racing, not to mention excelling at falconry. His artistic pursuits included the writing of plays and librettos for a number of operas and sponsoring the efforts of others, including not only Chesterton but Dylan Thomas.

De Walden became a board member of *GK's Weekly* but not surprisingly, in view of all his other commitments, he did not attend the board meetings, sending instead his solicitor, a Mr Thomson – 'quiet and businesslike', according to Titterton, 'determined not to give away what he thinks of the proceedings'. Other board members and benefactors included Maurice B. Reckitt, an earnest Anglo-Catholic and member of the wealthy family that produced a washing powder known as Reckitts Blue, and Cedric Chivers, the Mayor of Bath and founder of a famous firm of bookbinders. Chivers found the board meetings difficult because he was deaf, though not as deaf as another board member, the paper's business manager Mr Gander, who had the difficult job of soliciting advertisements for the paper. After his death Chesterton described Chivers as the only man he ever knew who really got any fun out of money: 'He lived,' he said, 'in an ugly villa that was full of beautiful things. He had the beautiful things because he liked looking at them and he did not mind the ugly villa because he lived inside the house and not in the front garden.'[4]

Bill Titterton, Chesterton's devoted deputy, also attended the board meetings, but he was, he says, 'present for reference only'. He describes Chesterton, the chairman and mainstay of the enterprise, endlessly doodling faces on his pad of blotting paper, puffing at a cheroot – 'and looking, without having a suspicion of it, tremendous. The truth is he would like to run away.' On the right sits Alderman Chivers – 'manly, simple and kind', Thomson, the solicitor, and Maurice Reckitt, 'very vital and eager but posing as negligent, and seeming to find the meeting an unpleasant necessity. It is always the same picture: the chairman thoughtful and embarrassed, Chivers brimming with zeal, Reckitt disdainfully semi-detached but on the pounce, Thomson, absolutely still, looking at the table. At every meeting Reckitt says, "Things can't go on like this, you know."'[5]

In September 1926, after only eighteen months, things had reached crisis point. Titterton now proposed to reduce the price of the paper from 6d to 2d and at the same time launch a Distributist League whose members would be subscribers. The idea was enthusiastically received and the League, an almost exclusively male organisation, was launched, with branches eventually forming throughout Britain. There was a regular meeting in London at the Devereux public house (adjacent to the *GK's Weekly* offices) with debates and speeches from a variety of speakers.

Although Chesterton became a Roman Catholic in 1922, the history of the Distributist League recalls, most strongly, the same eccentric atmosphere as the Christian Social Union of his pre-war Anglican days when he, Cecil and Masterman campaigned for social justice alongside clerics like Henry Scott Holland and Conrad Noel. Chesterton was to say as much himself when he wrote later in his paper: 'The Distributists are now the only representatives of all that was good in the just anger and disinterested compassion of the old Christian Socialists and the revolutionary companions of my youth.' It was no accident that the new movement attracted a great many from the Anglo-Catholic community, including two of its leading lights, Maurice Reckitt and Captain H. S. D. Went, one of the principal founders of the Distributist League. Chesterton himself was delighted by this and never wanted the League to be a specifically religious organisation, let alone a Roman Catholic one. 'No one except perhaps a devil worshipper would be banned,' he said.

The Catholic Church was represented most visibly in the person of the Dominican monk, that 'gaunt, bald, bony friar', in Brocard Sewell's description, Father Vincent McNabb, who had become a kind of unofficial chaplain to the *New Witness* and *GK's Weekly* as well as to the Belloc family. Conspicuous in a shabby white habit and cowl and a pair of heavy army boots which he claimed to polish with his sweat, McNabb, an Ulsterman who had emigrated to England in his youth, was a familiar figure to

Londoners, preaching from a soapbox in Hyde Park or Whitechapel. He was a regular attender at the Distributists' weekly gathering at the Devereux pub and a vehement supporter of the 'Back to the Land' faction, urging the Distributists: 'Why don't you *do* things?' He had taught himself to farm while at the Dominican priory at Rugeley in Staffordshire, and strongly disapproved of tinned food, typewriters and all machines. He wrote his frequent articles by hand, some on the backs of old envelopes, and walked everywhere, refusing to use public transport.

McNabb was the only person he had known, Ronald Knox wrote, 'who gives you some idea of what a saint must be like'. But though venerated by both Chesterton brothers and Belloc, he never shared their belief in the exclusivity of the Catholic Church. 'God knows how much I have striven and prayed to mend the shattered unity of Christendom,' he wrote. McNabb was equally emphatic in deploring anti-Semitism and never tired of quoting the words of Pope Pius XI: 'It is not possible for Christians to take part in anti-Semitism… Spiritually we are Semites.'[6] Yet he greatly admired Cecil and preached a fiery eulogy at his Requiem Mass in the Catholic Church in Maiden Lane, Covent Garden. In the course of this he levelled the charge of murder against those he held responsible for Cecil's death – presumably whoever ordered him to march several miles when he was ill.[7] Even from the pulpit it was a dangerous charge to make and may explain why no record of the sermon, described by Belloc as 'the finest piece of sacred oratory', survives.[8]

Chesterton, who shared McNabb's ecumenical views as far as the League was concerned, never managed to reconcile the very divergent politics of the membership, those like Maurice Reckitt who tried to link Distributism to the acceptance of a well-established modern industrial society, and the romantic radicals like Gill and McNabb, opposed to machinery and calling for a return to agriculture. With memories of the Christian Social Union he saw the movement as more of a 'political church' than a political party, a viewpoint that was to bring him into conflict with some of the younger, keener Distributists, who became increasingly impatient with their leader's other-worldly tendencies and his habit of making jokes about supposedly serious issues. For Chesterton it was enough that the League should spread the word – 'the only way to preserve liberty is to preserve property. The only way to preserve property is to distribute it much more equally among its citizens. This can only be done by breaking up the great plutocratic concentration of our time.'

As with the Christian Social Union, quite how this programme was to be put into effect was never explained by Chesterton. If he thought about it at all he would have been forced to advocate a revolution. Meanwhile his Distributist followers had a variety of solutions which led to often fractious disputes. Some favoured the formation of a political party, others advocated the establishment of communes. Campaigns were launched to support independent bus companies and small shops in preference to the chains and monopolies then growing in influence. A band of Distributists marching under McNabb's banner of 'Back to the Land' became so vociferous that they threatened a schism, forcing Chesterton to intervene in an attempt to restore harmony. Addressing the 1932 Summer Conference of the Distributist League at Douai Abbey in Berkshire, he told the delegates that there were 'a number of heroic headlong enthusiasts who exist in every movement, who had adopted austere ideals and wished at once to apply them'. As always, before launching into his criticism, Chesterton first expressed his admiration for his target – 'I have a profound admiration for such people, I feel humble in their presence' – but they had to realise that while 'Back to the Farm' might mean something to Americans, 'if you were to make that remark in London, to a man in the Tube, the man would probably conclude that one was a lunatic or a blackmailer, or ask what farm was being referred to. The Londoner has no farm to go back to. Nor had his father or his grandfather. The word "farm" might convey nothing to him except some vague identification with Chalk Farm.'9

The same year, 1932, saw another more serious threat to the unity of the Distributist movement. A. M. (Archie) Currie, a satirical writer who had been with *GK's Weekly* from the beginning and was a prominent supporter of the League, had long been agitating with a number of fellow members for the formation of a Distributist political party. Accusing the League of 'esoteric smugness' and being 'shot through with elitism', Currie proposed putting up Distributist candidates, and three constituencies were chosen. The movement had a great deal of support – an office was acquired and a manifesto prepared. But Chesterton himself, faithful to Belloc's principle that political parties were synonymous with corruption, was not in favour. After a few months, the movement collapsed when Currie became seriously ill, but not before it had caused a serious split in the ranks.

The formation of the League had created another bone of contention – was *GK's Weekly* to be the official organ of the League or would it enjoy a separate existence? A group of young Leaguers favoured the first alternative and were impatient with the chaotic way in which the paper was run. If the League was to prosper and recruit new members, *GK's Weekly* had to be made to pay its way and introduce more commercial methods. The old and deaf William Gander had retired, to be replaced by a friend of Titterton's, George Tyre, but the new recruits had no confidence in him and he was later dismissed – much to Chesterton's distress – for falsifying the accounts and concealing debts. Instead of settling their differences behind closed doors the new League members, led by two young brothers, Gregory and Edward Macdonald, organised a public debate, presided over by Chesterton, at which his faithful assistant Titterton defended the status quo and the earnest, American-born Macdonald brothers argued not only that the League should be the top priority but that a committee should be formed to be responsible for the running of the paper. After both sides had made their case Chesterton sided with the Macdonalds, much to the dismay of Titterton, who resigned, his place as assistant editor being taken by Edward Macdonald who was to slave away at his ill-paid post until Chesterton's death.

Drastic austerity measures were now introduced. The office was moved to two small rooms in Little Essex Street, one for the League, the other for the paper. Gregory Macdonald described 'a dingy room with one never-opened window', two tables pushed together to be shared by his brother Edward and V. N. Lucas, who doubled as business manager and music critic.

'Expense of all kind was simply cut out,' according to a later account by committee member Desmond Gleeson.[10] Spending was confined to the office rental and small salaries for a business manager and an assistant editor (Edward Macdonald was paid £2 a week). Contributors – apart, one assumes, from Belloc – were not paid anything.

The reforms may have kept *GK's Weekly* in existence but they imposed a heavy burden on the Macdonald brothers who were now having to write a great deal of the paper between them. Both were hard-working devotees of Chesterton and Belloc but they had none of the humour that Titterton had done his best to introduce. The letters in the correspondence column grew longer and more boring, the subscribers arguing among themselves about the economics of Distributism.

Chesterton himself was only an occasional visitor to the office. Looking back, a member of the editorial board, C. P. Smallwood, who wrote leaders and was later editor of the *Birmingham Mail*, described his arrival:

I can see Chesterton now, perhaps hear would be a better word, creaking up the stairs to the offices of *GK's Weekly* and the Distributist League that were over a pastry cook's in Little Essex Street. The rest of us were always there first and you heard this terrific creak of the staircase before you heard his footfall. Then you heard the puffing and blowing and he would come into the untidy attic with a high-pitched breathless apology for being, as usual, late. He was offered half a dozen chairs but never accepted one if there were more members of the editorial board present than chairs. I have seen him several times subside on to bundles of returned copies of the *Weekly*, throw off his cloak backwards and start discussing the week's leader or throw out some ideas for Notes[11] or, almost apologetically, tender to Edward Macdonald (the acting editor for many years) a dog-eared bit of typescript which he thought 'might tuck in somewhere, sometime'. Once Macdonald said he was 'stuck for a bit of something to end off a page'. Chesterton said, 'What, has the stock of poetry run out? Edward said it had and we had no useful 'shorts'. Then Chesterton took out a stub of pencil, poised himself on a rickety

stool at the table and knocked off in three or four minutes that delightful quatrain that appears in the Collected Editions of his own poems:

> If Brother Francis pardoned Brother Flea,
> There still seems need of such strange charity,
> Seeing he is, for all his gay goodwill,
> Bitten by funny little creatures still.

He had read in the tube coming along to the meeting an evening paper
account of the latest address by the then very loquacious Bishop Barnes
of Birmingham, ascribing the sacred stigmata of St Francis to flea bites.[12]

GK's Weekly continued under the new regime until Chesterton's death in
1936, and even for a short time afterwards, but with no firm leadership
from Chesterton, conflicts that already existed were never resolved and in
the end were to prove fatal. It is clear from Gregory Macdonald's letters
to his old headmaster and Chesterton's friend, the Benedictine monk
Father Ignatius Rice, that his brother Edward was under constant attack
from critics.

A good deal of my time has been taken up by Chesterton's potty
little paper. It is more apparent than ever that a spot of work elsewhere[13] would increase the revenue of that paper by about £250 a year
through advertisements and circulation which would relieve the strain
on Edward's menage of a wife and three kids. But the shabby tricks
continue and I am afraid that not even loyalty to Edward will tempt me
to go on after Chesterton's return to England.[14] The old man was plucky
to attempt a Mediterranean visit but he did not get as much out of it
as he wanted and is now on his way back... I suggested to Chesterton
that he should support Edward, appoint a secretary to the Company, get
some people on the board of directors who understand what the paper
stands for – J. B. Morton [Beachcomber] or Richard O'Sullivan[15] – stop
his attempt to win over by flattery, take a personal interest – the weekly

working of the thing and so on. Probably the womenfolk will turn on me for not treating him like a demi-god.[16]

In fact Frances Chesterton proved to be more than sympathetic to Macdonald's concerns. At the time of one of the periodic crises she actually came to a shareholders' meeting and asked whether it was worth carrying on the paper, 'whether it was serving any useful purpose, and if so, whether the same purpose might not be equally served in some less expensive manner'. She was shocked when the young Gregory Macdonald complained to her that his brother Edward was receiving a meagre salary of £2 a week, and promised to raise the issue with her husband. 'She talked the situation over with him,' Macdonald told Fr. Rice, 'arranging to give Edward an increase by a private monthly cheque.'[17]

What Chesterton replied to Frances when she queried the purpose of carrying on with his paper is not recorded. But it was a question that must have occurred to others apart from his wife. Both of the Macdonald brothers, who sacrificed almost everything to keep the paper going, subsequently regretted their actions. Chesterton must have been embarrassed by Frances's public intervention and no doubt made some jocular comments to justify his position, but without mentioning his primary motives – to continue Cecil's work, and at the same time provide his friend Belloc with a platform to promote his opinions.

This was especially generous as Belloc showed little gratitude, and had no particular regard for *GK's Weekly,* calling it, after Chesterton's death, 'a magnet for cranks'. Although it was he who had launched the notion of Distributism, he took little interest in the affairs of the League apart from speaking at an occasional meeting. His prime concern, now that his journalism was no longer in demand, was to maintain an outlet for his views on national and international events, and this Chesterton was determined to provide, even if it meant having to write more and more Father Brown stories to keep his paper afloat. 'Many a squire,' he wrote, 'has died in a dank garden arbour, transfixed by a mysterious dagger, many a millionaire has perished silently though surrounded by a ring of private secretaries, in order that Mr Belloc may have a paper in which he is allowed to point out that a great Empire does not default because it is growing richer.'[18] This was not the only thing that Belloc, who, thanks to his chronic restlessness, never became a regular contributor, wanted to point out. In a series of pieces in 1929 headed Current Affairs, he harped on the disastrous alliance of Britain with America, asserting that a combination of Jewish and American financiers were boosting the German economy for their own purposes – all the while deploring the decay of parliamentary democracy and the malign influence of Masons in France and Jews in Moscow. As always he wrote with an air of omniscience and self-importance, thus in April 1933: 'I am just returned from a few weeks on the Continent. It may be of interest to the readers of this paper to know what is being said and thought there by people who count in the West.'

By that stage, the possibility of another war with Germany was creating alarm. Hitler had become something of an obsession with the British public but though Belloc consistently warned of the danger of war, he never grasped the significance of Hitler. His stubbornly held view was that the real enemy was the Prussian General Staff which had brought about the First World War and was still in existence, threatening France and Poland. Hitler was a puppet in the hands of the military and was, in any case, merely a figurehead while the real mastermind was his adviser Alfred Rosenberg. 'Hitler is not thought to count for much,' Belloc informed his readers and Chesterton obediently followed his lead, at one point describing Hitler in 1934 as 'one of those stunted and stupid but very earnest little men who go to vegetarian restaurants'.

There is no evidence that Belloc ever bothered to study the nature of Nazism, or to read Mein Kampf. Even when it came to the Nazi persecution of the Jews, his tendency was to play it down: 'The anti-Jew business and all the spirit that goes with it,' he wrote following his Continental visit in 1933, 'is not thought to be of permanent effect.'[19] He even commended the Nazis on the grounds that they had 'brought the Jewish question out into the open'. What lay behind it all – and this would have come as no surprise to Belloc's followers – was the Dreyfus affair. Belloc had previously blamed the – mostly Jewish (in his view) – Dreyfusards for the French defeats in the first battles of the Great War, thanks to the damage they did to the French intelligence services. Now he was to accuse Dreyfus and his supporters of being responsible for Hitler's atrocities. The Nazi revolutionaries, he wrote, 'have access to all the archives'. They saw what damage had been done by Jewish agitators to France and the French army, hence the attack on the Jews: 'They feared to suffer as France had suffered and the result is before us.'[20] Belloc took comfort from reminding people that it was he and Cecil who had continually and courageously warned them of 'the Jewish problem' in the shape of a host of corrupt financiers and 'aliens' owing allegiance to a foreign 'nation'. Now Hitler, feeling the same way, was going to do something about it. He had a solution to the problem. But if people had only listened to Belloc's prophetic warnings and taken appropriate action this might never have happened.

There were echoes of 'Blare Hilloc' in the response of some readers to Belloc's controversial views. By no means all of them were impressed. One, signing himself 'The Atheist Reader', commented: 'It would be a great help to us all if Mr Belloc would state his sources of information so that our words may carry conviction to others when we quote him, especially with regard to international financial arrangements.' But Chesterton himself was always ready to leap to the defence of his friend and when another reader, Captain Blundell, suggested that Belloc had only attacked the Insurance Act to 'have a hit at Lloyd George' he reacted with untypical anger: 'To suggest that a man like Mr Belloc is so little interested in history and philosophy and the general destiny of Europe that he advances a whole theory about Christendom and pagan antiquity with his mind concentrated solely on one insignificant party politician, is to imagine a disproportion that could only exist in the mind of a maniac.'[21]

The ferocity of that response to what was just a harmless little dig at Belloc, the ridiculous description of Lloyd George as 'insignificant' and the final diagnosis of Captain Blundell as a maniac are further signs of Chesterton's compulsion to suppress his rational unease about Belloc's opinions, which were so much at odds with all his own instincts. In his early years Chesterton had mocked his friend George Bernard Shaw for his belief in the Superman, yet now he had been compromised by Belloc's devotion to the Italian Superman, Mussolini, who was supposedly restoring truth and decency to European politics. Equally difficult for Chesterton to stomach was Belloc's continuous harping on the merits of an aristocracy and his contempt for provincial or suburban attitudes. Reviewing Robert Speaight's biography of Belloc the historian A. J. P. Taylor writes, 'The trouble with Mr Speaight is that he thinks there is nothing wrong with the English upper classes. Belloc slipped into this view later on in life.'[22] But even as a young man Belloc had formed most of his close friendships with aristocrats and found himself a welcome guest in the houses of wealthy Conservatives like Lord Derby, who generously gave him the run of his library. Such associations helped to kindle Belloc's nostalgia for an age when England was ruled by earls and dukes, all well educated and familiar with the classics and the history of Europe, an age before the coming of upstarts like Lloyd George or Northcliffe and their Jewish backers. But such reverence for the old aristocratic ways was quite alien to Chesterton's philosophy, considering that long ago in the *Daily News* he had referred mockingly to 'the foolish accidental peers in the House of Lords', while in *Orthodoxy* (1908) he described aristocracy as a sin – 'generally a very venial one. It is merely the drift or slide of men into a sort of natural pomposity and praise of the powerful, which is the most easy and obvious affair in the world.'

As a criticism of Belloc's response to Mussolini, 'natural pomposity and the praise of the powerful' will serve very well. But Chesterton had now to ignore or find excuses for Belloc's reactionary views and his contempt for the working man – 'when he is cut off from religion his stupidity is intolerable'. As for snobbery, Chesterton had written, 'It is our great English vice; to be watched more fiercely than small-pox.'[23] Such a response was based partly on his personal reaction to high society and what he called 'the intense and awful thirst of the female upper class for verbal amusement and stimulus'. Unlike Belloc, who was sought after as a dinner guest by grand society hostesses like Lady Diana Manners (later Cooper), Chesterton had no great affection for 'the swells'. When he once stayed in a grand house he was horrified to discover that a valet had unpacked his pockets. 'There, laid out on the quilted silk eiderdown, were several stubs of pencils, a paperbacked murder story, some coloured chalks and a small cigar or two.'[24] By the expressionless face of the valet I could see he was thinking, "How different, how very different are these from the jewelled trifles that I am accustomed to removing from the tidy pockets of the well-to-do."'[25]

As for the 'vulgar press', deplored by Belloc, Chesterton had in the past often maintained that he preferred it. 'Even in the crudest and most clamorous aspects of the newspaper world,' he wrote in *Tremendous Trifles*, 'I still prefer the popular to the proud and fastidious. If I had to choose between taking in the *Daily Mail* and taking in *The Times* – I should certainly cry out with the whole of my being for the *Daily Mail*.'

Likewise, while Belloc sneered at the people in small suburban villas, these were the very people Chesterton had embraced. Suburbia might well be for Belloc the breeding ground of snobbery, but for Chesterton it was teeming with romance and adventure: 'The suburbs are commonly referred to as prosaic,' he wrote. 'That is a matter of taste. Personally I find them intoxicating.'

Yet the compulsion to keep in step with Belloc was to dog Chesterton and cast a shadow over the rest of his life, leaving him with the taint of Fascism. Even though the Fascist movement in Britain had been widely discredited after the ugly violence at Oswald Mosley's Olympia rally in 1934, Chesterton could still write the following year: 'Fascism is worth looking at whereas parliamentarianism is not worth looking at,'[26] and, the next month: 'That England is now tottering under terrible evils, its idiotic diplomacy, its brainless plutocracy, its corrupt incompetent politics, is one of the truths that bind us so far in sympathy with the Fascists of Great Britain.'[27]

That same year (1935) events were to make a mockery of the claim in his autobiography that, 'It was my instinct to defend liberty in small nations.' When Mussolini invaded Abyssinia in the autumn there was a widespread outcry in Britain, just as there had been when Germany invaded Belgium in 1914. Letters of protest poured into *The Times* reflecting a general feeling of anger at the unprovoked attack on a defenceless and impoverished country by a more powerful neighbour. Such feelings were strong, particularly among League members and readers of *GK's Weekly*. But Chesterton, whose instinctive response was to side with Abyssinia, was compromised by his loyalty to the Bellocian agenda. Just as in the Great War he had been unable to praise the achievements of Lloyd George, dismissed by Belloc as 'low-born... scum in office', so now he could not join in the general condemnation of Mussolini, hailed by Belloc as a great genius who had not only saved Italy but had given the world an example of how a corrupt parliamentary system could be replaced by dynamic uncorrupt dictatorship. Chesterton obediently accepted this version of events, writing that despite the patriotic feats of Déroulède in France, of Belloc and Cecil in England, political corruption had triumphed. But Mussolini was the man who had stopped the rot and when faced by the Abyssinian invasion, Chesterton felt compelled, if not openly to support Mussolini, to make excuses for him. He responded in much the same way as he had responded to Dreyfus in the early days of his friendship with Belloc. While his initial reaction had been to side with the mass of British opinion that Dreyfus was innocent, under the influence of Belloc he had later expressed his doubts and attacked the press, assured by Belloc that it was controlled by Dreyfus's fellow Jews.[28] Now, in 1935, whilst deploring Mussolini's aggression, his editorial simultaneously excused his lack of anti-Mussolini fervour by arguing that Britain, with its own imperial history, had no right to 'administer a moral rebuke' to Mussolini while the press was in the hands of plutocrats pursuing their own agenda when attacking the Italian dictator: 'It is one thing to condemn Italy in a limited quarrel with Ethiopia [Abyssinia] and another to encourage the English press in unlimited vainglory and vulgarity at the expense of Italy which it would be quite as ready to exhibit at the expense of Ethiopia.'[29]

These half-hearted opinions may have satisfied Belloc but they were anathema to a great many of Chesterton's followers. Protests flooded in, many from leading members of the League. Archie Currie, the man who had tried unsuccessfully to launch the Distributist political party, wrote: 'Twenty-five years ago when another small African people was being bludgeoned into submission, you were proud to be labelled pro-Boer by the gutter press of London. Today, when as I see it, the same dirty ploy is produced again with no important difference, save of cast, you appraise it coolly from the stalls and carefully abstain from condemnation.'[30]

This attack, it is safe to assume, must have caused Chesterton acute distress. Much the same opinion was to be voiced by Keith in her memoir: 'The voice of the defender of small peoples was silent. Gilbert's attitude was that, while he could have wished Mussolini had not made war, he felt Great Britain was the last country that could reproach him. It astounded me that this genius, who had built up a vast reputation as a protagonist of fundamental liberties, should sidetrack the issue by suggesting that, having once bullied, you had no right to protest against bullying.' She adds that his line on Mussolini had given rise to outrageous rumours that the paper was receiving 'Fascist support, monetary and otherwise'.

More serious from Chesterton's point of view was the angry reaction of Maurice Reckitt, a financial backer and a director of *GK's Weekly* from the beginning, one of Chesterton's most fervent admirers. Appalled by the paper's appeasement of Mussolini he wrote a letter of resignation from the board and was only restrained when Chesterton backtracked, seeming to change his tune: 'Between ourselves, and without prejudice to anybody, I do think myself that there ought to have been a more definite condemnation of the attack on Abyssinia. The whole thing happened while I was having a holiday...'[31] Seeking clumsily to divert attention from Mussolini he changed the subject. The letter continued: 'Very shortly, the mortal danger to me is the rehabilitation of Capitalism, in spite of the slump, which will certainly take the form of a hypocritical patriotism and glorification of England at the expense of Italy or anybody else. For the moment I only want you to understand that this is the mountainous peril that towers in my own mind.'[32]

Responding to Chesterton's appeal, Reckitt withdrew his resignation, but others felt differently. Both the League and *GK's Weekly* had been dealt a blow from which they never really recovered. A month before Chesterton's death, the League's AGM of 16 May 1936 reported 'a serious decline in membership'.

It is tempting to explain Chesterton's final illness in 1936 as a repeat of his collapse in 1913 brought about by the stress of the Marconi trial. The accusation that he had betrayed his youthful principles must have been especially painful for him. At the same time the violent reaction from many – mostly non-Catholic – members of the League threatened its continued existence. The difficulty is that once again, there is no evidence from Chesterton himself that he was suffering as a result of the Abyssinia uproar and the damage being done to the League. His biographers, in keeping with their generally uncritical approach, have no wish to deviate from their picture of a relatively serene final period in his life.

But the letters of Gregory Macdonald to his old headmaster tell a different story: 'Future generations will know nowt of the painful inside history and the less they know the better for everybody... a lot of the documents will have to be destroyed for the less known of the history of the paper the better.'[33] The depth of Macdonald's bitter disillusionment, and that of his brother Edward, can be gleaned from another letter to Father Rice dated 6 October 1937, over a year after Chesterton's death:

> Somehow I can't help feeling that there was a vast blot of snobbery, a laziness or pride in the whole menage. Patient Edward, reduced at last, said to me last night, 'I wish *GK's Weekly* had never been founded.' That is my own feeling and has been for some time. What finished him was the discovery, after years of being told that the paper was a terrible financial drain on him, that he earned up to the tune of £28,000.[34] We should not have had our noses rubbed in his poverty. No, there was something very wrong throughout, however it is over now. And I keep on praising him because of what he represented on the undoubtedly great other side of him.[35]

What people *don't* say is often more significant than what they do. If Chesterton said nothing about the disputes and schisms that erupted in 1935, that silence is itself an indication of his feelings. During the final months of that year, Chesterton had completed the autobiography which he had begun some years previously but then laid aside. He finished the book in 1936 though it was not to be published until after his death. It is noticeable that the autobiography contains several references to the *Eye-/New Witness* – 'There had never been anything like the *Eye-Witness* in England before... nor indeed has there ever been anything like it in England since.' But there is not a single mention either of *GK's Weekly* or the Distributist League. Considering that the paper had been published, against all the odds, for over ten years, and that the League, despite all the disagreements, had attracted loyal adherents all over the country, the omission is striking and must have come as a disappointment to the many people who had worked, mostly without payment. 'The autobiography surprised me,' Gregory Macdonald wrote to Father Rice, 'no single mention of *GK's Weekly.*' Chesterton himself may have been unaware of what he had done but it is hard to resist the conclusion that, subconsciously at least, he was well aware that both *GK's Weekly* and the League, the monuments to Cecil's memory, had been dealt a fatal blow. His long battle to keep his brother's flag flying whilst providing Belloc with his precious platform had ended in failure and recriminations. Once again it looks as if Chesterton suppressed all such thoughts, just as he had done with Marconi and Cecil's death, leaving his memoirs with a gaping hole, a mysterious lack of any reference whatever to a project to which he had devoted over ten years of his life. His example was to be followed by nearly all his biographers, who skate over the Mussolini debacle if they mention it at all. Very typically, Maisie Ward writes of the disputes at *GK's Weekly*, 'It would be hard today to say what it was all about,' when nothing would have been easier than to establish the facts – most of which she was probably well aware of in any case.

10

POST MORTEM

'THE DEATH OF CHESTERTON LEFT THE FATE OF *GK's Weekly* in suspense,' Belloc's biographer Robert Speaight writes. 'This was the old *New Witness* which Chesterton had taken over from his brother and renamed; and just as Gilbert had assumed its cares out of loyalty to Cecil, so Belloc felt obliged to assume them out of loyalty to Gilbert.' All this was consistent with Speaight's view of Belloc as 'a supremely good man', but it does not accord with reality. Belloc had a generally low opinion of *GK's Weekly*, and as for 'loyalty to Gilbert', he had never shown any awareness of the sacrifices his friend had made to provide him with his precious platform. In seeking to preserve *GK's Weekly* his only motive was to maintain a paper that would publish whatever he wrote – especially his views on politics, on Prussia, on the forthcoming war.

He wrote to his friend Evan Charteris, 'I am sweating blood to get the little review really interesting and readable and to put it on its legs again,'[1] and to the young Lord Oxford, Asquith's grandson, 'It will be interesting to see whether anybody buys *GK's Weekly* now that some trouble is being taken with it. The chances are that less people will buy it than before because the cranks will be put off and the cranks are always the standby of papers of that sort.'[2] The trouble was that many of those 'cranks' were cancelling their orders as a result of the Mussolini controversy and were not likely to be reassured by Belloc's takeover, considering his well known admiration for the Italian dictator. Typical was J. S. Cargill, a veteran of the League and one of those who had promoted the short-lived Distributist political party. He wrote to the paper demanding that Belloc should state without equivocation where he stood on Fascism: 'Hitler's brutality to the Jews, Mussolini's poison gas for the Abyssinians, General Franco's wholesale slaughter of his fellow-countrymen by the aid of his Moorish adherents are scarcely in accordance with the symbol of the cross. But perhaps Mr Belloc would say, with Cromwell, that the end justifies the means?'[3] Belloc replied, 'Do I like dictatorship? No. Nobody does for its own sake, but for a time it may be necessary in order to save the State.'[4]

Events in Abyssinia had done nothing to dampen Belloc's hero-worship of Mussolini – 'a man of genius who has all the inherited political talent of his race,' he wrote in September 1938, and again, in June 1939, calling him 'by far the most able statesman in Europe'. By then he had another hero in the shape of the Spanish dictator-to-be General Franco, a leader, he said, who combined the qualities of Charlemagne and Napoleon. Belloc met him on a visit to Spain in 1939: 'When I entered Franco's presence I entered the presence of one who had fought the same battle wherein Roland of legend died fighting.' So Franco had battled against the Communist hordes and their Russian/Jewish overlords just as Roland had gallantly fought and defeated the Saracens. When German bombers demolished the Spanish town of Guernica in April 1937, Belloc refused to believe the reports: 'The ruins of Guernica are not the ruins of a town levelled by heavy shelling or pitted by air bombs. They are the ruins of a town deliberately set on fire'[5] – by the Republicans, in other words, to promote their propaganda. As so often, Belloc wrote with the air of a man who knew all about such things, oblivious of the hypocrisy of accusing the Republicans of propaganda while himself writing propaganda for the other side, thus aligning himself with Dr Goebbels who was busily spreading the same lies about Guernica.

With many of the old Distributist guard, especially the non-Catholics like Archie Currie, falling by the wayside, Belloc appealed to his friends and disciples to help. Bernard Shaw wrote in defence of Stalin; Evan Charteris wrote a long article about the French Impressionists; Evelyn Waugh, who was made a director, gave his thoughts on Abyssinia where he had recently reported on the Italian invasion: 'Wrote free stuff for Belloc,' he noted in his diary, 'hope to get to heaven that way.'

The situation was only too reminiscent of the early days of the *Eye-Witness* when Belloc tried in vain to edit a paper while at the same time writing several books and delivering lectures all over the country. By August 1937 he had had enough of editing *GK's Weekly*. 'Devoted as I am to my connection with the paper,' he told the readers, 'I cannot be on the spot as continuously as is necessary for complete editorial work... It is just that my name should not still appear as being the permanently resident editor.' The implication seemed to be that while he might not be the permanently resident editor (which he never had been) he might quite like to continue to exercise some kind of editorial control or 'supervision', the word he had used to describe his relationship with Cecil Chesterton. But he needed a 'Miss Townsend' who would do all the day-to-day work, and now found one in the shape of his faithful son-in-law, R. D. (Rex) Jebb. In 1934, following the departure of his long-serving cook, Belloc had invited his daughter Eleanor, Rex and their four children to move into his Sussex home, King's Land. Belloc liked having children in the house and it suited both parties, as Eleanor could act as her father's housekeeper while Rex could assist Belloc, not only as nominal editor of *GK's Weekly*, now renamed the *Weekly Review*, but as an amanuensis at home, being on hand to take dictation whenever Belloc felt inspired. A veteran of the Great War, Jebb had not immediately commended himself to Belloc as a would-be son-in-law because he was a Protestant. But succumbing, as others had, to Belloc's powerful influence, Jebb converted to Catholicism and abandoning the prep school he was running, founded a Catholic alternative with Belloc's help. It was a disaster and was soon closed down, but the failure did nothing to diminish Jebb's uncritical admiration for Belloc, which rivalled even that of the faithful Beachcomber, and embraced not only Catholicism but all the shaky political principles of Bellocism. 'Every day Mussolini's policy and actions appear in a better light,' he wrote to Belloc in May 1936, 'he seems to make no mistakes and our politicians look sillier and sillier.'[6] Jebb was to write with equal enthusiasm of the South African Prime Minister D. F. Malan when he introduced apartheid in 1948.[7]

Belloc was playing his old game of 'supervising' and also trying to raise funds from backers whilst reassuring his grand friends that he had nothing much to do with the business. 'I no longer control or edit the paper,' he told Major General Guy Dawnay, 'I advise from time to time, especially as to what not to put in, there is always a danger in sheets of this kind that they will become cranky.'[8] Belloc had no intention of controlling his urge to be constantly travelling, and this made his task impossible: 'If I were in England all the time,' he told his friend Lady Phipps, 'and had the leisure and income to devote myself to it, I could make it a reputable organ of some effect; but constantly away and without capital that's impossible.'[9]

He was in exactly the same position he had occupied at the *New Witness*, 'supervising' and 'advising' while disowning responsibility for what was published, which he could always attribute to 'cranks'. He continued to contribute to the *Weekly Review* but the outbreak of war in 1939 and the subsequent events shattered him. As the biographer Hesketh Pearson, an occasional contributor to *GK's Weekly*, writes, 'Having firmly believed that the Catholic Civilisation was the only effective bulwark against barbarism, heresy and atheism, it must have been a dreadful shock for Belloc when Catholic France folded up before the German onslaught, when Catholic Italy joined forces with Germany and when Catholic Spain sided with Germany leaving Protestant Britain the sole barrier against savagery during the most critical phases of the struggle that began in 1940.'[10] What made it even more difficult for Belloc was his belief, reiterated over and over again in *GK's Weekly*, that the British people, Hitler or no Hitler, liked and admired the Germans above all other nations. He was even known to astonish fellow passengers on the train by announcing, 'Nothing will ever cure the English of their unconquerable love for the Prussians.'

But old age was catching up with him. 'The trouble is I get so fearfully tired nowadays,' he confided to Lady Phipps. He had always suffered from insomnia, apologising to Vincent McNabb for his poor handwriting: 'I write illegibly because I have hardly any sleep. Insomnia is becoming the burden of these ageing organs of mine... Pray for me that I may *sleep*.'[11]

What with insomnia and his hectic routine it was hardly surprising that Belloc's health had been rapidly declining, a fact that had been noted for some time. His fellow Catholic, Robert Bruce Lockhart, who had served in the Foreign Office and as a secret agent in Russia and who was later made editor of the Londoner's Diary in the *Evening Standard*, met Belloc, whom he greatly admired, on many occasions during the 1930s. He writes in his diary in October 1932:

> Went to Mass at Belloc's house at Shipley at nine… Mass was celebrated by missionary from Bombay – an English convert. The chapel is a tiny room on upper floor of Belloc's house and can hold about eight people. Old Belloc assisted as server. He is ageing very rapidly and now puffs and blows like a grampus. My last vision of him will be, as we all knelt, of him trying to blow out the candles. Or better still perhaps, downstairs, saying goodbye to us, fulminating against the politicians and running down D. H. Lawrence as filth.

'Old Belloc' was only sixty-two at the time – the same age at which Chesterton died in 1936. He managed to secure commissions to write no less than four obituaries of his friend. Later he was to commemorate Chesterton in a very short book with a very long title, *On the Place of Gilbert Chesterton in English Letters*, published in 1940. Despite the glowing references to Chesterton's brilliance, these tributes betray, better than any other evidence, Belloc's ignorance of his writing and his indifference to the personal circumstances of his life. Like Cecil in his earlier anonymous book, Belloc cannot conceal his jealousy of Chesterton's success, when measured against his own comparative failure, and falls back on the image of himself as a stoical crusader who has paid the price for his unpopular opinions while Chesterton basked contentedly in the sunshine of popular approval.

Belloc's keenness to show that Chesterton lacked his own varied experience sometimes led him to quite ludicrous comparisons. 'He had little experience of seafaring life,' he writes, conjuring up an unlikely picture of Chesterton clad in oilskins and sou'wester piloting an ocean-going yacht.

'He saw the sea not from a deck but as it is seen from the land: from an English cliff... though the English have a strong political and literary passion for the sea, they have as a people little personal familiarity with it, save on its shores. Thus you do not find among them the knowledge of the blind impersonal force of the sea which some have called the cruelty of the sea.'[12]

In other words, unlike Belloc, Chesterton was handicapped by being English. Inexperienced in nautical matters, Chesterton was not a historian as Belloc was: 'The English society in which he grew up – that of the public schools and the social classes formed by them – is not taught history seriously at all.'[13]

Belloc was perfectly prepared to salute his friend's charitable personality, but even this carried with it disadvantages – it was not just the cruelty of the sea but the cruelty of life in general that had passed him by:

> He was blessed in knowing nothing of the acerbities which bite into the life of writing men. The life of writing men has always been, since our remote fathers engaged upon it in the high Greek world, a bitter business. It is notoriously accompanied, for those who write well, by poverty and contempt... The writing man, I say, is a most unhappy beast of burden (and I know something about it)... Now Gilbert Chesterton enjoyed this singular, this very happy fate, that, though he was a writing man, the bitterness of the trade never approached him. He was spared its ignominies and its trials... [14]

So Chesterton was denied any chance of endurance, the 'permanence' of which Cecil had written some years earlier.

There is a brief reference to the Marconi campaign, now seen as a valiant but unsuccessful attempt to stamp out political corruption: 'no one was clearer in vision or harder in action during his vain struggle for purity in public life than these two brothers.' But when the campaign failed, 'Gilbert Chesterton turned more and more to the two living activities which should most occupy serious attention: social philosophy and religion.'[15]

Belloc is so determined to cast Chesterton as someone who, unlike himself, has never known the slings and arrows of the writer's life, that he is able to banish from his mind the true and tragic story of how, so far from retreating into philosophy and religion following the Marconi crusade, Chesterton had bravely, if misguidedly, committed himself to pursuing Cecil's campaigns, despite being utterly ill-equipped for the task. Not only that, he had founded *GK's Weekly* and persisted with it through thick and thin, partly so that Belloc himself could have an outlet to pontificate on the national and international situation, other outlets being denied to him. The effort involved put an immense strain on Chesterton, a strain which, in the view of two important witnesses, actually shortened his life. One was Maisie Ward, who was no doubt repeating what Frances Chesterton had told her.[16] The other was the faithful Bill Titterton, who writes in his memoir, 'It is probably true that in the end *GK's Weekly* killed him.'

Such thoughts, so much at odds with his vision of Chesterton as an innocent philosopher, passed Belloc by. In his mind, Chesterton could never earn a permanent place in the literary pantheon because he was too good a man:

> All men one may say, or very nearly all men, have one leading moral defect. Few have one leading Christian virtue. That of Gilbert Chesterton was unmistakably the virtue of Christian charity: a virtue especially rare in writing men…The drawback, however, of this virtue of charity as regards its action upon his fame was that it prevented the presence in what he wrote of that acerbity or 'bite' which gives an edge or rather a spearhead to every effort at persuasion. It preserved him from enmities. He had no enemies; and in a society such as ours in Modern England, a society which above all demands comfort and ease, this gave him a universality of appeal but furnished no occasion for attack. You do not rise from the reading of one of Chesterton's appreciations with that feeling of being armed which you obtain from the great satirists and particularly from the masters of irony [It is hard to avoid the conclusion that Belloc has himself in mind]… Of the personal advantage to himself

of so great and all-pervading a charity, too much cannot be said; but I believe it to be a drag upon his chances of endurance upon paper – for what that may be worth – and it is worth nothing compared to eternal things.[17]

So Belloc discounts the possibility that Chesterton's writing will survive but offers comfort to his admirers with the thought that he will have saved his soul and gone to heaven. In mitigation, when Belloc wrote in this vein he was old and tired and, as his remarks about Chesterton's lack of seafaring skills showed, inclined to semi-senility on occasion. But at the same time, old age had done away with discretion, and this critique of Chesterton exposes the reason for Belloc's failure to value him as a writer and his consequent tendency to over-value Cecil, a man who made wounding and killing (at least in words) his speciality. Here, perhaps, was the explanation why Belloc had refrained from editing Cecil's attacks on Masterman in *The Party System* – he might have thought them inadvisable, but at heart he couldn't but admire the young man's savagery and recklessness, even when it was directed against a man who regarded them both as his friends.

When Chesterton wrote his autobiography towards the end of his life, he devoted a whole chapter to Belloc with the title 'Portrait of a Friend'. He found it hard to conceal the contradictions, particularly as he felt obliged to point out that Belloc had started his career as a militant Republican and a fellow democrat and ended it as a 'monarchist' and lover of the aristocracy, without mentioning the fact that he himself had followed him down the same path, if not quite all the way. This involved him in a display of verbal gymnastics which would have made it hard for a reader, knowing nothing of Belloc, to gain any kind of picture of the man. Was he married? Did he have children? Where did he live? No answers were available.

Of all the many things that are not mentioned the most surprising is Belloc's religion, by far and away the greatest influence in his life. Considering that Chesterton had been a fellow Catholic for fourteen years when he wrote his book, the omission is surprising and must have come as a disappointment to many of his Catholic readers. But Chesterton was at pains not to criticise Belloc in any way, and he would have found it hard to avoid doing so when describing an attitude that was so profoundly different from his own.

It is never easy to define what religion means to a particular individual and Belloc was no ordinary individual. The world knew him as a devout Catholic, devout usually meaning no more than that the believer is a regular churchgoer. Belloc was certainly that. He went to Mass whenever he could though he seldom took communion and became impatient 'if the priest took more than 20 minutes saying Mass'.[18] At his local church at West Grinstead he would occasionally interrupt the priest as he was beginning to read out the notices by asking him in a loud voice which Sunday after Pentecost it happened to be. Robert Speaight also records the story of how a verger, seeing Belloc standing at the back of the church, urged him to sit down. 'Go to hell!' was Belloc's response. 'I beg your pardon, sir,' the verger replied, 'I didn't know you were a Catholic.'

He always carried his wife Elodie's rosary with him, Speaight writes, 'and he once became nearly distraught in the middle of Holborn because he thought he had lost it. If he wanted something for himself or a friend, he would put up a candle before a statue of a saint, like a child or the humblest of the faithful.' Speaight adds that Belloc 'never read "spiritual" books, but the essential passages of Scripture were familiar to him from their reproduction in the Missal. He did not read them elsewhere.' This may be taken as yet another example of the evasion with which the biographers write about Belloc and Chesterton, 'elsewhere' referring to the Gospels, the reader being informed almost as an afterthought that Hilaire Belloc, the great Catholic spokesman who wrote endlessly about Church matters, the 'Catholic Dr Johnson' as Father Martin D'Arcy once called him, was unfamiliar with the New Testament.

In focusing his attention on the Church and ignoring scripture as far as he could, Belloc was hoping to bypass those elements of his religion which he was unable to reconcile with his anti-Semitism, in particular the inescapable links between Judaism and Christianity and, most obviously, the fact that Jesus, his mother and his disciples were all Jews. It was this obstacle that led Charles Maurras, the French monarchist and Fascist, greatly admired by Belloc, to reject Christianity whilst at the same time praising the Church as a unifying social force. Belloc, though he must have been tempted, could not go so far, taking comfort instead by dismissing the Old Testament as 'Yiddish folklore' only valued by Protestants, and insulting St Paul: 'If you find St Paul difficult,' he wrote to his one-time secretary Bonnie Soames, 'it's not your fault. The old Yid (saving his holy office) had a most turgid and muddy mind. But every now and then he squeezed out a fine lapidary sentence – sometimes Pantheist, sometimes Patriotic.'[19]

Belloc seems aware of his anti-Jewish prejudice and is trying to pass it off as a joke, though there is always difficulty in deciding how seriously to take some of his most provocative statements as he quite liked shocking people, and when engaged in controversy was not averse to telling lies. This he admitted in his long argument with the anti-Catholic Cambridge historian Professor G. G. Coulton: 'If you go about it in the right way,' he wrote in the *Weekly Review*, 'you can tell a particular kind of lie which will infallibly make the dead bones of the pedant spring to life, and once that is accomplished you have before you an infinite vista of jest, irony and downright fun such as compensate us poor hacks for the many weary days in which we have to labour at one silly sentence after another dealing with the silly subject of some silly and utterly unimportant controversy.'

Belloc's eccentric Catholicism gave him an alibi for his failure to succeed as a don, an MP and even as a journalist – he could speak of himself as the victim of anti-Catholic prejudice. The more knocks he had the more he clung to his faith, reassuring himself that it was the lot of the good Catholic to endure neglect and exile, so 'paying the price'.

Feeling as he did, it was natural that Belloc should be lukewarm about Chesterton's interpretation of Christianity and his Catholicism in particular. As Father Ker notes, his letter to Chesterton following his reception in 1922 is noticeably lacking in any word of congratulation, any expression of pleasure on Belloc's part. Rather than welcoming Chesterton into his

Church he appeals for his sympathy, sounding a very typical note of self-pity and bewailing his loss of any religious emotion: 'It is my misfortune. In youth I had it: even till lately. Grief has drawn the juices from it. I am alone and unfed.'[20]

He was more outspoken in a letter to Maurice Baring, lecturing him on the nature of faith and Chesterton's failure, as he saw it, to live up to the demands of the Church:

> People said he might come in at any time because he shared such a Catholic point of view and so much affection for the Catholic Church. That always seemed to me quite the wrong end of the stick. Acceptation of the Faith is an act not a mood. Faith is an act of will and as it seemed to me the whole of his mind was occupied in expressing his liking for and attraction towards a certain mood, not at all towards the accepta-tion of a certain Institution as defined and representing full reality in this world. There is all the difference between enjoying military ideas and even joining the volunteers, and becoming a private soldier in a common regiment.[21]

But it was not just that Belloc did not like the idea of Chesterton becom-ing a Catholic; there is evidence that he even made a half-hearted attempt to prevent it happening, according to a curious story related by John O'Connor,[22] the priest who inspired the character of Father Brown and who had always been a close friend of Frances Chesterton. As he neared conversion, Chesterton had been writing to Father O'Connor, whose parish was in Yorkshire, asking for his advice and inviting him to come to Beaconsfield to help him. O'Connor agreed to come, and in the meantime wrote to Belloc to tell him of his plan, adding, presumably, the good news that Chesterton was on the point of converting to Rome. The sequel was mysterious and reminiscent of a Father Brown story.

Two days before he was due to travel south to Beaconsfield, O'Connor received a typical Belloc telegram: 'Appointment meet me today London.' Showing, once again, the power that Belloc was able to exert over less forceful citizens, even when they were Catholic priests, O'Connor replied: 'Westminster Cathedral 3.30.' He caught a train to St Pancras and reached the cathedral well before the appointed time. He then waited for over an hour but there was no sign of Belloc, and he was now forced to spend two days in London before he was due at Beaconsfield.

He later received two or three letters from Belloc expressing his surprise at Chesterton's conversion but saying nothing about his failure to come to the cathedral. O'Connor asked him about it when they eventually met some weeks later. 'I wanted to keep you from going to Gilbert,' he said. 'I thought he would never be a Catholic' – a baffling reply suggesting that he wanted to stop O'Connor from wasting his time by going to Chesterton. But why then tell him to come all the way to London and then fail to make the appointment? (O'Connor records that Belloc had been seen in the capital that morning.) Is it possible that Belloc actually wanted to persuade O'Connor not to go to Beaconsfield because he didn't want Chesterton to join the Church, then thought better of it, decided not to meet the priest and later fobbed him off with a spurious explanation?

Whatever the truth, Belloc showed no sign of wanting to celebrate the event with his fellow Catholics. Chesterton's reception into the Catholic Church, when it eventually took place, involved three separate services. The first, his baptism, was held in an annexe of the Railway Hotel in Beaconsfield (there being no Catholic church in the village) on 30 July 1922. Only two priests and Frances Chesterton were present and to avoid the inevitable publicity the occasion was kept secret, not even Chesterton's best friends Belloc and Baring being told about it. Baring only learned what had happened when he read the story in his newspaper. It was followed in September by his first communion (also at the Railway Hotel) and his confirmation later the same day at the Church of St Augustine, High Wycombe. Belloc had been expected at this particular service and the small congregation waited patiently for his arrival. But, as with his tryst with Father O'Connor in Westminster Cathedral, Belloc failed to appear, and after waiting an hour the Bishop decided to go ahead without him.

According to Ronald Knox, who had come over from Oxford to take part, the occasion had been spoilt by the absence of Belloc.[23]

Belloc's lack of enthusiasm was partly based on the inevitable reservations which the cradle Catholic feels about the convert. Unlike Belloc, the child of Catholic parents, educated at Catholic schools, Chesterton was brought up in a family without any specific religious beliefs apart from what was then defined as the 'New Theology':

> I was brought up in the New Theology and so were most of my friends. It was the great established convention of the late Victorians. Queen Victoria believed in the New Theology. Lord Tennyson, poet laureate, believed in the New Theology... Disraeli believed in the New Theology, if he believed in anything, that is what he meant by such a misty phrase as being 'on the right side of the angels'. The New Theology is the admirable religion of one's aunts and uncles. It is merely the vague Victorian optimism in which we all grew up... Since some years before I was born the New Theology has been the general and reputable creed.[24]

One consequence of this, he wrote, was that anyone like General Gordon or Gladstone who 'retained a dogmatic Christianity were in that respect regarded as magnificent but a little mad'. So in the same way, he maintained, Belloc as an avowed Catholic was regarded as, if not mad, then definitely eccentric. In stating that the New Theology was the religion of his aunts and uncles Chesterton was probably thinking more of his parents, who had no fixed religion apart from the New Theology or what has been described as 'a vague utilitarianism'. He must have encountered Christianity in its public-school form at St Paul's but says nothing about it. The process of his slow conversion began when he was an art student at the Slade and went through a period of acute depression during which he had 'an overpowering impulse to record or draw horrible ideas and images'. Evelyn Waugh has mentioned rumours of homosexuality at this period in his life, and Wilfrid Blunt refers in his diary to an attempt by Lord Alfred Douglas to blackmail him which he and Belloc managed to prevent. Whatever his experiences were, they left Chesterton with an abiding sense of evil – 'I had dug quite low enough to recognise the devil' – an experience previously prompted by playing with an ouija board with Cecil. This frightened him so much that he vowed never to touch it again 'with a bargepole'.[25]

His wife Frances, whom he married in 1901 when he was twenty-seven, was more responsible than anyone for Chesterton's conversion to Christianity. She was, he writes, the first person he knew who lived a religious life. He presumably meant regular churchgoing and acts of charity but as with almost all aspects of his personal life he supplies few details, presumably out of deference to Frances who had asked to be kept out of his memoir.

Apart from Frances, the most compelling religious influence on the young Chesterton was an eccentric aristocrat and Anglo-Catholic clergyman, Conrad Noel, famous for flying the red flag from his church at Thaxted, who combined religion and socialism with humour and tomfoolery – for Chesterton an irresistible combination. An Old Etonian and the grandson of the Earl of Gainsborough, 'He took great pleasure in appearing in correct clerical clothes,' Chesterton recalled, 'surmounted with a soft sort of hairy or furry cap, making him look like an aesthetic rat-catcher.'[26] It was this eccentricity of Noel's that drew him and Cecil to what he calls 'the serious consideration of the theory of a church', adding, 'I was considerably influenced by Conrad Noel, and my brother, I think, even more so.'[27]

This is one of those evasive statements of Chesterton's about his brother that borders on dishonesty, in particular the use of the words 'I think' to suggest that he cannot be sure of the facts. The most significant fact, which he knew very well, was that Cecil, who had hitherto been an atheist, was confirmed in 1905 as a member of the Anglican Church by Conrad Noel, who describes the event in his autobiography:

> I prepared Cecil for confirmation, for his parents had brought him up
> in the vague beliefs of Unitarians and ethical societies and through our
> friendship he had become convinced of the truth of the Catholic faith.

I had given him a long preparation in which humour was blended with a liberal interpretation of the creeds. I took him to St Mary's Primrose Hill for the sacrament of confirmation. Unhappily the ponderous and Protestant Bishop of Islington was confirming and gave the addresses. As the bishop droned on Cecil's face drooped in dejection and discouragement. The situation was saved by the vicar, Dr Percy Dearmer, handing down from the stall a note which referred us to the Twenty-Sixth Article of the Thirty-Nine, and Cecil revived with a chuckle when he read, 'The unworthiness of the ministers which hinders not the effect of the Sacrament.'[28]

It is likely that Chesterton would have been present on this occasion, along with Frances, yet he never mentions it in his memoir or ever referred to his brother's conversion when writing about him. His reticence is followed by Chesterton's biographers Maisie Ward and Ian Ker. All concerned are Roman Catholics and it could be that wishing only to emphasise Cecil's conversion to Rome in 1912 they suppressed the fact, deliberately or not, that he had undergone a previous and more fundamental conversion from militant atheism to orthodox Christianity.

Chesterton's silence is understandable if he was most reluctant publicly to confront the obvious question which a reader of his autobiography might very well ask: if Cecil presented himself for confirmation, why didn't he do the same? On the face of it he was the more likely convert, being a devoted friend of Conrad Noel's and married to a practising Anglo-Catholic.

Despite that, he remained, as Cecil put it, the man who stayed outside the church ringing the bell. This would seem to have been almost literally true, as prior to his becoming a Roman Catholic in 1922 Chesterton, the most influential Christian apologist of his day, was not a churchgoer. The vicar of Beaconsfield testified that he had been 'a very bad Anglican' and was glad that he had gone over to Rome and might now be more conscientious. From this, and similar evidence, it would seem that Frances fulfilled her religious duties on her own.

Branding himself as an exile 'alone and unfed', the victim of anti-Catholic prejudice, Belloc was most reluctant to empathise with Chesterton. Just as he did not read the Gospels in case they disturbed his anti-Semitism, so he avoided Chesterton's best-known religious books, *Orthodoxy* and later *The Everlasting Man*, which had little in common with his view of Catholics, condemned, like himself, to a life of inevitable exclusion and exile. There is nothing to suggest that he ever read either of these books, nor that he had any acquaintance with Father Brown, whose adventures had made an obscure Catholic priest into a much-loved figure, thereby upsetting Belloc's view of a nationwide hostility to, and ignorance of, Catholicism. He wrote later:

> His name and writings were already familiar before his conversion to a general public which had no idea of the Faith. They were thus familiar and accepted long before he threw down the last challenge by fully accepting the Creed, the Unity and the temporal disabilities of Catholic allegiance. He had before his reception acquired, as it were, a privileged position which permitted him to be still listened to after he had crossed that frontier of the Faith beyond which lies all that his fellow-countrymen oppose. Herein he was blessed and may be justly envied by those who are condemned by their Faith to exclusion and exile.[29]

In describing Belloc's hounding of Charles Masterman, H. G. Wells had observed that Masterman was Belloc's rival, the man whose political career had flourished while Belloc's floundered on the rocks, provoking envy and resentment – and it is legitimate to infer that Belloc's attitude towards Chesterton in the religious sphere was based on similar emotions. Hitherto Belloc had seen himself as the best-known Catholic in the country (his disciple J. B. Morton describes him as the 'leader' of the Catholic community, albeit one who had been let down by the feebleness of his followers) and he must have been aware that Chesterton, who was a much better-known and more popular figure, was likely now to usurp his role.

When Belloc referred to those people who said 'he might have come in at any time', he could have added that a great many of Chesterton's readers must have been under the impression that he had come in already. The confusion arose thanks to the way Anglo-Catholics – Conrad Noel for example – always referred to themselves as Catholics, Chesterton being no exception. Long before his reception in 1922, he wrote continually of his loyalty to the Catholic Church and was frequently referred to as a Catholic by agnostics and non-believers. It followed that his 1922 reception must have come as a surprise to many of his readers who had assumed that he had been a member for some time. The fact that he was best known as the creator of a famous detective in the person of the Catholic priest Father Brown will only have confirmed that impression.

If Belloc failed to read Chesterton's *Orthodoxy* and *The Everlasting Man* (written after his conversion) that was because he had little or no interest in a defence of religion in general and Christianity in particular. Unlike Belloc, Chesterton believed that the religious instinct was natural to man and that it was the agnostic and the atheist who was the odd man out. 'Atheism,' he wrote, 'is abnormality. It is not merely the denying of a dogma. It is the reversal of a subconscious assumption in the soul; the sense that there is a meaning and a direction in the world it sees.'[30] Again, 'Religion is the sense of ultimate reality, of whatever meaning a man finds in his own existence or the existence of anything else.'[31] With this sense, on his part, went an unconditional acceptance of the supernatural: 'The incredible thing about miracles is that they happen.'[32]

The Everlasting Man was written as a riposte to Chesterton's great friend H. G. Wells and his best-selling book *The Outline of History*. Belloc had already engaged in a long and bitter controversy with Wells over the book, but as so often, he spoiled the effect of his attack with his strong sense of grievance, in this case his ill-concealed jealousy of Wells's commercial success, *The Outline of History* having sold 100,000 copies in a year – far more than all of Belloc's many historical works taken together. If his jealousy was ill-concealed, his intellectual snobbery was not concealed at all, Belloc continually referring, as he had always done, to Wells's failure to be among the 'educated and travelled', being a man of provincial background and suburban tastes who lacked the benefit of a university education and who was woefully ignorant of modern European scholarship – 'an Englishman of the Home Counties and the London Suburbs'.

Chesterton's approach could not have been more different. He was aware, as Belloc was not, that Wells's obsessive hostility to religion was the product of deep-seated doubts, and that he would not be able to argue his case without becoming irrational.

Wells's central thesis, a strange one to put forward just after the terrible slaughter of the First World War, was that mankind was engaged in a steady progress towards a world state. This notion of a slow and permanent process of evolution meant picturing the prehistoric age as one of primitive savagery. Like Father Brown finding a simple solution to a mystery, Chesterton answered Wells by pointing to the prehistoric cave paintings at Pech Merle in France's Midi Pyrénées, which had been discovered by two boys and a priest in 1922. It was natural that Chesterton, who had once written of his urge when lying in bed to have a pencil long enough for him to be able to draw on the ceiling, should feel at one with the Pech Merle cavemen. As an artist who compulsively covered any available surface with his drawings, he was inspired to write one of his most memorable passages by these cave paintings:

> They were drawings or paintings of animals; and they were drawn or painted not only by a man but by an artist. Under whatever archaic limitations, they showed that love of the long sweeping or the long wavering line which any man who has ever drawn or tried to draw will recognise... They showed the experimental and adventurous spirit of the artist, the spirit that does not avoid but attempts difficult things; as where the draughtsman had represented the action of the stag when he swings his head clear round and noses towards his tail, an action familiar enough in the horse. But there are many modern animal painters who would set themselves something of a task in rendering it truly.[33]

That was enough for Chesterton to demolish the notion of 'crude evolutionism', of man slowly progressing from the primitive.

When it came to Christianity, Belloc, partially on account of his antipathy to Jews, shied away from scripture. Chesterton confronted it head-on in conformity with his genius for looking at anything, however insignificant, as if for the first time. The difficulty with the Gospel story, he argued, is that it is too familiar – 'no man of our civilisation, whatever he thinks of our religion, can really read the thing as if he had never heard of it before.'[34] In looking at it as he tried to do from the point of view of an 'imaginary man from the moon', the first thing he would notice is that 'it is in some ways a very strange story' – 'The Strangest Story in the World' is his chapter heading. The word 'strange' recurs in this chapter nearly continually in Chesterton's account of the life of Jesus. But no one who read the story could possibly reconcile the thesis advanced by non-believers like Wells, who accepted that Christ was a historical figure but portrayed him as 'a wandering teacher', with a message of peace and love.

Jesus could be said to have preached such a message but unlike all the other founders of religion – 'Mahomet, Buddha, Confucius' – he combined his teachings with claims to be divine, claims that would normally be ascribed to lunacy: 'It is possible to find here and there human beings who make this supremely superhuman claim. It is possible to find them in lunatic asylums; in padded cells; possibly in strait waistcoats.'[35]

Just as Chesterton had seen the caveman from the point of view of a fellow artist, he focused on the language used by Jesus as someone who himself excelled in the use of exaggeration, paradox and simile to make his points:

> Even in the matter of mere literary style... there is a curious quality to which no critic seems to have done justice. It had among other things a singular air of piling tower upon tower by the use of the *a fortiori*; making a pagoda of dreams like the seven heavens... There is perhaps nothing so perfect in all language or literature as the use of these three degrees in the parable of the lilies of the field; in which he seems first

to take one small flower in his hand and note its simplicity and even its innocence; then suddenly expands it in flamboyant colours into all the palaces and pavilions full of a great name in national legend and national glory; and then, by yet a third overturn, shrivels it to nothing once more with a gesture as if flinging it away, 'and if God so clothes the grass that today is and tomorrow is cast into the oven – how much more'...[36]

There was something very appropriate in Chesterton's emphasis on this famous passage and its message – 'Take no thought for the morrow.' It was the same spirit in which he had rebuffed Cecil's old charge that he had no concern with his legacy. There is no sign that Chesterton ever concerned himself with his reputation, present or posthumous, insisting that he was and remained a journalist and quoting with approval Stevenson's observation that 'whatever we are intended to do we are not intended to succeed'. He added his own thought that failure may be one step towards becoming a saint. By contrast Belloc's thoughts turned frequently to the theme of permanence, comforting himself with the idea that sales were not the test of immortality: 'It matters little whether strong permanent work finds a thousand or fifty thousand or a million readers. Rock stands and mud washes away.'

Belloc was to live until 1953 but his final years were unproductive and sad. 'My heart so often aches for him' his sister Marie wrote in her diary in February 1947. He had suffered a stroke in 1941 and apart from an occasional piece in the *Weekly Review* wrote nothing afterwards. His travels were finally over. Walking became difficult, he grew a long beard and his mind wandered as he struggled to keep a hold on life. One son Louis had been killed in the First War and Peter, who had joined the Marines, died of septicaemia in the early days of the Second. A third son Hilary had emigrated to America after quarrelling with his father, and his youngest daughter Elizabeth, in the words of A. N. Wilson, 'remained like an emaciated ghost clad invariably in a dark blue cloche hat until the end of her days'. Only the faithful Eleanor stayed at her father's side at King's Land, though she was unable to give him the round-the-clock care he needed.

His clothes were dirty, his fingernails untrimmed. And always the same lifelong obsessions rose to the surface of his drink-fuddled mind: 'Do they still think Dreyfus was innocent?' he asked the visiting Dom Aelred Watkin, later Abbot of Downside, who knew nothing of the matter. 'Poor darling, he was guilty as sin.'[37]

Most of his circle were dead. On 12 July 1953 Eleanor smelt burning and found her father lying on the floor of his study with live coals from the fire burning him and his clothing. He was taken to hospital with severe burns to his back and shoulders and died three days later.

In the brave new post-war world of the 1950s Hilaire Belloc seemed an anachronistic figure, a rare survivor from the remote Edwardian era. He received many tributes, almost all of them from fellow Catholics. At his Requiem Mass in Westminster Cathedral, Monsignor Ronald Knox (once dismissed by Belloc as 'insufficiently coarse')[38] hailed him as a great prophet: 'Here was a man that interpreted divine things for us – have no fear, he will be remembered.'

But if Belloc had prophetic gifts they were not shared by Ronald Knox, as Belloc has not been remembered except as the author of his *Cautionary Tales* and other satirical verse. He himself had previously written his own comic epitaph: 'When I am dead, I hope it may be said / His sins were scarlet but his books were read.' Yet even in his lifetime Belloc had been aware of the fact that compared with those of his contemporaries like Chesterton and Wells, his books had not been read. It might have been tempting for him to characterise the public's indifference as yet another consequence of anti-Catholicism, the same prejudice that had barred him from All Souls, but he was well aware that he had written too much and too quickly – 'one silly sentence after another' – and that a good deal of it was hack work – 'I am writing a book about the crusades,' he once informed a friend, 'so dull I can scarcely write it.'

When it came to Chesterton, both Belloc and Cecil had underestimated him from the beginning, remaining blissfully unaware of their damaging influence upon him. While Belloc persuaded himself that Chesterton was too charitable a man to be a good writer, Cecil, in his anonymous book about his brother published in 1908, had speculated that though his books, marred by tastelessness and lack of technical skill, might not survive, it was perhaps possible that he could well live on as a famous personality like Dr Johnson, whose books might be forgotten but whose sayings would be remembered – always assuming that a Boswell would be on hand to record them.

Though no Boswell materialised, there was an element of truth in Cecil's prophecy. With the exception of the Father Brown stories Chesterton's books have never achieved the status of classics, yet he has remained one of the most frequently quoted of authors whose sayings, culled from his voluminous writings, reflect a Johnsonian wisdom expressed often in the form of a memorable paradox, occasionally via the medium of Father Brown. These insights, covering almost all aspects of life, past and present, are like precious stones embedded in a covering of often muddy prose or, as the anonymous *TLS* reviewer put it, 'grains of purest Chestertonian corn' buried in a quantity of chaff.[39] Chesterton's 'incidental remarks' John Gross writes, 'are more important than his grand conclusions.'[40]

Chesterton's autobiography ought to have clarified his life but there is very little personal disclosure in it. Perhaps he would have argued that someone of his generation was not given to making revelations about his more private feelings, yet the true explanation is that there was a great deal in his story, particularly concerning Cecil, that he was incapable of confronting. When it came to confession, more than once Chesterton wrote that he became a Catholic to get rid of his sins, his followers deducing, probably correctly, that he harboured some deep-seated feelings of guilt dating from his experiences at the Slade, which left him, as he said, with a strong sense of the physical nature of evil. Whatever may have been those sins, they must seem trivial when compared to his treatment of his friends Gardiner, Masterman and Cadbury, his lies about Cecil's death and his vicious and unprovoked attack on Rufus Isaacs. Yet Chesterton, despite his strong sense of sin and the value of confession, could not even acknowledge these failings, let alone the many inexcusable examples of anti-Semitism in his writings. 'The unfortunate man,' Professor Dudley Edwards writes, 'hardly realised that the sins that he committed were as injurious to the Christianity that he loved as the wildest charges of its gravest traducers.'

Such blindness to his own failings went hand in hand with his extreme reluctance to confront antagonism, disputes and unpleasantness. Chesterton's father Edward, Keith writes, had a neurotic aversion to illness and death. His own heart condition, which had brought about his early retirement, was 'never mentioned in the family circle', or, for that matter, in Chesterton's memoir. Likewise with his first child, Beatrice, who died aged eight. Her portrait was turned to the wall and Edward forbade any mention of her name. Maisie Ward makes no mention either of this prohibition or of Edward's early retirement and morbid fears.

Chesterton, who idolised his father, inherited his neurosis along with his artistic gifts. Ronald Knox once said that he shared Dr Johnson's morbid obsession with the terrors of death and it was only with the greatest difficulty, Keith records, that he visited his father when he was dying. Such squeamishness may seem puzzling in a writer like Chesterton who, in his Father Brown stories, described a number of often quite gruesome murders. But it was a squeamishness reserved for all personal problems which, whenever possible, were best left in the dark. 'Non-interference was the family motto,' Keith writes. So it was not only their loyalty to the Catholic Church that restrained his biographers when describing Chesterton's life. It was as if in deference to his genius, they felt obliged to follow in his footsteps and play down or ignore altogether unpleasant or jarring elements in the story – even the likelihood, referred to only in passing, that his personal conflicts had resulted not only in a serious breakdown but may well have helped to bring about his premature death.

This whitewashing of Chesterton did him no favours as it left the world with an unreal figure, the figure that Belloc had described, an innocent uncomplicated man blessed with almost permanent happiness and having no experience of suffering – hence an ideal candidate for canonisation.

Whatever his failings they cannot detract from Chesterton's undoubted genius, least of all his humility. As his great friend Father Vincent McNabb wrote: 'He could not defend himself. He seemed to feel that everywhere he was a misfit and that even his coming into existence was a mistake. He was shaming to God and apologetic to his fellow men for having been born.'[41]

Writing of his beloved wife Frances he had used the phrase 'in many ways a very heroic tragedy' to describe her life – seemingly unaware of how aptly those words described his own.

Notes

Introduction

1 *Spectator*, 20 April 1944
2 Robert Speaight, *The Life of Hilaire Belloc* (1957)
3 Letter to Brocard Sewell, 23 October 1973
4 Brocard Sewell, *Cecil Chesterton* (1975)
5 Dudley Barker, *G. K. Chesterton: A Biography* (1973)
6 She was received into the Church in 1942.

1. A Legend in the Flesh

1 Frank Swinnerton, *The Georgian Literary Scene* (1935)
2 Christopher Hollis, *The Mind of Chesterton* (1970)
3 'The Twelve Men', *Tremendous Trifles* (1909)
4 'The Travellers in State', *Tremendous Trifles*
5 'The Riddle of the Ivy', *Tremendous Trifles*
6 'The Quick One', *The Scandal of Father Brown* (1935)
7 Years later in 1930 the *Daily News* merged with the *Daily Chronicle* to become the *News Chronicle*.
8 A. G. Gardiner, *Prophets, Priests and Kings* (1908) and *Pillars of Society* (1914)
9 Barbara W. Tuchman, *The Proud Tower: A Portrait of the World Before the War* (1966)
10 A. G. Gardiner, *Pillars of Society*
11 G. K. Chesterton, *Autobiography* (1936)
12 E. C. Bentley and G. K. Chesterton, *Biography for Beginners: Being a Collection of Miscellaneous Examples for the Use of Upper Forms* (1905)
13 A. G. Gardiner, *Prophets, Priests and Kings*, (2nd edition, 1914)
14 Stephen E. Koss, *Fleet Street Radical: A. G. Gardiner and the Daily News* (1973)

2. The Indulged Younger Brother

1   A fact that neither Chesterton nor his biographer ever referred to.

2   Mrs Cecil Chesterton, *The Chestertons* (1941)

3   Ibid.

4   Denis Conlon (ed.), *G. K. Chesterton: A Half Century of Views* (1987)

5   Maisie Ward, *Gilbert Keith Chesterton* (1943)

6   Denis Conlon (ed.), *G. K. Chesterton: The Critical Judgements* (1976)

7   Thomas Beecham, *A Mingled Chime: Leaves from an Autobiography* (1944)

8   Kate Carew, *New York Tribune*, 15 September 1912

9   Conlon (ed.), *G. K. Chesterton: The Critical Judgements*

10 An obvious reference to A. J. Balfour.

11 Chesterton was not a Catholic when he launched the Father Brown stories.

12 Obituary of Chesterton, *Tablet*, 20 June 1936

13 *Tremendous Trifles* (1909)

14 Nicolas Bentley, *A Version of the Truth* (1960)

15 Conlon (ed.), *G. K. Chesterton: The Critical Judgements*

16 *GK's Weekly*, 17 October 1925

17 'The Invisible Man', first published in the *Saturday Evening Post*, 28 January 1911

3. Keith and Frances

1   See note 1, Chapter 8

2   In her biography, Maisie Ward states that Frances was 'the daughter of a diamond merchant some time dead. The family was of French descent, the name de Blogue having been somewhat unfortunately anglicised into "Blogg".' (Neither Ward nor, later, Ker names Frances's father.) Subsequent biographers Alzina Stone Dale (1982) and Ian Ker (2011) add that the de Blogues were Huguenots. This account has since been faithfully repeated by almost all of Chesterton's biographers. However, in her book *Chesterton and the Jews* (2015), Ann Farmer queries Ward's facts. She points out that Frances's father and grandfather, both called George Blogg, were well-known diamond merchants in London and that the worldwide diamond trade has always been almost exclusively in the hands of Jews. Going back three generations there is no evidence of a de Blogue in the family tree. The name Blogg, on the other hand, is found in England and is not an uncommon Jewish family name, a variation of the name Bloch. It is therefore highly likely that the Bloggs were Christianised Jews (George F. Blogg, Frances's grandfather, was baptised in 1842 in London). Had Chesterton been aware of this background, not dissimilar to that of Rufus Isaacs, whose family

were fruit merchants in East London, he might then have modified his anti-Jewish pronouncements, in particular with regard to what he called 'the folly of the fashion by which Jews often concealed their Jewish names'. By an appropriate coincidence Hilaire Belloc's ancestry has also been traced back to a Moses Bloch, a seventeenth-century wine merchant in Nantes, according to A. N. Wilson, a shipbuilder according to Speaight.

3   E. C. Bentley, *Those Days* (1940)

4   Marie Belloc Lowndes, *Diaries and Letters, 1911–1947* (1971)

5   Christopher Hollis, *The Mind of Chesterton* (1970)

6   Masterman Papers, Birmingham University

7   *Autobiography* (1936)

8   *What's Wrong with the World* (1910)

9   Ibid.

10 *William Cobbett* (1925)

11 Brocard Sewell, *Cecil Chesterton* (1975)

12 See Chapter 5 below.

13 *What's Wrong with the World*

14 Mrs Cecil Chesterton, *The Chestertons* (1941)

15 *Spectator*, 17 July 1941, reprinted in Graham Greene, *Collected Essays* (1969)

16 Greene's review concludes: 'Mrs Cecil Chesterton may consider that this passage of her book disposes of Frances Chesterton once and for all; it disposes far more destructively of the author who is ready to print it… One is left contrasting these badly-written, expansive, discretionless memoirs with the silence of Frances Chesterton, the wife of the greater brother, who will be remembered in her husband's verse long after these spiteful anecdotes are forgotten.'

17 Rupert Hart-Davis (ed.), *Max Beerbohm's Letters to Reggie Turner* (1964)

18 Denis Conlon (ed.), *G. K. Chesterton: The Critical Judgements* (1976)

4. Baskets and Dead Cats

1   *Autobiography* (1936)

2   A. J. P. Taylor, *Politicians, Socialism and Historians* (1980)

3   From Belloc's poem 'The South Country'

4   Hilaire Belloc, *On the Place of Gilbert Chesterton in English Letters* (1940)

5   Marie Belloc Lowndes, *Diaries and Letters, 1911–1947* (1971)

6   *New Witness*, 26 April 1917

7   D. J. Conlon (ed.), *G. K. Chesterton: A Half Century of Views* (1987)

8   J. B. Morton, *Hilaire Belloc: A Memoir* (1955)

9 Letter from Maurice Baring to Hilaire Belloc, 4 January 1934

10 Nicolas Bentley, *A Version of the Truth* (1960)

11 Robert Speaight, *The Life of Hilaire Belloc* (1957)

12 A. G. Gardiner, *Pillars of Society* (1914)

13 Maisie Ward wrote: 'Belloc himself told me he thought the chief thing he had done for Chesterton when they first met was to open his eyes to reality.'

14 Gardiner, *Pillars of Society*

15 Barbara Tuchman, *The Proud Tower: A Portrait of the World Before the War* (1966)

16 Hilaire Belloc, *The Cruise of the 'Nona'* (1925)

17 *New Witness*, 26 November 1914

18 Cecil Chesterton was faithfully to echo this view, writing in the *New Witness*: 'It is in silence and darkness that evil things thrive and flourish.'

19 G. K. Chesterton also echoed Belloc, referring to Bolsheviks as 'the Jew Socialist Minority' in Russia (*Illustrated London News*, 24 July 1920).

20 *Weekly Review*, 19 September 1940

21 Cecil Chesterton had a similar habit of assuming villains with suspicious-looking names to be Jews, for example Leon Czolgosz, the Polish–American anarchist, son of Catholic parents, who assassinated US President McKinley in 1901. Similarly G. K. Chesterton assumed that Brahms was a Jew purely on the basis of his name.

22 *Weekly Review*, 1 July 1938

23 *Weekly Review*, 18 May 1939

24 Gardiner, *Pillars of Society*

25 Ann Farmer, *Chesterton and the Jews* (2015)

26 Letter to *The Nation*, 18 March 1911

27 See pp 156 below.

28 Compare historian James Joll in *The Anarchists* (1964): 'Large numbers of people were arrested and executed or deported.' Belloc's ill-informed conclusions on Ferrer are accepted *in toto* by his biographer Speaight, who writes (at pp. 238–9) that Belloc 'analysed the case very carefully' and that Ferrer, an educational crank and libertine, was guilty as charged: 'The campaign had revealed Belloc's force and courage in controversy'.

29 *New Witness*, 3 November 1922, quoted by Tom Villis in *Reaction and the Avant-Garde: The Revolt Against Liberal Democracy in Early Twentieth-Century Britain* (2006) and *British Catholics and Fascism: Religious Identity and Political Extremism Between the Wars* (2013)

30 Belloc, *The Cruise of the 'Nona'*

31 Ibid.

32 'In Memoriam PD'

33 The French equivalent of 'wogs'

34 Quoted by Carmen Callil in *Bad Faith: A Story of Family and Fatherland* (2006)

35 *GK's Weekly*, 8 March 1934

36 Even after the man's public disgrace at the end of the war, Eccles, Professor of French Literature at London University from 1920 to 1934, maintained his admiration for Maurras, writing: 'However deeply we may regret the error of judgement, largely explained by his horror of communism, which led Charles Maurras to support the ambiguous policy of Marshall Pétain... his good faith and sincerity remain unquestioned.' (*Tablet*, 31 July 1948).

37 *The Resurrection of Rome* (1930)

38 *Bernard Shaw* by Hesketh Pearson

39 *G. K. Chesterton: A Criticism* (1908)

40 A favourite theme of Belloc's, this refers to the leading figure in the Marconi scandal, Herbert Samuel (see Chapter 6 below). His great-uncle Nathan Samuel was a pawnbroker in Liverpool and the founder of the family fortune. His uncle and guardian the banker Samuel Montagu – his parents reversed his two names – became a Liberal MP and major backer of the party. He was created Lord Swaythling in 1907. Belloc was convinced that Herbert Samuel owed his position *solely* to his uncle's donations to the Liberal Party.

41 *GK's: A Miscellany of the First 500 Issues of GK's Weekly* (1934)

42 Mrs Cecil Chesterton, *The Chestertons* (1941)

5. Going into the Other Camp

1 C. F. G. Masterman, *From the Abyss* (1902)

2 Beatrice Webb, *Our Partnership* (1948)

3 Lucy Masterman, *C. F. G. Masterman* (1939)

4 Ford Madox Ford, *Return to Yesterday* (1931)

5 A. G. Gardiner, *Prophets, Priests and Kings* (1908)

6 Lucy Masterman. Churchill may have been referring to his narrow escape when fighting in the Boer War.

7 Piers Brendon, *Winston Churchill: A Brief Life* (1984)

8 Lucy Masterman, *C. F. G. Masterman* (1939)

9 A. J. P. Taylor, *British Prime Ministers* (1999)

10 The National Insurance Act received royal assent in December 1911.

11 This was straightforward hypocrisy on the part of Belloc, a Liberal MP who on his visits to his Salford constituency stayed in the palatial house of his great friend the High-Tory MP George Wyndham, formerly secretary to Prime Minister Arthur Balfour, and at other times accepted the hospitality of the former Tory Lord Derby who gave him 'the full-hearted free run of his library'.

12 *The Party System*, pp. 40–1

13 *The Party System*, pp. 196–7

14 Lucy Masterman, in *C. F. G. Masterman* (1939)

15 *Tablet*, 29 July 1911

16 Ibid.

17 See Chapter 6 below.

18 H. H. Asquith, *Letters to Venetia Stanley* (1982)

19 Frank Swinnerton, *An Autobiography* (1936)

20 Ignoring the usual procedures, Lloyd George had dispatched a civil servant, W. J. Braithwaite, to Germany to investigate the workings of their social security system and then report to him in the South of France where he was on holiday. In the course of four hours Braithwaite outlined what he had learned, and on that basis Lloyd George, with Masterman's substantial input, produced a Bill, Part 1 of which introduced national health insurance. In 1913 Masterman himself followed in Mr Braithwaite's footsteps when he too was sent to Germany with his friend Ford Madox Ford as his interpreter to interview waiters about their insurance policies. Ford recalled that Masterman – 'that large, sleepy, always smiling, crooked-nosed statesman' – soon wearied of the task, deciding to explore the battlefields of the Franco-Prussian War instead.

21 Gardiner, *Pillars of Society* (1914)

22 Ibid.

23 *GK's Weekly*, 29 October 1932

24 Robert Speaight, *The Life of Hilaire Belloc* (1957)

25 Despite his obvious failings, Masterman was much liked by his contemporaries. Belloc's sister Marie records: 'Among the liberals of that time I had a special regard and respect for Charles Masterman,' while Gardiner called him 'one of the most generous souls of his generation'.

26 *New Witness*, 21 May 1914

27 *Eye-Witness*, 5 September 1912

28 *New Witness*, 10 August 1916

29 The words 'I will not betray' had been crossed out.

30 The Masterman Papers, University of Birmingham, Cadbury Research Library

31 See note 29 above.

32 The manuscript of this letter, quoted by Bernard Wasserstein in his 1992 biography of Herbert Samuel, is now unaccountably missing from the Samuel Archive in the House of Lords.

33 1839–1922

34 George Bernard Shaw, *Platform and Pulpit* (1961)

35 A. G. Gardiner, *Life of George Cadbury* (1923)

36 The *Daily News* Sweated Industries' Exhibition 1906 was the brainchild of Gardiner who had seen a similar event in Berlin. The Princess of Wales not only attended but 'went everywhere and spoke to the workers', stimulating public interest in the event. See David W. Gutzke (ed.), *Britain and Transnational Progressivism*, at p. 172.

37 This was a typical Cecil smear, as Cadbury's wealth had been accumulated by his own efforts and those of his brother.

38 Cecil Chesterton, *The Prussian Hath Said in His Heart* (1914)

39 Gardiner, *Pillars of Society*

40 *New Witness*, February 1913

41 Stephen E. Koss, *Fleet Street Radical: A. G. Gardiner and the Daily News* (1973)

42 Maisie Ward quotes only lines 3 and 4, describing the context as 'one of Gilbert's poems in praise of wine'.

43 Professor Owen Dudley Edwards has speculated that the offending cocoa verse may actually have been written by Cecil. He writes: 'The *New Witness* under Cecil's editorship had been including poems as space fillers and these poems seem often to have been written in committee. W. R. Titterton indicates that they might begin as songs with different members of the Belloc-Gilbert-Cecil group adding new lines or new verses... I suspect that the verse against cocoa was Cecil's and not Gilbert's and that Gilbert's return to Beaconsfield prevented his knowing that so savage an attack on the Cadburys, owners of the *Daily News*, was being printed under his own name' (*Chesterton Review*, May 1992). Aside from the savagery, the repetition of 'cad' is foreign to Chesterton's normally careful choice of words.

44 Koss, op. cit.

45 Ibid.

46 See Chapter 1, p. 25 above.

47 See Chapter 6 below.

48 *New Witness*, 13 September 1917

49 *Autobiography* (1936)

50 Ibid.

51 Chesterton's views are faithfully echoed by his biographer Maisie Ward who writes: 'The funds of the Liberal Party actually depended chiefly on Quaker millionaires who were noted pacifists and at whose bidding national honour was jeopardised by our delay in declaring our support of France.'

6. A Real Smash-Up

1 A. N. Wilson, *Hilaire Belloc: A Biography* (1984)

2 *Eye-Witness*, 27 June 1912

3 Godfrey Isaacs's full name is given in several books as Godfrey du Buillon Isaacs, Godfrey du Buillon being a famous French crusader. This was a Belloc joke which seems to have been taken seriously by a great many commentators including Belloc's official biographer Robert Speaight. His actual name was Godfrey Charles Isaacs.

4 They did make a profit, though not on the scale that was later claimed by their critics. The boom in American Marconi stock was not simply a by-product of the UK Government contract: other factors included the United Wireless deal and the role of wireless telegraphy in mitigating the *Titanic* death toll.

5 See John Grigg, *Lloyd George: From Peace to War – 1912–1916* (1985)

6 A. G. Gardiner, *Pillars of Society* (1914)

7 Belloc Archive, British Library

8 He was the managing director. Belloc made the same mistake in his letter to Haynes.

9 See Professor Owen Dudley Edwards, *Chesterton Review*, November 1985.

10 The Select Committee on Marconi's Wireless Telegraph Company Ltd Agreement. See p. 121.

11 Maisie Ward, *Return to Chesterton* (1952)

12 *Eye-Witness*, 4 July 1912

13 A. G. Gardiner, *Prophets Priests and Kings* (1908)

14 Ibid.

15 Ibid. Beatrice Webb used the same word about Samuel in her diary, 3 February 1939.

16 Samuel subsequently succeeded in securing a ban on children in licensed premises, legislation which he framed and introduced when Under-Secretary at the Home Office under Gladstone.

17 *Eye-Witness*, 15 August 1912

18 *Eye-Witness*, 22 August 1912

19 See note 10 above.

20 In 1912 the Liberals and Conservatives both had 272 MPs, and the Liberals governed with the support of the Irish Nationalist and Labour MPs. The Liberals and Conservatives therefore had equal representation on the Committee (six members each), and the rest of the Committee consisted of two Irish Nationalist members and one Labour, weighting the Committee in favour of the Government.

21 Not strictly correct: see note 20 above.

22 Ford Madox Ford, *Selected Memories and Poems* (1915)

23 Arthur Ransome, *The Autobiography of Arthur Ransome* (1976)

24 See Chapter 4 above.

25 Granville was later to inform the Committee that Cecil had offered his solicitor £5.00 in exchange for the paper, explaining, 'I was out of the way at the time.'

26 Mrs Cecil Chesterton, *The Chestertons* (1941)

27 Dudley Barker, *G. K. Chesterton* (1973)

28 *New Witness*, 16 January 1913

29 'Song of Cosmopolitan Courage', Ker, *G. K. Chesterton: A Biography*, p. 312

30 *The Times*, 28 May 1913.

31 Ibid.

32 The misspelled word appeared on a handwritten calling card that Queensberry left at Wilde's club.

33 The policy paid off though its success had more perhaps to do with the intense reluctance of lawyers to proceed against their fellow lawyers. Rufus Isaacs went on to become Lord Chief Justice and Smith Attorney General and later Lord Chancellor. In 1916 both men, one as prosecutor the other as judge, successfully secured the conviction of Sir Roger Casement for treason for supplying German weapons to the Irish rebels in the Easter Rising of that year. In his final speech Casement referred to the contrast in his career with that of Smith: 'The Unionist champions chose a path they felt would lead to the woolsack while I went a road I knew must lead to the dock.' Casement was condemned to death by Rufus Isaacs and was hanged on 3 August 1916. G. K. Chesterton was one of a group of authors who appealed to the Home Secretary, in vain, for a reprieve. Belloc refused to sign, claiming that Casement was bound to be reprieved because unlike the leaders of the Easter Rising he was a Protestant.

34 *Chesterton Review*, August 1985

35 First published in the *Eye-Witness*, 30 May 1912

36 Frederick Winston Furneaux Smith, 2nd Earl of Birkenhead, *FE: The Life of F. E. Smith, First Earl of Birkenhead* (1960)

37 Reprinted in *Pillars of Society*

38 Mrs Cecil Chesterton, *The Chestertons*

39 Granville was later sentenced to fifteen months hard labour, a penalty that Belloc insisted had been engineered by the Government, telling Chesterton, 'The politicians only put him in prison in revenge for Marconi.' In his memoirs, Ford Madox Ford, another writer to suffer financial loss at Granville's hands, refers to 'a man, the bearer of a very honoured name, in whose faith too many had reposed their trust. He subsequently committed suicide.'

40 This was a realistic assessment: later on, the Prime Minister Asquith, when speaking in defence of Isaacs and the others, told the Commons that 'the most disgraceful appeals were made from the beginning to racial and religious animosity'.

41 See note 53 below.

42 *New Witness*, 1 May 1913

43 Eleanor and Reginald Jebb, *Testimony to Hilaire Belloc* (1956)

44 Mrs Cecil Chesterton, *The Chestertons*

45 Belloc Archive, British Library

46 Jocelyn Hillgarth and Julian Jeffs (eds), *Maurice Baring: Letters* (2007), p. 109

47 Frank Hugh O'Donnell, a former MP, had written flagrantly anti-Semitic pieces for the *New Witness*: see Chapter 7 below. Belloc does not mention the fact that he himself recruited him as a contributor.

48 Hillgarth and Jeffs (eds), *Maurice Baring: Letters*

49 The judge made only a passing reference to it in his summing-up. 'The defendant and those behind him [possibly a reference to Belloc] were partly activated by racial prejudice.'

50 H. Montgomery Hyde, *Lord Reading: The Life of Rufus Isaacs* (1967)

51 Quoted by Maisie Ward in *Gilbert Keith Chesterton* (1943)

52 In private he amused himself and his followers with satirical verses, e.g. 'Marconi Isaacs, dead and turned to clay / Will make a clout to keep the wind away. / I am not fond of draughts and yet I doubt / If I could get myself to touch that clout.'

53 Hilaire Belloc's introduction to Cecil Chesterton's *The Perils of Peace* (1916)

54 Belloc dedicated this work 'To Miss Ruby Goldsmith, my secretary for many years at King's Land and the best and most intimate of our Jewish friends, to whom my family and I will always owe a deep debt of gratitude.'

55 A corrupt scheme to raise funds for Ferdinand de Lesseps, builder of the Suez Canal, to build another canal in Panama.

56 *GK's Weekly*, 6 March 1926

57 *GK's Weekly*, 5 November 1932

58 Hugh Kingsmill (ed.), *More Invective* (1930)

59 *GK's Weekly*, 5 September 1932

60 Gardiner, *Pillars of Society*

61 *GK's Weekly*, 5 September 1932

7. The Art of Stirring Mud

1 'The Trumpet in the Night', *Daily Herald*, 24 May 1913, reprinted in A. L. Maycock, *The Man Who Was Orthodox* (1963)

2 *The End of the Armistice* (1940)

3 Pro-German French premier 1911–12, later tried for treason and imprisoned

4 Quoted in Maisie Ward, *Return to Chesterton* (1952)

5 In 1906 in the *Daily News* he had written a denunciation of the view that wealthy men forming a government 'would not think it worthwhile to be directly or indirectly bribed': 'This statement is so frantic in its innocence as almost to have a wild,

unworldly charm about it... To say that governments consisting of successful men will not be corrupt is simply to say that no governments on the face of the globe ever have been corrupt. For it does not require a painful effort of the intellect to perceive that the government of a country in any age will be likely to consist of successful men.'

6 *Autobiography* (1936)

7 *Eye-Witness*, 5 September 1912

8 See pp. 130–2 above.

9 *Daily Herald*, 25 April 1913

10 Ibid.

11 *Manchester Guardian*, 9 June 1913

12 Mrs Cecil Chesterton, *The Chestertons* (1941)

13 Belloc Archive, British Library

14 Mrs Cecil Chesterton, *The Chestertons*

15 Quoted by Tom Villis in *Reaction and the Avant-Garde: The Revolt Against Liberal Democracy in Early Twentieth-Century Britain* (2006)

16 In July 1914 he informed Chesterton that he had not written in the paper for a year.

17 *New Witness*, 9 October 1913

18 'The New Name', *Daily Herald*, 15 April 1914, reprinted in *Utopia of Usurers*

19 Maisie Ward, *Gilbert Keith Chesterton* (1943)

20 Addressing Cecil after the verdict, Mr Justice Phillimore said: 'When I consider the cruelty of some of these charges and the fact that they might have rendered Godfrey Charles Isaacs a beggar and driven him from his employment, as well as from the fame and respect of good men; when I remember the sending of those placards along the front of his place of business in the Strand, it is extremely difficult to refrain from sending you to prison.'

21 John O'Connor, *Father Brown on Chesterton* (1937)

22 *New Witness*, 6 August 1914

23 *New Witness*, 12 April 1917

24 'We can only judge men today when we have met them,' he announced after meeting Foch. He was, he wrote in a letter to Mrs Reginald Balfour dated 26 June 1917, a '*really* delightful man full of genius and movement'. Chesterton faithfully echoed this opinion: 'He was to be counted on to stand for the ancient and normal morals of Christendom.'

25 *Life for Life's Sake* (1968)

26 *New Witness*, 30 March 1916

27 Letter to Maurice Baring, 13 April 1916

28 Belloc's introduction to Cecil Chesterton, *The Perils of Peace* (1916)

29 *Autobiography* (1936)

30 Millions of native Congolese suffered terrible mutilation and massacre at the hands of the Belgian occupiers of what was then known as the Congo Free State.

31 'When the conspiracy against Dreyfus was exposed, his [Belloc's] voice rose like a hurricane in defence of the anti-Dreyfusards. When the Congo horrors shocked the world, he braved the storm on behalf of the wretched Leopold.' (*Pillars of Society*)

32 *Hansard*, 22 July 1909

33 Cecil Chesterton, *Perils of Peace*, p. 102

34 Douglas Goldring, *The Nineteen Twenties* (1945).'The most forged charge ever trumped up against a critic even by the British Government' (A. J. P. Taylor).

35 Gardiner, *Pillars of Society*

36 *Autobiography* (1936)

37 *New Witness*, 10 August 1916

38 Ibid.

39 Ibid.

40 *Spectator*, 7 July 1939

41 Masterman was the head of Britain's War Propaganda Bureau (known as Wellington House) set up by Lloyd George in 1914.

42 *New Witness*, 13 January 1916

43 *New Witness*, 20 January 1916

44 As a further sign of the censorship that has marred Chesterton studies, his biographer Maisie Ward, who prints this correspondence, replaces the name Prothero with a dash, so does not reveal to her readers that the Ford review was written by Cecil's deputy and wife-to-be.

45 Maisie Ward, *Gilbert Keith Chesterton*

46 Ibid.

47 *New Witness*, 16 October 1916. McNabb's reference to 'miles of bleak sodden road' was eerily prophetic in view of the circumstances of Cecil's death (see pp. 173–6 below).

48 Belloc Archive, Boston

49 Kitchener had drowned in 1916.

50 *New Witness*, 9 December 1916

51 See Chapter 2 above.

52 Thomas Beecham, *A Mingled Chime: Leaves from an Autobiography* (1944)

53 Ibid.

54 *New Witness*, 4 October 1917

55 *New Witness*, 11 October 1917

56 Mrs Cecil Chesterton, *The Chestertons*, pp. 166–7

57 *Ibid*, p. 200

58 *Ibid*, p. 205

59 See below, pp. 177–80.

60 Ffinch, M, *G. K. Chesterton* (Weidenfeld); 1986. W. R. Titterton, *G. K. Chesterton: A Portrait* (1936)

61 *New Witness*, 27 September 1917

62 The Army Records of the First World War at the National Archive in Kew contain no details of Cecil Chesterton's service record.

63 Bright's Disease is a historical medical term no longer in use. It refers to nephritis – inflammation of the kidneys.

64 *New Witness*, 27 December 1918

65 W. R. Titterton: *G. K. Chesterton: A Portrait* (1936)

66 H. Montgomery Hyde, *Lord Reading: The Life of Rufus Isaacs, First Marquess of Reading* (1967)

67 Any antipathy to Poles and Poland was interpreted by Belloc and Chesterton as a sign of anti-Catholic bias.

68 Gerald Rufus Isaacs, *Rufus Isaacs: First Marquess of Reading (1960–1914) by His Son* (1942). The Marconi scandal had had an even more dramatic effect on Lloyd George, according to his biographer: 'He had lost weight, lost vitality, fell ill again, and his black hair grew grey, the lines began to mark his face and for the first time in public he was seen to use spectacles. A great life on the ledge.' Frank Owen, *Tempestuous Journey* (1954).

69 See pp. 193–4 below.

8. The Death of the New Witness

1 These words appeared in an appendix attacking Keith's memoir *The Chestertons*. Ward must have had second thoughts about the appendix as she omitted it entirely from subsequent editions of her book, possibly more concerned with preserving a generally serene account of Chesterton's life than with causing offence to Keith.

2 The 'Chesterbelloc' tag was originally coined by George Bernard Shaw.

3 *Tablet*, 25 July 1953

4 Ian Ker, *G. K. Chesterton: A Biography* (2011)

5 Ibid.

6 Ibid.

7 Belloc Archive, Boston

8 Ibid.

9 *New Witness*, 17 September 1920

10 Ibid.

11 W. R. Titterton, *G. K. Chesterton: A Portrait* (1936)

12 *New Witness*, 17 September 1920

13 Ker, op. cit.

14 *The New Jerusalem* (1920)

15 Ibid.

16 Maisie Ward, *Gilbert Keith Chesterton* (1943), p. 478

17 *New York Times*, 31 January 1921

18 *William Cobbett* (1925)

19 Maisie Ward, *Gilbert Keith Chesterton*

20 Belloc Archive, Boston

21 Mrs Cecil Chesterton, *The Chestertons* (1941)

22 Ibid.

23 Ibid.

24 Ibid.

25 Ibid.

26 Ibid.

27 Ibid.

28 Ibid.

29 12 July 1924

30 The Caves of Harmony was a fashionable dance club in Charlotte Street: 'Some people came in fancy dress, some in evening clothes, others in tweeds.' Alec Waugh, *The Early Years of Alec Waugh* (1962)

31 Hugh Lygon, a close friend of Waugh's, is thought to have inspired the character of Lord Sebastian Flyte in *Brideshead Revisited*.

32 *GK's Weekly*, 15 May 1926

33 Mrs Cecil Chesterton, *The Chestertons*

9. Chesterton's 'Potty Little Paper'

1 W. R. Titterton, *G. K. Chesterton: A Portrait* (1936)

2 Reprinted in *One Hundred and One Ballades* (1931)

3 Maisie Ward, *Gilbert Keith Chesterton* (1943)

4 Brocard Sewell, *GK's Weekly: An Appraisal* (1990)

5 Titterton, *G. K. Chesterton: A Portrait*

6 The Pope spoke these words to a group of Belgian pilgrims on 6 September 1938, though his attitude to anti-Semitism was not as unequivocal as his words suggest; (see *The Dark Valley* by Piers Brendon (2000), pp. 471–2.

7 W. R. Titterton: *A Candle to the Stars* (1932)

8   A similar allegation is recorded in Brocard Sewell's memoir *My Dear Time's Waste* (1966): 'His colleagues [in the *New Witness*] maintained that Cecil had been passed as medically fit for a long route march in bad weather at a time when he was very unwell and further that someone in the Government had given instructions that something of this kind should be done when a suitable opportunity occurred.' When Hilaire Belloc himself was convinced that Charles Granville had been punished with imprisonment for publishing the *Eye-Witness*, such a bizarre rumour is not surprising.

9   Chalk Farm is a station on the London Underground.

10 Maisie Ward, *Return to Chesterton* (1952)

11 Notes of the Week

12 *Chesterton Review*, 2009

13 Presumably a reference to Chesterton.

14 He was on holiday in France.

15 An Irish-born barrister, later made a director.

16 Gregory Macdonald to Ignatius Rice, 28 May 1934, Douai Abbey Archive

17 Gregory Macdonald to Ignatius Rice, 28 December 1934

18 Maisie Ward, *Gilbert Keith Chesterton*

19 *GK's Weekly*, 27 April 1933

20 *GK's Weekly*, 18 May 1933

21 *GK's Weekly*, 16 July 1927

22 A. J. P. Taylor, *Politicians, Socialism and Historians* (1980)

23 *Tremendous Trifles* (1909)

24 A similar assortment was found in Chesterton's pockets after his death.

25 Maisie Ward, *Return to Chesterton*

26 *GK's Weekly*, 29 August 1935

27 *GK's Weekly*, 5 September 1935

28 'Jewish financial power has prevented people from knowing the truth about most famous foreign trials where Jews were concerned.' (Letter to Maurice Baring, 30 October 1913)

29 *GK's Weekly*, 26 September 1935

30 *GK's Weekly*, 12 September 1935

31 Letter to Maurice Reckitt, 19 September 1935

32 Ibid.

33 Gregory Macdonald to Ignatius Rice, 3 July 1936, Douai Abbey Archive

34 Chesterton left £28,389 in his will. Considering his lack of interest in money it is likely that Macdonald was blaming Frances for the misleading excuses about his poverty.

35 Douai Abbey Archive

10. Post Mortem

1 21 October 1936, quoted in Robert Speaight, *The Life of Hilaire Belloc* (1957)
2 A. N. Wilson, *Hilaire Belloc: A Biography* (1984)
3 *GK's Weekly*, 20 August 1936
4 *GK's Weekly*, 27 August 1936
5 *GK's Weekly*, 24 June 1937
6 A. N. Wilson, op. cit.
7 *The Register*, March 1949
8 Letters of Hilaire Belloc
9 Ibid.
10 Hesketh Pearson, *Lives of the Wits* (1962)
11 30 June 1935
12 Hilaire Belloc, *On the Place of Gilbert Chesterton in English Letters* (1940)
13 Ibid.
14 Ibid.
15 Ibid.
16 See p. 185.
17 Hilaire Belloc, *On the Place of Gilbert Chesterton in English Letters*
18 Robert Speaight, *The Life of Hilaire Belloc* (1957)
19 A. N. Wilson, op. cit.
20 Speaight, op. cit.
21 *Letters of Hilaire Belloc*. Belloc's military allusion was a direct and cruel comparison – possibly subconscious – between himself, who had served as a private soldier in the French army, and Chesterton, who with his physical bulk and poor eyesight could never have been a soldier – or, for that matter, a sailor, as Belloc was later to point out (see p. 225).
22 John O'Connor, *Father Brown on Chesterton* (1937)
23 This incident, told to him by Auberon Herbert, who in turn was told it by Ronald Knox, is recorded by A. N. Wilson in his biography of Belloc. There is no mention of it in any Chesterton biography – another sign perhaps of a general tendency to suppress discordant details. Maisie Ward makes no mention whatever of the confirmation service – a surprising omission, considering the importance she attaches to Chesterton's conversion.
24 *Daily News*, 10 December 1910
25 *Autobiography* (1936)
26 Ibid.
27 Ibid.
28 Conrad Noel (ed. Sidney Dark), *An Autobiography* (1945)

Notes

29 Belloc, *On the Place of Gilbert Chesterton in English Letters*

30 *The Everlasting Man* (1925)

31 *Orthodoxy* (1908)

32 Ibid.

33 *The Everlasting Man*

34 Ibid.

35 Ibid.

36 Ibid.

37 A. N. Wilson, op. cit.

38 Penelope Fitzgerald, *The Knox Brothers* (1977)

39 *TLS*, 24 February 1940

40 *Rise and Fall of the Man of Letters*

41 Dominican Archive

Bibliography

Chesterton wrote over a hundred books (some published posthumously) in addition to articles and essays in a variety of newspapers and magazines.

The late John Sullivan catalogued his oeuvre in three bibliographies:

G. K. Chesterton, A Bibliography, ULP, 1958
Chesterton Continued, ULP, 1968
Chesterton Three, Vintage Publications, 1980

The Chesterton Review, edited by Fr. Ian Boyd, was launched, originally as a quarterly, in Saskatoon, Canada, in 1974. Now appearing twice yearly, it has published a host of articles by and about Chesterton, as well as pieces of general Catholic interest.

The Ignatius Press (San Francisco) has meanwhile undertaken the Herculean task of reprinting all of Chesterton's writings, including his uncollected journalism.

Biographies of G. K. Chesterton

Barker, Dudley, *G. K. Chesterton: A Biography*. Constable, 1973
Coren, Michael, *Gilbert: The Man Who Was G. K. Chesterton*, Jonathan Cape, 1989

Dale, Alzina Stone, *The Outline of Sanity: A Life of G. K. Chesterton*, W. B. Eerdmans, 1982

Ffinch, Michael, *G. K. Chesterton*, Weidenfeld, 1986

Ker, Ian, *G. K. Chesterton: A Biography*, OUP, 2011

Pearce, Joseph, *Wisdom and Innocence: A Life of G. K. Chesterton*, Hodder and Stoughton, 1996

Ward, Maisie, *Gilbert Keith Chesterton*, Sheed and Ward, 1943

Ward, Maisie, *Return to Chesterton*, Sheed and Ward, 1952

Selected Memoirs and Studies of Chesterton

Ahlquist, Dale, *Knight of the Holy Ghost*, Ignatius Press, 2018

Belloc, Hilaire, *On the Place of G. K. Chesterton in English Letters*, Sheed and Ward, 1940

Chesterton, Cecil (Anon.), *G. K. Chesterton: A Criticism*, Alston Rivers, 1908

Conlon, D. J. (ed.), *G. K. Chesterton: The Critical Judgements, Part 1*, Antwerp Studies, 1976

Conlon, D. J. (ed.), *G. K. Chesterton, A Half Century of Views*, OUP, 1987

Hollis, Christopher, *The Mind of Chesterton*, Hollis and Carter, 1970

Maycock, A. L (ed.), *The Man Who Was Orthodox*, Dennis Dobson, 1963

O'Connor, Fr. John, *Father Brown on Chesterton*, Muller, 1937

Sewell, Brocard, *GK's Weekly*, Aylesford Press, 1990

Sprug, J. W. (ed.), *An Index to G. K. Chesterton*, CUA Press, Washington, 1966

Titterton, W. R., *G. K. Chesterton: A Portrait*, Alexander Ouseley, 1936

Biographies and Memoirs of Hilaire Belloc

Belloc, Hilaire, *Letters of Hilaire Belloc*, R. Speaight (ed.), Hollis and Carter, 1958

Jebb, Eleanor and Reginald, *Testimony to Hilaire Belloc*, Methuen, 1956

Morton, J. B., *Hilaire Belloc*, Hollis and Carter, 1955

Bibliography

Pearce, Joseph, *Old Thunder: A Life of Hilaire Belloc*, Harper Collins, 2002
Speaight, Robert, *The Life of Hilaire Belloc*, Hollis and Carter, 1957
Wilson, A. N., *Hilaire Belloc*, Hamish Hamilton, 1984

Cecil Chesterton

BIOGRAPHY

Sewell, Brocard, *Cecil Chesterton*, Saint Albert's Press, 1975

BOOKS BY CECIL CHESTERTON

Gladstonian Ghosts, S. C. Brown Langhan, 1905
The Party System (with Hilaire Belloc), Stephen Swift, 1911
The Prussian Hath Said in His Heart, Chapman and Hall, 1914
The Perils of Peace (Introduction by Hilaire Belloc), T. Werner Laurie, 1916
A History of the United States (Introduction by G. K. Chesterton), Chatto and Windus, 1919

BOOKS BY MRS CECIL CHESTERTON

In Darkest London, Stanley Paul, London, 1926
I Lived in a Slum, Gollancz, 1936
The Chestertons, Chapman and Hall, 1941

Other Books Referred To

Archer, William, *The Trial and Death of Francisco Ferrer*, Chapman and Hall, 1911
Baring, Maurice, *Letters* (selected and edited by J. Hillgarth and J. Jeffs), Michael Russell Publishing, 2007

Beecham, Thomas, *A Mingled Chime: Leaves from an Autobiography*, Hutchinson, 1979

Beerbohm, Max, *Letters to Reggie Turner*, Hart-Davis London, 1964

Belloc Lowndes, Marie, *Diaries and Letters*, Chatto and Windus, 1972

Belloc Lowndes, Marie, *A Passing World*, Macmillan, 1948

Bentley, E. C., *Those Days*, Constable, 1940

Brendon, Piers, *Winston Churchill: A Brief Life*, Pimlico, 2001

Brendon, Piers, *The Dark Valley: A Panorama of the 1930s*, Knopf, 2000

Callil, Carmen, *Bad Faith*, Jonathan Cape, 2006

Camp, William, *The Glittering Prizes*, Macgibbon and Kee, 1960

Dangerfield, George, *The Strange Death of Liberal England*, Constable, 1936

Donaldson, Frances, *The Marconi Scandal*, Rupert Hart-Davis, 1962

Farmer, Ann, *Chesterton and the Jews*, Angelico Press, 2015

Ford, Ford Madox, *Return to Yesterday*, Victor Gollancz, 1931

Ford, Ford Madox (with Violet Hunt), *Zeppelin Nights*, John Lane, 1916

Gardiner, A. G., *Prophets Priests and Kings* (2nd edition), J. M. Dent, 1914

Gardiner, A. G., *Pillars of Society*, James Nisbet, 1913

Gardiner, A. G., *Life of George Cadbury*, Cassell, 1923

Goldring, Douglas, *The Nineteen Twenties*, Nicholson and Watson, 1945

Greene, Graham, *Collected Essays*, Bodley Head, 1969

Grigg, John, *Lloyd George: From Peace to War 1912–1916*, Harper Collins, 1985

Gross, John, *The Rise and Fall of the Man of Letters*, Weidenfeld, 1969

Hopkins, Eric, *Charles Masterman Politician and Journalist*, Edwin Mellon Press, 1999

Hyde, H. Montgomery, *Lord Reading*, Heinemann, 1967

Isaacs, Gerald Rufus, *Rufus Isaacs: First Marquess of Reading (1860–1945) by His Son* (2 vols), Hutchinson, 1942

Kingsmill, Hugh (with Hesketh Pearson), *Talking about Dick Whittington*, Eyre and Spottiswoode, 1947

Koss, Stephen, *Fleet Street Radical – A. G. Gardiner and the Daily News*, Allen Lane, 1973

Masterman, C. F. G., *From the Abyss: Of its inhabitants, By one of them*, Brimley Johnson, 1902

Bibliography

Masterman, Lucy, *C. F. G. Masterman*, Frank Cass, 1939

Pearson, Hesketh, *Lives of the Wits*, Heinemann, 1962

Ransome, Arthur, *The Autobiography of Arthur Ransome*, Cape, 1976

Reckitt, Maurice, *As It Happened*, Dent, 1941

Squire, J. C. (ed.), *One Hundred and One Ballades*, Cobden–Sanderson, 1931

Swinnerton, Frank, *An Autobiography*, Hutchinson, 1937

Swinnerton, Frank, *The Georgian Literary Scene*, Dent Everyman, 1935

Symons, Julian, *Horatio Bottomley*, Cresset Press, 1955

Taylor, A. J. P., *English History 1914–45*, OUP, 1965

Taylor, A. J. P., *Politicians Socialism and Historians*, Stein and Day (New York), 1982

Taylor, A. J. P., *The Troublemakers*, Hamish Hamilton, 1964

Taylor, A. J. P., *British Prime Ministers*, Allen Lane, 1999

Titterton, W. R., *A Candle to the Stars*, Grayson and Grayson, 1932

Villis, Tom, *Reaction and the Avant-Garde*, Tauris, 2006

Wasserstein, Bernard, *Herbert Samuel: A Political Life*, Clarendon Press, 1992

Watt, Richard M., *Dare Call it Treason*, Chatto and Windus, 1963

Waugh, Alec, *My Brother Evelyn and Other Profiles*, Cassell, 1967

Waugh, Evelyn, *Diaries* (ed. M. Davie), Weidenfeld, 1976

Wells H. G., *Mr Belloc Objects*, Watts, 1926

Woolf, Leonard, *Sowing*, Hogarth Press, 1960

Index

Index

Chesterton, G. K. (Gilbert
Keith)
appearance 13, 26–7, 28, 46,
103, 194
and Belloc: on Belloc and
Cecil 133–4; as Belloc
illustrator 38, 69; Belloc
influence 4, 6, 61–2,
68–9, 72, 76, 84, 220,
241, 248nn13; Belloc on
legacy 32, 221, 225–8, 243;
chapter on Belloc 228–9;
defence of Belloc 214–16;
Flambeau character 37,
38; meets Belloc 57, 61;
underestimation by Belloc
241
birth 1, 9
canonisation campaign 2, 3,
5, 243
and Cecil: arguments 26–7,
31, 32, 52, 104; Cecil's
death 7, 173–81, 182,
183, 185, 186, 197, 242;
Cecil's *G. K. Chesterton*
29–33; Cecil's influence
4, 6, 49, 84, 241–2; Cecil's
legacy 199, 200, 211, 220,
221, 227; Cecil's religion
234–5; closeness with 26;
GKC autobiography 9;
GKC character 13; GKC
health 151; GKC move

to Beaconsfield 48–9, 53;
GKC's fame 29; relationship
advice to GKC 54;
underestimation by Cecil
241–2
character: absent-mindedness
13, 100; aversion/
squeamishness 243;
Christian charity 227–8;
crusading nature 144;
emotions 143; fame/
reputation 1, 29, 30,
32, 41; gentleness 104;
humility 244; humour
9, 20; intelligence 150;
jolly journalist 58;
laziness 30; needing help
of others 14; neurosis
243; other-worldliness
9, 23–4; overview 1–4,
13–14; popularity 28, 29;
reliance on Frances 47–8;
Smallwood profile 210–11;
sociability 51, 52
childhood 38–9
death of 8, 173, 209, 211, 212,
219–21, 225–8, 240, 243,
259n34
education 28, 39, 233
and F. E. Smith 126
finances 27, 49–51, 197, 219,
259n34
First World War 152